Poetry and the Anthropocene

T0360890

This book asks what it means to write poetry in and about the Anthropocene, the name given to a geological epoch where humans have a global ecological impact. Combining critical approaches such as ecocriticism and posthumanism with close reading and archival research, it argues that the Anthropocene requires poetry and the humanities to find new ways of thinking about unfamiliar spatial and temporal scales, about how we approach the metaphors and discourses of the sciences, and about the role of those processes and materials that confound humans' attempts to control or even conceptualise them.

Poetry and the Anthropocene draws on the work of a series of poets from across the political and poetic spectrum, analysing how understandings of technology shape literature about place, evolution and the tradition of writing about what still gets called Nature. The book explores how writers' understanding of sciences such as climatology or biochemistry might shape their poetry's form, and how literature can respond to environmental crises without descending into agitprop, self-righteousness or apocalyptic cynicism. In the face of the Anthropocene's radical challenges to ethics, aesthetics and politics, the book shows how poetry offers significant ways of interrogating and rendering the complex relationships between organisms and their environments in a world increasingly marked by technology.

Sam Solnick is the William Noble Research Fellow in the Department of English at the University of Liverpool, UK.

Sam Solnick has written an indispensable account of the concept of ecopoetry, its meanings, history, and vicissitudes, giving the term a sharp and valuable focus. Better than that, he has instantiated its force in informed, engaged close readings.

Timothy Clark, Durham University, UK

Sam Solnick has written a compellingly mobile, unpredictable and multi-dimensional study of contemporary poetry within the context of current debates about literature, ecology, systems theory and environmental crisis. It operates on two fronts. In the first place, Solnick offers a brilliant critique of modern thinking about ecology, ecopoetry, ecocriticism, and the poetry associated with it, provocatively rethinking current assumptions about environment-oriented poetry and theory. In the second, he offers scintillating and authoritative readings of three major contemporary poets no-one else would have dreamed of bracketing together: Ted Hughes, Derek Mahon and J.H. Prynne. Claiming that poetry is particularly useful for thinking about the 'biological, ecological and social systems important to the Anthropocene', Solnick has not only written a highly original study of the three poets in their intellectual contexts but a uniquely self-reflexive map of current thinking about the fate of the human, the natural and the ecological in our period of acute environmental crisis.

Hugh Haughton, University of York, UK

As Solnick says, we are living in an age when humanity has 'the capacity to disrupt (but not control) biological and ecological process'. This thoughtful and timely book addresses what it means to read and write poetry in this context.

Robert Hampson, Royal Holloway, University of London, UK

Routledge Environmental Humanities

Series editors: Iain McCalman and Libby Robin

Editorial Board

Christina Alt, St Andrews University, UK
Alison Bashford, University of Cambridge, UK
Peter Coates, University of Bristol, UK
Thom van Dooren, University of New South Wales, Australia
Georgina Endfield, University of Nottingham, UK
Jodi Frawley, University of Sydney, Australia
Andrea Gaynor, The University of Western Australia, Australia
Tom Lynch, University of Nebraska, Lincoln, USA
Jennifer Newell, American Museum of Natural History, New York, US
Simon Pooley, Imperial College London, UK
Sandra Swart, Stellenbosch University, South Africa
Ann Waltner, University of Minnesota, US
Paul Warde, University of East Anglia, UK
Jessica Weir, University of Western Sydney, Australia

International Advisory Board

William Beinart, University of Oxford, UK
Sarah Buie, Clark University, USA
Jane Carruthers, University of South Africa, Pretoria, South Africa
Dipesh Chakrabarty, University of Chicago, USA
Paul Holm, Trinity College, Dublin, Republic of Ireland
Shen Hou, Renmin University of China, Beijing
Rob Nixon, University of Wisconsin-Madison, USA
Pauline Phemister, Institute of Advanced Studies in the Humanities, University of Edinburgh, UK
Deborah Bird Rose, University of New South Wales, Australia
Sverker Sorlin, KTH Environmental Humanities Laboratory, Royal Institute of Technology, Stockholm, Sweden
Helmuth Trischler, Deutsches Museum, Munich and Co-Director, Rachel Carson Centre, LMU Munich University, Germany
Mary Evelyn Tucker, Yale University, USA
Kirsten Wehner, Head Curator, People and the Environment, National Museum of Australia

The *Routledge Environmental Humanities* series is an original and inspiring venture recognising that today's world agricultural and water crises, ocean pollution and resource depletion, global warming from greenhouse gases, urban sprawl, overpopulation, food insecurity and environmental justice are all *crises of culture*.

The reality of understanding and finding adaptive solutions to our present and future environmental challenges has shifted the epicenter of environmental studies away from an exclusively scientific and technological framework to one that depends on the human-focused disciplines and ideas of the humanities and allied social sciences.

We thus welcome book proposals from all humanities and social sciences disciplines for an inclusive and interdisciplinary series. We favour manuscripts aimed at an international readership and written in a lively and accessible style. The readership comprises scholars and students from the humanities and social sciences and thoughtful readers concerned about the human dimensions of environmental change.

Poetry and the Anthropocene

Ecology, biology and technology in contemporary British and Irish poetry

Sam Solnick

Routledge
Taylor & Francis Group

LONDON AND NEW YORK

First published 2017
by Routledge
2 Park Square, Milton Park, Abingdon, Oxon OX14 4RN

and by Routledge
711 Third Avenue, New York, NY 10017

First issued in paperback 2018

Routledge is an imprint of the Taylor & Francis Group, an informa business

© 2017 Sam Solnick

The right of Sam Solnick to be identified as author of this work has been
asserted by him in accordance with sections 77 and 78 of the Copyright,
Designs and Patents Act 1988.

All rights reserved. No part of this book may be reprinted or reproduced or
utilised in any form or by any electronic, mechanical, or other means, now
known or hereafter invented, including photocopying and recording, or in
any information storage or retrieval system, without permission in writing
from the publishers.

Trademark notice: Product or corporate names may be trademarks or registered
trademarks, and are used only for identification and explanation without
intent to infringe.

British Library Cataloguing in Publication Data
A catalogue record for this book is available from the British Library

Library of Congress Cataloging in Publication Data
A catalogue record has been requested for this book.

ISBN 13: 978−1−138−59745−7 (pbk)
ISBN 13: 978−1−138−94168−7 (hbk)

Typeset in Bembo
by Taylor & Francis Books

For Esme and Lewis, and in memory of Jacqueline and Harry.

Contents

Acknowledgement

I am grateful to the archivists and librarians at the Stuart A. Rose Manuscript, Archives, and Rare Book Library, Emory University, The University of Essex's Albert Sloman Library, The Wellcome Library and The University of Connecticut's Thomas J. Dodd Research Center who were all incredibly helpful. Melissa Watterworth at UConn deserves special thanks for the lifts and tours, and for showing me the goats.

Thanks to J.H. Prynne and to Bloodaxe, for the generous permission to quote from the third edition of *Poems* (2015) and from his correspondence; to Jonty Tiplady for allowing me to quote from his poetry; to One Little Indian records for the permission to quote 'Anchor Song' by Björk; to Faber & Faber and the estate of Ted Hughes for their permission to quote from his published and unpublished writings. 'Crowego', excerpt from 'A Horrible Religious Error', excerpt from 'Creation; Four Ages; Flood; Lycaon', and excerpt from 'Snake Hymn' taken from *Collected Poems* by Ted Hughes. Copyright © 2003 by The Estate of Ted Hughes. Reprinted by permission of Farrar, Straus and Giroux, LLC. Excerpts from 'Positive Feedback Loop' from *Sea Change* by Jorie Graham. Copyright © 2009 by Jorie Graham. Reprinted by Permission of HarperCollins Publishers and Carcanet Press Limited (excerpts appear on pages 205–209 of this volume). Quotations from the writings of Derek Mahon appear by kind permission of The Gallery Press, Loughcrew, Oldcastle, County Meath, Ireland.

Thanks are also due to my friends and colleagues – Beci Carver, Jane Darcy, Ben Eastham, Patrick Goddard, Dan O'Gorman, Alex Harris, Deborah Lilley, Simon Morley, Ben Poore, Stephen Quincy-Jones, Orlando Reade and John Redmond – for their care and time in reading sections of the manuscript when it was thrust upon them (often without warning and occasionally accompanied by a guilt trip); to my PhD examiners, for their illuminating comments and feedback on the thesis from which this book evolved; to the UCL MA students who took my 'Arts and the Anthropocene' course and provoked a range of new conundrums and solutions; to the department at Liverpool for giving me the impetus to finish this stage of my research off, so that I can take it into a new phase; to Helen Bell at Routledge for her help and patience; to Joe Luna and Dan Eltringham for helpfully sending me draft copies of their work; to my family who have been a constant source of encouragement and support and whose influence on the direction of my studies runs deeper than they probably imagine; to Kate Wills without whose love, indulgence and eagle-eyed editing I, as ever, wouldn't have got very far; to everyone who took me out of myself and the library over the last few years to remind me what my work emerges from.

There are many teachers and colleagues to whom I owe a debt of thanks for helping me on my way over the years, but particular mention has to be made of Gerald Dawe for first convincing me that pursuing graduate work on British and Irish poetry wouldn't be such a bad idea, Pete Swaab for seconding him when my nerve and attention were wavering, Clair Wills for her ever-incisive comments and Annie Janowitz for her theory reading group which inspired several of the critical investigations which inform this project. I would also like to thank the Queen Mary English Department and the AHRC; without their support this book would not have got off the ground.

The biggest debt of gratitude is owed to Peter Howarth: for taking a chance on what must have seemed an interesting but quite strange project, for patiently helping form order out of chaos but, most of all, for constantly challenging my sense of how and why we read poetry.

This book is dedicated to my grandparents, great accelerators and Anthropocene explorers in their own ways.

The spring, the summer,
The childing autumn, angry winter, change
Their wonted liveries, and the mazèd world,
By their increase, now knows not which is which:
And this same progeny of evils comes
From our debate, from our dissension;
We are their parents and original.
— William Shakespeare, *A Midsummer Night's Dream*

Introduction

Poetry and science

A WEEKLY ILLUSTRATED JOURNAL OF SCIENCE

"To the solid ground
Of Nature trusts the mind which builds for aye."—WORDSWORTH

THURSDAY, NOVEMBER 4, 1869

NATURE : APHORISMS BY GOETHE

NATURE ! We are surrounded and embraced by her : powerless to separate ourselves from her, and powerless to penetrate beyond her.

Without asking, or warning, she snatches us up into her circling dance, and whirls us on until we are tired, and drop from her arms.

She is ever shaping new forms : what is, has never yet been ; what has been, comes not again. Everything is new, and yet nought but the old.

We live in her midst and know her not. She is incessantly speaking to us, but betrays not her secret. We constantly act upon her, and yet have no power over her.

The one thing she seems to aim at is Individuality; yet she cares nothing for individuals. She is always building up and destroying ; but her workshop is inaccessible.

all-comprehending idea, which no searching can find out.

Mankind dwell in her and she in them With all men she plays a game for love, and rejoices the more they win. With many, her moves are so hidden, that the game is over before they know it.

That which is most unnatural is still Nature ; the stupidest philistinism has a touch of her genius. Whoso cannot see her everywhere, sees her nowhere rightly.

She loves herself, and her innumerable eyes and affections are fixed upon herself. She has divided herself that she may be her own delight. She causes an endless succession of new capacities for enjoyment to spring up, that her insatiable sympathy may be assuaged.

She rejoices in illusion. Whoso destroys it in himself and others, him she punishes with the sternest tyranny. Whoso follows her in faith, him she takes as a child to her bosom.

Undermining *Nature*'s solid ground

In his introduction to the first issue of *Nature*, which follows a quotation from Wordsworth and a set of aphorisms he attributes to Goethe, Thomas Huxley claims that the journal 'aims to mirror the progress of that fashioning by Nature of a picture of herself, in the mind of man, which we call the progress of science' (1869: 11). Science speaks for Nature and is part of it. Though writing two years before *The Descent of Man*, Huxley does not make it explicit, he is positioning science as a method and discourse through which a highly evolved animal reflects back on itself and its environment. As Huxley recognises, aspects of the way he locates the 'mind of man' within Nature correspond with the way the poets he quotes link mind and world, thinking things and objects of thought. As Huxley's translation of what he takes to be Goethe puts it, 'Mankind dwells in her [Nature] and she in them [...] she creates tongues and hearts by which she feels and speaks' (1869: 10).[1]

This correspondence between poetry and science is not simply felicitous. Huxley suggests that Goethe's exultation of the natural whole emerges through his attendance to its parts – pointing out that while Goethe was having these pantheistic musings he was also occupied with comparative anatomy, particularly the human intermaxilliary bone (a body part which provided anatomical evidence linking humans and other animals).[2] Though not a poet-scientist in the vein of his German counterpart, Wordsworth was also aware of the discourses of eighteenth-century science. As he puts it in the preface to *Lyrical Ballads* in 1800, the 'remotest discoveries of the Chemist, the Botanist, or Mineralogist, will be as proper objects of the Poet's art as any upon which it can be employed, if the time should ever come when these things shall be familiar to us' (1984: 607).

This notion of familiarity is part of a broader issue of scientific communication which neither the Romantic poets nor the Victorian scientist who quotes them acknowledge. Communication technologies – such as poetry books and scientific journals – disseminate and mediate remote discoveries to professional and lay audiences. A 1969 centenary editorial in *Nature* looking back on Huxley's article asserted the importance of the communication of research – '*Nature* has stuck fast to this positivist doctrine that discoveries are only discoveries when they are recognized as such outside the circle in which they are first made [...] when they are insinuated into the minds of others' (Maddox, 1969: 420). Because the information amongst its reports, not to mention its letters, adver-tisements and comment pieces, potentially plays a role in commercial, industrial and (neo)imperial applications of science, *Nature* is not always, as Huxley suggests, a passive mirroring of Nature. Rather, like so many of the texts I discuss here, it is involved in a process of feedback: the reflection in *Nature*'s mirror sometimes shapes the Nature it reflects.

Huxley closes his article with the suggestion that when a 'half-century has passed' readers may remember 'back numbers' with a 'smile' that acknowledges that, though theories in the articles may well have become obsolete, it might be that 'the vision of the poet will remain as a truthful and efficient symbol of the wonder and the mystery of Nature' (1869: 11). In some ways Huxley was right. Surprisingly, that first masthead designed to accompany the poet's 'wonder and mystery' lasted for well over a 'half-century'. The starry sky, billowing clouds, twiggy font and rising globe – that anticipates the famous 'Earthrise' photos – stayed on the cover until 1959. And it would actually be ninety-four years until Wordsworth's poem was removed from the front cover in 1963.

That same year, Rachel Carson – whose 1962 book *Silent Spring* had done much to modify the perception of Nature's solid ground – gave the feedback loop between the perception of Nature and its material health a darker twist. Expanding on her book, which itself relied on a fusion of science and poetry for its popularity, Carson argued on national television that 'Man's attitude toward nature is now critically important simply because we have now acquired a fateful power to alter and destroy nature. But man is part of nature and his war on nature is inevitably a war against himself' ('The Silent Spring of Rachel Carson', 1963). Since 1963 this sense of the potential for not only destruction, but also alteration in general has grown.

When the environmentalist Bill McKibben famously proclaimed 'the end of nature' in 1989 he referred not only to ecosystems and the entities within them (though many of these face extinction) but to a 'certain set of human ideas about the world and our place within it', particularly the idea of 'the world apart from man to which he adapted' (1989: 8). Concerns about emergent technologies and the global impact of human activity mean that even the word Nature – a term which might well be applied to genes, individual organisms, species, local ecosystems, national parks or the planetary biosphere – becomes increasingly problematic, perhaps to be avoided. For Bruno Latour, the idea of Nature is often used to paralyse a genuine political ecology. It is a slippery concept, 'nature is not "wilderness" nor the outside, nor the harmonious providential balance, nor any sort of cybernetic machine, nor the opposite of artificial or technical', hence he suggests that 'it would be much more expedient to forget entirely the word "nature" or to use William James's definition: "nature is but a name for excess"' (Latour, 2015: 221). Even assuming this to be desirable, it is easier said than done; the term Nature and its associations are too fundamental to be so easily divested. However, I do think it is worth capitalising the word, as Timothy Morton does, 'to reinforce a sense of its deceptive artificiality' (2013: 42).

The concept of the Anthropocene provides a further radical challenge to cherished ideas of the natural. As one of the key papers in disseminating and popularising the term explains, the Anthropocene describes an epoch where the impacts of 'human activities have become so pervasive and profound that they rival the great forces of Nature and are pushing the Earth into planetary *terra incognita*' (Steffen et al., 2007: 614). As the next section shows, debate about the Anthropocene's starting point, and indeed the validity of the concept itself, are not yet settled. Even so, the term, and its rapid rise in popularity, speaks to the moment Wordsworth imagined when the 'remotest discoveries of the Chemist, the Botanist, or Mineralogist' might become 'manifestly and palpably material to us as enjoying and suffering beings'. For Wordsworth, if

> the labours of Men of science should ever create any material revolution, direct or indirect, in our condition, and in the impressions which we habitually receive, the Poet will sleep then no more than at present; he will be ready to follow the steps of the Man of science, not only in those

general indirect effects, but he will be at his side, carrying sensation into the midst of the objects of the science itself.

(1984: 606–607)

This is a book about how poetry responds to the challenges of the Anthropocene epoch: how it addresses the revolutions the Anthropocene creates in humanity's condition and impressions, how it carries sensation into the midst of the objects of the science itself.

The poetry discussed in this book flows from a period beginning with Carson's polluted landscapes and extending to the present fear that rising sea levels might leave underwater what had seemed solid ground. Looking at poetry through the lens of the Anthropocene sharpens the focus on how awareness of the central features of the epoch, if not the word itself, inflects the ways that ecologically concerned and scientifically informed poetry conceives of life (in the broadest sense) and how some humans might live theirs. In the first chapter I address a variety of different types of poetry alongside the broad range of critical paradigms that engage with the shifts in ecological awareness of the last half century (a period which, by some reckonings, coincides with the start of the Anthropocene, or at the very least the crucial so-called 'Great Acceleration' that occurs after the Second World War). In the later chapters I conduct detailed readings of three major poets from across the poetic and political spectrum – Ted Hughes, Derek Mahon and J.H. Prynne – each of whom provides interesting ways of rendering the Anthropocene: not just in terms of well-known environmental issues such as climate change, but the fundamental questions the Anthropocene poses about the relationships between local and global, individual and collective, economy and ecology, thought and technology.

This book asks what it means to read and write poetry now that humanity and its technologies have the capacity to disrupt (but not control) biological and ecological processes across multiple scales, to 'rival the great forces of Nature', now that the stability of Wordsworth's solid ground is undermined and Huxley's 'wonder and mystery' is mapped, modelled and (co)modified. My contention is not just that the Anthropocene provides a challenge to poetry, but that poetry provides significant modes of interrogating and inhabiting the Anthropocene.

Welcome to the Anthropocene

When is the Anthropocene and who invented it? There are different proposals for when the Anthropocene might be said to have begun. Although scientists recognise that the Anthropocene is informally used to describe massive ecological, sociological and anthropological changes, it is ultimately a geological term, albeit one whose formalisation, unlike other 'prior subdivisions of geological time [...] reaches well beyond the geological community' (Waters et al., 2016: 137). Part of the difficulty of formalising the term involves finding either a suitable date (a 'Global Standard Stratigraphic Age') or an agreed-upon stratigraphic marker (a 'Global Boundary Stratotype Section and Point' or 'golden spike' that is visible in the geological record).

As Schwägerl points out, despite the recent flurry of activity and interest, the notion of man as a geological agent has a long history. Important forerunners include Antonio Stoppani's 1871 description of an 'anthropozoic era' with humanity as a 'new telluric force', Ernst Fischer's 1915 essay 'Der Mensch als geologischer's Faktor [man as a geological factor]', and the 1920s claims Vladimir Vernadsky made for mankind becoming 'a powerful geological force' (all quoted in Schwägerl, 2014: 55–57). However, the term 'Anthropocene' itself was coined by Eugene F. Stoermer in the 1980s and arrived at, apparently independently, by Nobel Prize-winning atmospheric chemist Paul Crutzen in discussions at a conference in 2000. The two published a co-written article later that year and the term became increasingly visible after Crutzen's subsequent commentary in *Nature* which suggested that it 'seems appropriate to assign the term "Anthropocene" to the present, in many ways human-dominated, geological epoch, supplementing the Holocene [recent whole]' (2002: 23).

The Anthropocene was initially proposed to have started with the Industrial Revolution (Crutzen highlighted the importance of James Watts's 1784 work on the steam engine). Other important proposed beginnings include an 'early-Anthropocene' caused by factors such deforestation (c. 8,000 years ago) and changes in agriculture (c. 5000 years ago), the 'Columbian Exchange' of different species, and the increasingly prevalent claims for a boundary point which works with the mid-twentieth century 'Great Acceleration' in human activity, population growth and industrialisation (see Monastersky, 2015; Waters et al., 2016 for summaries). With the great acceleration in mind some scientists, including Jan Zalasiewicz – the head of the 'Anthropocene Working Group' currently considering the formalisation of the term for the International Commission on Stratigraphy – have proposed 1945, after which a layer of identifiable radioactive material shows up in the geological record thanks to the emergence of nuclear military technologies (Zalasiewicz et al., 2015).

In proposing two possible dates for the Anthropocene, Lewis and Maslin highlight the intriguing challenge of designating an appropriate stratigraphic marker. They have proposed that the Anthropocene might be dated as beginning in either 1610 (after changes stemming from the conquest of the Americas took hold) or 1964 (the peak in fallout from nuclear testing which begin to decline thanks to the nuclear test ban treaty in 1963). The geological markers Lewis and Maslin foreground for the 1610 date include the 'mixing of previously separate biotas, known as the Colombian Exchange' which is partly visible due to the fact that pollen preserves well in certain sediments. More strikingly they highlight a notable dip in atmospheric CO_2 as evinced by ice core signatures and other stratigraphic markers. The authors link this decline to the massive reduction in the pre-1492 population of the Americas (from 54–61 million to as little as 6 million) caused by disease, war, enslavement and famine. The accompanying 'near-cessation of farming and reduction in fire use resulted in the regeneration of over 50 million hectares of forest, woody savanna and grassland', leading to greater carbon absorption (Lewis and Maslin, 2015: 174–175). Although it was swiftly challenged by Zalasiewicz (2015), the proposed 1610 Anthropocene provides a stark, early reminder of the way the concept brings together questions of geology, technology (including military and transport innovations), globalisation, (neo)colonialism, ecology and, potentially, death on unprecedented scales.

Across these proposed dates the central premise remains familiar: human activities have changed the 'biological fabric of Earth', the 'stocks and flows of major elements in the planetary machinery' (e.g. carbon, nitrogen) and the energy balance of the Earth's surface (leading to warming and so on) (Steffen et al., 2007: 614). The effects become more pronounced and pervasive during the 'Great Acceleration' following the Second World War, a period 'marked by a major expansion in human population, large changes in natural processes, and the development of novel materials from minerals to plastics to persistent organic pollutants and inorganic compounds' (Lewis and Maslin, 2015: 176). This acceleration has had significant implications, not just for climate change which, while hugely important, is not the sole feature of the Anthropocene, but also for other ecologically crucial 'planetary boundaries' including biodiversity loss, chemical pollution and ocean acidification (Steffen et al., 2011: 861).

It is remarkable how a proposed geological term which, at the time of writing in early 2016, has yet to be formalised by the International Commission on Stratigraphy, should have had such an immense impact beyond the sciences. The Anthropocene concept has snowballed, resulting in articles, conferences and monographs across the disciplines. It has been on the front page of popular magazines, there are Anthropocene Twitterfeeds, Facebook pages and underwater sculptures, not to mention a host of related terms playing on its popularity, including Misanthropocene (Clover and Spahr, 2014), Capitalocene (see Moore, 2015: Chapter 7), and Sustainocene (Faunce, 2014). My personal favourite is Donna Haraway's 'Chthulucene', which nods to H.P. Lovecraft's octopus-monster to describe 'the diverse earth-wide tentacular powers and forces' which entangle 'myriad temporalities and spatialities and myriad intra-active entities-in-assemblages' (2015: 160).[3]

'Anthropocene' is a powerfully suggestive term which, while strikingly effective in communicating the impact of humanity on planetary systems, also risks becoming totalising and also encouraging of a renewed anthropocentricism. After all, to influence is not to control (assuming human activities could ever be so coordinated). Rob Nixon asks:

> [does] the very notion of an Age of Humans risk encouraging species narcissism? It's one thing to recognize that *Homo sapiens* has accrued massive bio- and geomorphic powers. But it's another thing altogether to fixate on human agency to a degree that downplays the imperfectly understood, infinitely elaborate webs of non-human agency, from the microbiome to the movement of tectonic plates, that continue to shape Earth's life systems.
>
> (2014)

With this in mind it is worth noting that, almost from its inception, the Anthropocene has been discussed alongside the possibility of geoengineering – a form of technological mastery of the organic on a global scale which begs questions about governance, oversight and so on. Who would geoengineer, and for whom?[4] The collective impact of humanity may be global, but its effects are not uniform and will affect different communities and populations with varying degrees of severity; no doubt, some will prosper. As those politicians from island nations that risk being submerged by a rise in sea levels know all too well, we may 'all be in the Anthropocene but we're not all in it in the same way' (Nixon, 2014). Ironically, it is frequently those populations who are the least responsible for pollution and greenhouse gas emissions who are most likely to suffer and who have the fewest technological and financial resources to adapt.

The current fascination with all things Anthropocene perhaps reflects the idea's catchiness rather than its geological worth. In fact, as Whitney J. Autin and John M. Holbrook point out, geologists are placed in a somewhat odd position where they are 'left to map a unit conceptually rather than conceptualizing a mappable stratigraphic unit' (2012: 61). The speed and scale of the concept's take-up amongst the humanities and social sciences indicates a powerful, adaptable and also problematic concept for addressing some of the myriad related concerns about the ways humanity and its technologies influence biological, ecological and geological processes.

The ways poets in this book address the ecological issues of the Anthropocene often need to be considered alongside their approaches to technology and biology. Questions of ecology – the study of the relations between organisms and their environments – include questions of (co)evolution and adaptation, the ways in which species shape and are shaped by their environments. In some ways this is a biological issue – mutation in genomes leads to different phenotypic characteristics which partially determine an organism's survival within an ecosystem. However, for humans, environmental adaptation is now primarily via technology which itself is predicated upon a range of evolved capabilities (not least language) that make them technological animals. The poets in this book address the ways technology helps constitute the human and shape its environments. Their poetry challenges fantasies of the non-technological human and, in the Anthropocene, the unmodified landscape or globe.

The significance of how scientific ideas are communicated across different discourses is demonstrated by the tellingly optimistic claim in *Nature*'s centenary editorial that looks back to Huxley and his poeticising:

> it is possible to hope if not to count on the certainty that the potential excesses of science and technology will be combated and probably headed off by the human instincts of liberal societies. In short, there is no need to pretend that science is always safe. It is enough to know that it is what ordinary people wish to make of it.
>
> (Maddox, 1969: 422)

Maddox's claims about the conscious agency of ordinary people (whoever they may be) are problematic. Not least because, by this reckoning, 'ordinary people' and their elected representatives have consciously made 'science and technology' into a prime contributor to the sixth mass extinction event.[5] The poets in this book concern themselves in different ways with the relation of science to society and the questions this raises about authority, scientism and the exercise of power. Their different engagements with certain branches of ecology and biology (including evolutionary biology, biochemistry and earth systems science) lead them to bring their poetry to bear on the way scientific discoveries and models play out in the popular imagination. They address the ways that the popular dissemination of scientific ideas is bound up with the constitutive mythologies of societies, with concepts and metaphors drawn from other discourses, with sensory experience, with our awareness of our own (and other animals') embodiment and the ways that these features recombine and mutate in the practice of everyday life.

Such concerns form an important part of the field commonly called 'ecocriticism' or 'literature and the environment'. While ecocriticism is far from a unified discourse, and itself can be seen as part of the broader emergent field of the 'environmental humanities', my study can be located, for the most part, within Timothy Clark's 'working definition' of ecocriticism as 'a study of the relationship between literature and the physical environment, usually considered from out of the current global environmental crisis and its revisionist challenge to given modes of thought and practice' (2011: xiii). One thread which runs through ecocriticism suggests that, as for Huxley, 'the vision of the poet' has a particular importance.

The form of ecology

How does poetry fit with the concerns of the Anthropocene, not least the pragmatics of the environmental movement? Jonathan Bate writes that 'a manifesto for ecological correctness will not be poetic because its language is bound to be instrumental' (2001: 42). David Gilcrest, in his ecocritical explorations of American poetry, goes so far as to say that poetry about environmental crisis 'forecloses ontological possibilities and sacrifices degrees of truthfulness' and 'risks its own relevance by sacrificing literary value on the altar of certitude' (2002: 9, 34).

This line of argument that, to appropriate André Gide's words, 'it is with fine sentiments that bad literature is made' also applies to ecocriticism; ecocritical work has to be more than environmentalist agitprop (2000: 44). Yet, particularly within early ecocriticism, resistance to instrumentality led to critical approaches overly focused on landscape or renewed sensory engagement which were often inappropriate for addressing the complexity of contemporary ecology. As I show in the next chapter, the coordinates for writing and reading ecologically engaged poetry have shifted as poets and ecocritics have addressed the conceptual challenges of thinking about ecology. This first chapter draws on ecocriticism, posthumanism and systems theory to explore the key critical categorisations of ecologically engaged poetry, including 'radical landscape poetry', 'post-pastoral' poetry and 'ecopoetics'. It also explores why issues such as non-human agency, the role of technology in shaping humans and their environments, and an awareness of scale effects of human behaviour must be considered in any discussion of ecologically engaged poetics.

The Romantics' understanding of life, particularly its flourishing and inter-relation, was central to their subject-matter and also their poetics. Their notions of 'organic form' are fascinating precisely because, as M.H. Abrams (1953) and more recently Denise Gigante (2009) have shown in detail, their interest in the life sciences intersects with their aesthetic theory. For Coleridge, perhaps the most attentive to these questions of how artistic creation reflected the processes of life, 'imaginative unity is an organic unity: a self-evolved system, constituted by a living interdependence of parts' (Abrams, 1953: 175). This view of Nature's generative capacity repeated in the mind of the individual is the aesthetic counterpart to his holistic vision:

> Our noontide Majesty, to know ourselves
> Parts and proportions of one wondrous whole!
> This fraternizes man, this constitutes
> Our charities and bearings.
> ('Religious Musings', 1997: lines 24–27)

Coleridge's words here still resonate surprisingly strongly with aspects of contemporary environmentalism. Cognisance of global interrelation does partially formulate human 'charities and bearings' – though not always with the effects that might be expected or desired by the ecologically concerned. But such an approach struggles to cope with those contemporary conceptualisations which posit the Earth as a dynamic, even evolving, entity. The Earth's conditions shift in response to technological and social conditions that are not easily described in organicist terms, not least what the next chapter describes as the 'scale effects' that mean that relations between local and global are often typified by contra-diction rather than co-adaptation. Coleridge employs the image of the plant to describe how the mind assimilates material from without. But his figuration cannot properly account for humanity's 'originary technicity' where the emergent techniques and tools of the human-animal shape its mind's power to assimilate and communicate.[6]

And yet, something pertinent lingers in the Romantic conception of human part within organic whole, something more useful than a hasty hiving-off of the cultural from a reified sense of Nature. Contemporary descriptions of the biosphere return us to Goethe and Coleridge's whole with the twenty-first century twist of the feedback loop. Musing on the problematic figure of James Lovelock's Gaia, Bruce Clarke reminds us that 'we cannot look at Gaia as a planetary whole without looking, self-referentially, at ourselves, a part of Gaia, looking at Gaia'. Objectivity is 'surpassed by participation'. Here Bruce Clarke's description of global ecology – which stems from a tradition of systems theory – combines biological systems with the emergent metabiotic systems which partly shape them: 'organizations of consciousness and communication' which have emerged from the 'evolution (or Gaian proliferation) of living systems' (2012: 59, 75).[7] One of the more significant aspects of the systems theory approach, which helps establish the theoretical backdrop of my study, is its reorientation 'from interest in design and control to an interest in autonomy and environmental sensitivity, from planning to evolution' (Luhmann, 1995: 10).

Many of the poems I analyse deal with those technologies that physically shape landscapes and their inhabitants – from pesticides and wind farms to abattoirs and genetics laboratories. But the use and development of these technologies is linked to those communicative or social systems which help construct human consciousness and its relationship toward the environment, and are therefore central to the state of local and global ecosystems. Like the biosphere, these communicative systems are inimical to design and control; the intricacies of technologically mediated communication mean that individuals' environmental awareness is not only a matter of education but dynamically bound up with beliefs, sensations, memories, prejudices and patterns of consumption.

Hughes, Mahon and Prynne partially resuscitate one of the most significant aspects of Romantic poetics – the relation of poetic form to life's operations. However, they do so at a time when the solidity of 'Nature' has dissolved into interlinked assemblages of biological systems and inorganic materials currently shaped on a global scale by the emergence of human technology. The myths of the state of nature and the noble, non-technological human who dwells there are supplanted by the Anthropocene and the posthuman.

This book tracks some of the afterlives of organic form in the Anthropocene. I ask how various poetries' formal strategies can interrogate, model or even attempt to enact ecologically and biologically significant processes at a time when ecological thinking means engaging with the feedbacks and relationships within and between the organic, abiotic materials, the technological and the social.

The evolution of Ted Hughes

> When something abandons Nature, or is abandoned by Nature, it has lost touch with its creator, and is called an evolutionary dead-end. According to this our civilization is an evolutionary error.
>
> (Hughes, 'The Environmental Revolution', 1994: 129)

The above words are from perhaps the most often-quoted section of Hughes's prose: a 1970 book review for *Your Environment*. The piece marks some of the key aspects that make Hughes such a significant figure for ecology in poetry, setting out an environmentalist stance that had crystallised throughout the 1960s (particularly since his reading of Carson). Like so much of Hughes's work, the article sees him shuttling between science, politics and the sort of bombastic mythologisation of the natural world that has left him vulnerable to criticism and even ridicule, and which can make it easy to forget that Hughes kept himself scientifically informed.[8]

With its environmentalist underpinnings and its engagement with landscape and non-human animals, Hughes has remained amongst the most popular contemporary poets for ecocritical study, especially as his work does not just fit with certain ecocritical positions, but also helps constitute them. Most of the major figures in Hughes studies – Leonard Scigaj, Keith Sagar and Terry Gifford – have also authored ecocritical volumes, and it is striking that Jonathan Bate, the most important early voice in British ecocriticism, has recently published a major biography that includes assessments of Hughes's environmentalism. As Gifford has pointed out, Hughes is often the only contemporary British poet considered in broader American ecocritical studies such as Lawrence Buell's *Writing for an Endangered World* (2001) and John Felstiner's *Can Poetry Save the Earth?* (2009).

No study of post-war British poetry and ecology can sensibly ignore its most influential and divisive figure, but my reasons for beginning with Hughes stem from an interest in the way aspects of his work have been (mis)read or elided by both his many critics, and his staunchest supporters too. Chapter Two will show how neither group have fully teased-out the ways his environmental concern is bound up with his deceptively sophisticated rendering of evolution and technology. This speaks to a more general failure of some ecocriticism to interrogate technology on a fundamental level.

Reading Hughes's vast correspondence, it becomes clear how his campaigns against pollution, lobbying of politicians and education projects for children were counterpart and complement to the work he saw himself doing in mending the way people experienced and conceptualised their environment. Gifford has probably done more than anyone else to highlight the relationships between Hughes's poetry and his advocacy, but his description of Hughes's sense of ecology and poetry skates over an often-ignored aspect of the Laureate's work that is a starting point for my argument. Gifford presents the poetry's exploration of the relations between cognition, sensation and environment as a 'healing' where poetry engenders a kind of imaginative reunion between a series of binaries – male/female, rational/animal, culture/nature – so that the imagination becomes 'a tool for healing the errors of culture' (2011: 12). In doing so he follows Hughes, who was interested in the bio-evolutionary foundations of culture, in describing the imagination as 'the psychological component of the autoimmune system', where the artist's imagination draws on inner psychological resources to respond to a crisis in its environment. However, Hughes also states that this autoimmunity 'works on others like a medicine' (interview with Heinz, 1995). Medicines are not part of the autoimmune system. Intentionally ingested with a curative objective in mind, they are better described as a thing 'added to make good a deficiency or as an enhancement', a (sometimes dangerous) supplement ('supplement, n.1', *OED*).

Gifford, like many other ecocritics working on Hughes, may locate the evolution of human culture in relation to the rest of the organic world but he cannot account for this logic of supplementarity. The ways in which we conceptualise the relationship of technology to humans or their environments have evolved. Building on the posthumanist criticism of Bernard Stiegler, Bruce Clarke, Carey Wolfe and David Wills I will argue that Hughes's challenging of the rational human by foregrounding its animal impulses is matched by a technological rupturing. His poetry frequently positions the human, at its root, as a technological animal. The chapter will develop this question of technicity to show how Hughes tracks the influence of communicative, agricultural and martial technologies on our relations to our own, and other animals', environments, bodies and behaviours.

A posthumanist reappraisal of Hughes can only go so far without exploring how his most distinctive poetic strategy – the use of myth(opoeia) – relates to his ideas about technological and evolutionary adaptation. I will show how Hughes approaches myth and symbol as a series of culturally determined codifications of a society's environment. For Hughes the body of myths (and the mythologised body) not only evolves, but is itself an evolutionary-adaptive mechanism – a form of what Stiegler calls 'epiphylogenetics' – through which humans adapt and misadapt (to) their environment.

Derek Mahon's ironic ecology

Derek Mahon's work is (self-)described as ironic, liberal and humanist. It lacks the destabilising force of either Hughes's or Prynne's posthumanist perspectives, but this is precisely what makes his work so significant to a study of ecological thinking. His poetry highlights what happens when the liberal-humanist individual, even one keenly attuned to place, politics and history, addresses the emergent concerns of the Anthropocene, particularly those related to climate change.

Mahon's trademark irony partly developed as a strategy for resisting the snares of nationalist violence. I show how this position evolves in his later attacks on the depredations of corporate modernity and their role in environmental crisis. While Mahon acknowledges the resistive potential of spaces beyond economic forces and the rationalising glare of modernity, where there is no 'Google goggling at our liminal lives', any restorative effect is limited and partial ('Dreams of a Summer Night', 2011: 342). His work on economic and environmental crisis is beset by a creeping awareness that, as Tom Cohen puts it, we cannot 'place the blame at the feet of an accidental and evil "1%" of corporate culture alone, since an old style revolutionary model does not emerge from this exitless network of systems' (2012: 15). Mahon refers to the globe's interpenetrating economic and ecological processes as 'a chaos of complex systems' and is anxious about the ramifications of any aesthetic or social retreat into dwelling.

Chapter Three interrogates that perspective embodied by the 1963 *Nature* editorial according to which 'science and technology' are what 'ordinary people' and their 'liberal societies' wish to make of them. While acknowledging the limits of individual agency the chapter uses Mahon's poetry to explore the crucial role irony and cynicism play in political and ecological inactivity. I read his work in the light of Morton's theory of the 'ecological beautiful soul' and Clark and Ingolfur Blühdorn's description of 'simulative politics'. Mahon, like many environmentally concerned writers and members of humanities departments, knows the inadequacy of his eco(poetic)-interventions and the contradictions of his environmentalist stance. His work forms a compelling arena in which to explore the issues that typify what Clark has recently termed 'Anthropocene disorder'. This term describes a kind of psychology emerging from the mismatch between 'familiar day-to-day perception and the sneering voice of even minimal ecological understanding' (including the 'scale effects' discussed in my first chapter). Anthropocene disorder also exists

> in the gap between the human sense of time and slow-motion catastrophe and, finally, in a sense of disjunction between the destructive process at issue and the inadequacy of the arguments and measures being urged to address them.
>
> (Clark, 2015: 140)

The ironic stance Mahon uses so effectively to puncture dangerous notions of authenticity and to remove the individual from the lures of nationalist fervour stutters in the face of global ecological issues which require complex forms of (dis)engagement with contemporary capitalist society. Mahon's work includes poems touching on the technologies related to climate change – the cars and planes, solar panels and wind farms so central to notions of ecological responsibility and complicity. But what makes his work so interesting is the way that addressing the impact of human technologies on a changing planet leads to him ironising a too-easy environmentalism. What he offers instead is a more realistic, troubling and sometimes blackly comic form of ecological consciousness. Yet at the same time, Mahon remains aware of the debilitating force that irony can exert on individual and political will and therefore is constantly negotiating both the critical possibilities and inertial drag that irony engenders. Mahon's work forces the reader to think of ecological consciousness as dynamic and capricious.

Rematerialising Prynne

Throughout Prynne's work we find engagements with the complex relationships between humans, their environment(s) and the technologies that impact both. For example, his poems include material on hydroelectric dams and the electric grid (in 'Die a Millionaire'), the tools and currency enabling farming and trading in early societies ('A Note on Metal'), techniques for bitumen extraction from the Athabasca Tar Sands ('Beyond the Wall') and the genotoxic chemicals used by agribusiness (*High Pink on Chrome*).

Sometimes accused of wilful obscurantism, Prynne's notorious difficulty partly stems from his poems' inclusion of a range of specialist discourses which foreground the forces – sociological, technological, geomorphic, evolutionary, economic and climatic – through which the figure of the human arises. Prynne, in a valuable description of his poetics, says that it

> has mostly been my own aspiration, for example, to establish relations not personally with the reader, but with the world and its layers of shifted but recognisable usage; and thereby with the reader's own position within this world.
>
> (epigraph to Riley, 1992)

In their book, N.H. Reeve and Richard Kerridge (the latter also an important figure within British ecocriticism), describe how the shifting scope of Prynne's poetry provides a challenge to 'the humanist paradigm and its place in late-capitalist culture by imposing shifts of scale which immediately disrupt any sense of personal, unmediated perception' (1996: 4). The significant and sudden shifts in spatial and temporal scale, and the inclusion of specialist languages disorientate the reader and necessitate a different sort of reading practice, one which often requires a philological dictionary and, more recently, a search engine. John Wilkinson describes this as a kind of 'General Poetic Theory out of which human consciousness can be seen to struggle as a by-product of specific environmental conditions, the chief interest being the interlocking of an array of systems from quantum physics to geopolitics to biochemistry to language' (2014: 102).

Writing on Prynne and Allen Fisher, Peter Middleton explains why their investigation of scientific language plays a particularly important role. These poets, Middleton argues, see the work of the sciences as an 'active political force' requiring engagement

> with the claims being made on the wider community or attention, action and reconceptualization. What distinguishes the writings of Prynne and Fisher is their recognition that this work of the concerned citizen requires an understanding of the new science on its own terms. They ask what is being claimed, and what the implications are for its own domain and for other areas of knowledge outside that domain.
>
> (2013: 391)

Prynne's poetry includes work brain physiognomy, database systems, pharmacology, spacetime, geology and, crucially for my work, biochemistry.

My intervention into the debates surrounding Prynne is rooted in his continued interrogation of the relationship between information and materiality, particularly as it relates to genetics (often figured as the transfer of information on a biomolecular level). Prynne's prose and the letters indicate that information theory is central to his interest in genetics, but it is seldom if ever treated as such.

I use Prynne's approach to the idea of quantifiable 'information' as a means through which to frame the questions of materiality, intelligibility and quantification that permeate his approaches to biology, environment and poetics.

The chapter begins by highlighting Prynne's interest in the co-evolution of the human subject with technologies and techniques of quantification and exchange as they structure relations to place across (pre)history. The idea of quantifiable information developed by Claude Shannon and taken up by biologists – including Prynne's college acquaintance Francis Crick – provides a springboard to show how Prynne addresses his concern with the qualitative/material and the quantitative/informational at a formal level, something Prynne himself explored in the lectures collected in *Stars, Tigers and the Shape of Words*. I will show how Prynne remains concerned with what lies outside these formulations of transaction and exchange at multiple scales, what cannot be reduced to efficiency, what is significant without necessarily being meaningful. Middleton describes Prynne as paying scrupulous attention to certain scientific concepts because of their 'epistemological, rhetorical, and metaphorical generativity' (2013: 390). Information is one such concept and it is a significant one because, as Derrida puts it,

> information does not inform merely by delivering an information content, it gives form '*in-formiert*', '*formiert zugleich*'. It installs man in a form that permits him to ensure his mastery on earth and beyond.
>
> (1983: 14)

Prynne's concern about the rendering of human biology into something mappable, adaptable and consumable on an ontological level finds a key parallel in his approach to the ways different environments are conceptualised and manipulated. Of particular interest is his work's depiction of carbon and the way its commodification has ramifications for different landscapes and communities – an issue I show him examining in both the 1960s and the 2010s. In Prynne's work, the ways that technology and the logics of exchange have inflected conceptions of materiality and biology is intimately related to a misplaced notion of human control over the different substances that form bodies, landscapes and also poems. His writing provides a way of thinking, at micro and macro scales, about the ways we conceive of materiality and technology in the Anthropocene

The poetry in this book does not simply, as Morton's Shelleyan suggestion would have it, look to the aesthetic to help us 'imagine that which we know' about ecology, but asks us why we are prone to certain (re)imaginings (2010: 1). Through their various poetic strategies these writers question what sorts of change are desirable, or even possible, within the communicative systems which, through their impact on human thought and behaviour, ultimately have an ecological function. Poetry can no longer 'sing the song of the earth'. In the Anthropocene, poetry is forced to find new ways of rendering, recalibrating and mutating the complex relationships between human organisms and the environments that their behaviours and technologies have shaped.

Notes

1 While the aphorisms' sentiment and perhaps even the phrasing are Goethe's, the actual text was written by a Swiss scholar called G.C. Tobler. Goethe himself confirmed that Tobler's words are closely based on the conversations about natural science and natural theology Tobler and he had in 1781 (see Boyle, 1992: 338–339).
2 See George Wells (1967) for a broader discussion of this aspect of Goethe's work.
3 Haraway is careful to distinguish her concept from some of the less-savoury aspects of Lovecraft's Cthulhu, which is part of the reason for the spelling difference.
4 In his first *Nature* article Crutzen argued that coping with the Anthropocene 'may well involve internationally accepted, large-scale geo-engineering projects, for instance to "optimize" climate' (Crutzen, 2002: 23). He has more recently said that he would not geoengineer at present and has pointed out some of his fears regarding a sense of technocratic control of the biosphere (interview with Schwägerl, 2013).
5 Barnosky et al. (2011) posit the rise in atmospheric CO_2 as a key contributory factor to a mass extinction event that the authors suggest is likely already underway.
6 'Technicity, n. Technical quality or character, technicality; the extent to which a people, culture, etc., possesses technical skills or technology' (*OED*).
7 I follow Clarke in using the term 'metabiotic' to refer to non-living autopoetic systems (i.e. communication systems). I am aware that Clarke's appropriation of the term differs from its normal use as an adjective for metabiosis – the alteration of the environment by one organism so that another organism can flourish. Clarke's coinage appears to be a contraction of Habermas's description of Niklas Luhmann's 'metabiological' systems. See Habermas (1990: 372).
8 One undated letter defends his right to claim the *New Scientist* on Laureate expenses. Hughes states the magazine is 'relevant to my job as Poet Laureate and the business of writing poems' ('Letter', n.d.).

References

Abrams, M.H. 1953. *The Mirror and the Lamp: Romantic Theory and the Critical Tradition*. Oxford: Oxford University Press.

Autin, Whitney J., and John M. Holbrook. 2012. 'Is the Anthropocene an Issue of Stratigraphy or Pop Culture?' *GSA Today*, July, 60–61.

Barnosky, Anthony D., Nicholas Matzke, Susumu Tomiya, Guinevere O.U. Wogan, Brian Swartz, Tiago B. Quental, Charles Marshall *et al.* 2011. 'Has the Earth's Sixth Mass Extinction Already Arrived?' *Nature* 471(7336): 51–57.

Bate, Jonathan. 2001. *The Song of the Earth*. First paperback edition. London: Picador.

Boyle, Nicholas. 1992. *Goethe: The Poetry of Desire (1749–1790)*. Oxford: Oxford University Press.

Buell, Lawrence. 2001. *Writing for an Endangered World: Literature, Culture, and Environment in the U.S. and Beyond*. Cambridge, MA: Harvard University Press.

Clark, Timothy. 2011. *The Cambridge Introduction to Literature and the Environment*. Cambridge: Cambridge University Press.

Clark, Timothy. 2015. *Ecocriticism on the Edge: The Anthropocene as a Threshold Concept*. London: Bloomsbury Academic.

Clarke, Bruce. 2012. 'Autopoiesis and the Planet'. In *Impasses of the Post-Global*, edited by Henry Sussman. Ann Arbor, MI: Open Humanities Press. 58–76.

Clover, Joshua, and Juliana Spahr. 2014. *#Misanthropocene: 24 Theses*. Oakland, CA: Commune Editions.

Cohen, Tom. 2012. 'Introduction'. In *Telemorphosis: Theory in the Era of Climate Change, Vol. 1*, edited by Tom Cohen. Ann Arbor, MI: Open Humanities Press. 13–42.

Coleridge, Samuel. 1997. *The Complete Poems of Samuel Taylor Coleridge*. Edited by William Keach. London: Penguin.

Crutzen, P.J. 2002. 'Geology of Mankind'. *Nature* 415(6867): 23.

Derrida, Jacques. 1983. 'The Principle of Reason: The University in the Eyes of Its Pupils'. Translated by C. Porter and E.P. Morris. *Diacritics* 13(3): 3–20.

Faunce, Thomas Alured, ed. 2014. *Nanotechnology Toward the Sustainocene*. Boca Raton, FL: CRC Press.

Felstiner, John. 2009. *Can Poetry Save the Earth?* New Haven, CT: Yale University Press.

Gide, André. 2000. *Journals: 1939–1949*. Translated by Justin O'Brien. Champaign, IL: University of Illinois Press.

Gifford, Terry. 2011. *The Cambridge Companion to Ted Hughes*. Cambridge: Cambridge University Press.

Gigante, Denise. 2009. *Life: Organic Form and Romanticism*. New Haven, CT: Yale University Press.

Gilcrest, David W. 2002. *Greening the Lyre*. Reno: University of Nevada Press.

Habermas, Jürgen. 1990. *The Philosophical Discourse of Modernity*. Translated by Frederick Lawrence. Cambridge, MA: MIT Press.

Haraway, Donna. 2015. 'Anthropocene, Capitalocene, Plantationocene, Chthulucene: Making Kin'. *Environmental Humanities* 6: 151–165.

Heinz, Drue. 1995. 'The Art of Poetry 71: Ted Hughes'. *Paris Review* 134. Available at: http://www.theparisreview.org/interviews/1669/the-art-of-poetry-no-71-ted-hughes [accessed 24 March 2016].

Hughes, Ted. 1994. *Winter Pollen: Occasional Prose*. London: Faber & Faber.

Hughes, Ted. *'Letter [unknown date and addressee]'*. Box 56, Folder 20. Ted Hughes papers, Stuart A. Rose Manuscript, Archives, and Rare Book Library, Emory University.

Huxley, T.H. 1869. 'Nature: Aphorisms by Goethe'. *Nature* 1(1): 9–11.

Latour, Bruno. 2015. 'Fifty Shades of Green'. *Environmental Humanities* 7: 219–225.

Lewis, Simon L., and Mark A. Maslin. 2015. 'Defining the Anthropocene'. *Nature* 519 (7542): 171–180.

Luhmann, Niklas. 1995. *Social Systems*. Translated by John Bednarz and Dirk Baecker. Stanford, CA: Stanford University Press.

Maddox, John. 1969. 'Is It Safe to Look Back?' *Nature* 224(5218): 417–422.

Mahon, Derek. 2011. *New Collected Poems*. Oldcastle, County Meath: Gallery Press.

McKibben, Bill. 1989. *The End of Nature*. New York: Random House.

Middleton, Peter. 2013. 'The "London Cut": Poetry and Science'. In *The Oxford Handbook of Contemporary British and Irish Poetry*, edited by Peter Robinson. Oxford: Oxford University Press. 384–406.

Monastersky, Richard. 2015. 'Anthropocene: The Human Age'. *Nature* 519(7542): 144–147.

Moore, Jason W. 2015. *Capitalism in the Web of Life: Ecology and the Accumulation of Capital*. New York: Verso Books.

Morton, Timothy. 2010. *The Ecological Thought*. Cambridge, MA: Harvard University Press.

Morton, Timothy. 2013. *Realist Magic: Objects, Ontology, Causality*. Ann Arbor, MI: Open Humanities Press.

Nixon, Rob. 2014. 'The Anthropocene: Promise and Pitfalls of an Epochal Idea'. *Edge Effects*, 6 November. Available at: http://edgeeffects.net/anthropocene-promise-and-pitfalls/ [accessed 31 March 2016].

Prynne, J.H. 1993. *Stars, Tigers and the Shape of Words*. The William Matthews Lectures 1992, delivered at Birkbeck College, London. London: Birkbeck College.

Reeve, N.H., and Richard Kerridge. 1996. *Nearly Too Much: The Poetry of J. H. Prynne*. Liverpool: Liverpool University Press.

Riley, Peter. 1992. *Reader*. London: n.p.

Schwägerl, Christian. 2013. '"Es macht mir Angst, wie verletzlich die Atmosphäre ist" [It scares me how fragile the atmosphere is: interview with Paul Crutzen]'. *Frankfurter Allgemeine Zeitung*, 20 November. Available at: http://www.faz.net/aktuell/wissen/heute-in-der-zeitung-es-macht-mir-angst-wie-verletzlich-die-atmosphaere-ist-1267 2803/die-seite-n2-der-ausgabe-von-12672819.html [accessed 12 December 2015].

Schwägerl, Christian 2014. *The Anthropocene: The Human Era and How It Shapes Our Planet*. Santa Fe, NM: Synergetic Press.

Steffen, Will, J. Crutzen and John R. McNeill. 2007. 'The Anthropocene: Are Humans Now Overwhelming the Great Forces of Nature?' *Ambio* 36(8): 614–621.

Steffen, Will, Jacques Grinevald, Paul Crutzen and John McNeill. 2011. 'The Anthropocene: Conceptual and Historical Perspectives'. *Philosophical Transactions of the Royal Society of London A: Mathematical, Physical and Engineering Sciences* 369(1938): 842–867.

'The Silent Spring of Rachel Carson'. 1963. CBS Reports.

Waters, Colin N., Jan Zalasiewicz, Colin Summerhayes, Anthony D. Barnosky, Clément Poirier, Agnieszka Gałuszka, Alejandro Cearreta *et al.* 2016. 'The Anthropocene is Functionally and Stratigraphically Distinct from the Holocene'. *Science* 351 (6269).

Wells, George A. 1967. 'Goethe and the Intermaxillary Bone'. *British Journal for the History of Science* 3: 348–361.

Wilkinson, John. 2014. 'Silicon Versets at Work, Blue Slides at Rest'. *Hix Eros* 4: 101–112.

Wordsworth, William. 1984. *William Wordsworth*. Edited by Stephen Gill. Oxford: Oxford University Press.

Zalasiewicz, Jan. 2015. 'Epochs: Disputed Start Dates for Anthropocene'. *Nature* 520 (7548): 436.

Zalasiewicz, Jan, Colin N. Waters, Mark Williams, Anthony D. Barnosky, Alejandro Cearreta, Paul Crutzen, Erle Ellis *et al.* 2015. 'When Did the Anthropocene Begin? A mid-Twentieth Century Boundary Level is Stratigraphically Optimal'. *Quaternary International*, The Quaternary System and its formal subdivision, 383 (October): 196–203.

1 Evolving systems of (eco)poetry

Gary Snyder's book *Earth House Hold* is sometimes taken as an example of ecocriticism (and ecopoetry) *avant la lettre*. The title plays on the etymology of *oikos* (as house) and one section posits 'Housekeeping on Earth' as a mode of ecological survival, envisioning Earth as a household and the Earth as a house that we must hold onto, i.e. save for the future (1969: 127).[1] But the connotations of house or household are not necessarily appropriate to thinking about ecology – who is in the household, who is its head, does anyone leave home, are there neighbours, who built the family home and, if damaged, should it be restored or improved? These questions are only half facetious. The tensions in Snyder's title between local and global, care and control, inclusion and exclusion, are reminders that while ecocriticism and ecopoetics have both proved popular neologisms, the direction that they take very much depends on what sense of eco, of *oikos*, is brought to bear by poet or critic. It is a problematic root – as we know all too well from analyses of that other *oikos*, the economy.

As both poetry and ecocriticism have developed, becoming more theoretically sophisticated and scientifically aware as they draw on other disciplines, descriptions of the *oikos* have evolved (Snyder's work itself is a case in point). This chapter charts those changes and some of their implications. The first section tracks the key developments in ecocriticism (and related fields) as it has expanded its purview. Ecocriticism's early focus on phenomenological engagement and specific places has been modified by more refined considerations of the complex relationships between local and non-local. Humanity's enmeshment with different materials, objects and processes on multiple scales means that we have to consider what can be described as 'non-human agency' alongside more familiar issues such as environmental justice, sustainability or pollution, particularly when it comes to climate change. Also discussed in this section are the ways different poets and theorisations of poetry have responded to, or in some cases anticipated, these matters of concern. The second section focuses on technology, arguing that the ecological impact of technology is intimately related to the fact that, on a fundamental level, technologies always structure humans' relationships with, and conceptualisations of, their environments. I then build on this posthumanist appraisal of technology to highlight some of the psychological, political and poetic challenges arising from an awareness of the 'scale effects' of quotidian technology use. In the third section I use systems theory to explore how ecology is communicated across different parts of society, and how this poses questions about disciplinarity, aesthetics and the sorts of claims we might make for poetry.

Thinking about the Anthropocene requires a constant consideration of different scales, systems, materials, discourses and technologies. Its interrelated concerns are rendered in contrasting ways by various types of writing. Perhaps it is unsurprising then that reading and writing about poetry in the Anthropocene often requires – to use another derivative of *oikos* that Snyder also highlights – a relatively ecumenical criticism. In order to explore how poetry's diverse ways of happening articulate the Anthropocene and its discontents, we have to be prepared to negotiate multiple disciplines, theoretical paradigms and poetic traditions and to ask what sorts of awareness are facilitated, or indeed diminished, through any particular approach.

A non-local habitation and a name

Discussions about ecologically orientated poetry and poetics are marked by questions of terminology and focus. Various associations accrue around critical terms such as 'post-pastoral' poetry, 'radical landscape poetry' and 'ecopoetics'. These questions of nomenclature are related to issues of scale – that is how different poetries address different spatial frames (landscape, global environmental systems, microscopic but ecologically significant substances) and different temporal spans (human, geological, evolutionary and so on).

Wordsworth's line, discussed in the introduction, which graced the first issue of *Nature* has a peculiar resonance with early ecocriticism's approaches. His 'solid ground of Nature', as Gillian Beer points out, 'condenses the senses "earth" and "argument"' (1999: 174–175). An association of Nature with a particular way of thinking and writing permeated the work of those academics such as Cheryl Glotfelty and Scott Slovic who helped formalise the study of literature and ecology in the 1990s by setting up ASLE (The Association for the Study of Literature and the Environment). This organisation grew out of subscribers to 'The American Nature Writing Newsletter' and early issues of ASLE's journal *ISLE* paid significant attention to the American tradition of literary representations of landscape and wilderness – to figures such as John Muir and Henry David Thoreau as well as their inheritors such as Annie Dillard and Barry Lopez. Lawrence Buell's (2005) survey of the field called such work 'first wave' ecocriticism. Reading it often conveys the sense that through literary re-engagements with 'earth' an 'argument' emerges: a better mode of being, outside the domination of industrial modernity – and often critical theory too. Richard Kerridge described the first wave as characteristically asserting that 'physical contact with wilderness is the antidote to modes of critical thinking that have become too abstract, theoretical and cultural-constructionist' (2012: 26). It is important to highlight the dominant role that place, and its related category, landscape, played in the field, as indicated by Glotfelty's introduction to *The Ecocriticism Reader* which asks whether in 'addition to race, class, and gender, should place become a new critical category?' (1996: xix).

While, particularly in America, the realism of Nature Writing often appeared to be the natural aesthetic partner for early ecocriticism, there was also an interest in poetry. Critics such as Jonathan Bate, Karl Kroeber, Kate Rigby and James McKusick focused on Romantic ecology, and McKusick in fact highlights the sometimes-unacknowledged influence of British Romanticism on American wilderness writing (2000: 5). Also, as Ursula Heise points out, ecocriticism was more interested in poetry 'than other schools of criticism' had been 'in recent decades', suggesting that possibly this was because 'metaphor is a particularly easy way of establishing such connections between mind, body, and place' (2006: 511)

From relatively early on there was an interest in poetry which in some way went beyond depictions of Nature into an engagement with contemporary ecological issues. Terry Gifford who, along with Bate, was one of the most influential early UK and Ireland-based, and orientated, scholars working in the field, spoke in the 1990s of 'green poetry' as 'those recent nature poems which engage directly with environmental issues' (1995: 3). Gifford's statement was echoed in 2002 by J. Scott Bryson in a volume which brought together a variety of approaches to poetry and the environment that included essays on some of the most popular poets for ecocritical study such Snyder, A.R. Ammons, W.S. Merwin and Wendell Berry. Bryson describes this burgeoning field of 'ecopoetry' as 'a subset of nature poetry that, while adhering to certain conventions of romanticism, also advances beyond that tradition and takes on distinctly contemporary problems and issues'. He goes on to posit three pervasive characteristics. The first is 'an ecocentric [i.e. not anthropocentric] perspective recognizing the interdependent nature of the world; such a perspective leads to a devotion to specific places and to the land itself'. Second, 'an imperative toward humility in the relationships with both human and nonhuman nature', particularly in the face of that which might be said to exceed human agency. The third aspect Bryson identifies is 'an intense skepticism concerning hyper-rationality, a skepticism that usually leads to an indictment of an over-technologized modern world and a warning concerning the very real potential for ecological catastrophe' (2002: 5–6).

Bryson's description is fairly typical of poetry-orientated ecocriticism of the period, and sketches out some of the issues that are still very much of interest to this book: how does the possibility of environmental catastrophe change how we address the tradition of poetry about Nature? How do we think about interconnection, interdependence and a corresponding sense of responsibility? What is the nature of non-human agency and the relationship between humans and their technologies? However, aspects of Bryson's claims are also problematic, not least the emphasis on certain types of emotive response such as 'humility', or the supposition that ecological awareness in poetry is primarily a distinct subset of a tradition of 'nature poetry'. Bryson's vision is one that returns us to 'specific places and to the land itself', to the solid ground of Nature.

It is interesting that one of the key touchstone-texts for studies of poetry-orientated ecocriticism was published in the same year the as Crutzen and Stoermer's first article on the Anthropocene. The coordinates for ecologically engaged readings of British and Irish poetry have shifted dramatically since Jonathan Bate's arguments for the peculiar importance of poetry to ecology in *The Song of the Earth* (first published in 2000) and before that in *Romantic Ecology* (1991). While aspects of his work still resonate, others have become problematic. Both the focus and the terminology for poetry relating to ecological issues have evolved.

Although Bate's concerns range from political issues like postcolonial eco-justice to aesthetic categorisations of Nature such as the picturesque, the core supposition across both his ecocritical books is essentially that poetry enables 'readers better to enjoy or to endure life [...] by teaching them to look and dwell in the natural world' (1991: 4). Working off Heidegger's notion that poetry 'is the original admission of dwelling', Bate argues that poetry offers better modes of thinking because it attunes humans to the Earth, enabling them to care for it (2001: 261). For Bate, Romanticism 'regards poetic language as a special kind of expression which may effect an imaginative reunification of mind and nature'. In response to humans' alienation from Nature, Bate positions poems as 'imaginative parks in which we may breathe an air which is not toxic and accommodate ourselves to a mode of dwelling that is not alienated' (2001: 45, 64). He models a deep-ecological integration, an imaginative return to Nature in order to save it:

> Let us begin by supposing that we cannot do without thought-experiments and language experiments which imagine a return to nature, a reintegration of the human and the other. The dream of deep ecology [i.e. a state of Nature] will never be realized upon the earth, but our survival as a species may be dependent on our capacity to dream it in the work of the imagination.
>
> (2001: 37–38)

Bate privileges this dream of reunion, 'the controlling myth of ecopoetics is a myth of the pre-political, the pre-historic: it is a Rousseauesque story about imagining a state of nature prior to the fall into property, into inequality and into the city' (2001: 266). For Rousseau this fall into culture is a fall into language and into meat eating. The ur-myth of return underscores Bate's vision of what a poem does. His Heideggerian argument proposes that, in the face of the alienation wrought by modern technology – where Nature is enframed (*Gestell*) and shows up as standing-reserve (*Bestand*) – there are types of *technē* which can reconnect the human with the rest of natural world. For Heidegger, '*technē* is the name not only for the skills and activities of the craftsman, but also for the arts of the mind and the fine arts. *Technē* belongs to bringing forth, to *poeisis*' (Heidegger, 1977: 13). In Bate's work poetry goes back to a type of *technē* which was 'attuned to the natural unfolding of things', it 'unconceals' Nature. The work of the poem on a formal level is part of this unconcealing:

it could be that *poesis* in the sense of verse-making is language's most direct path of return to the *oikos*, the place of dwelling, because metre itself – a quiet but persistent music, a recurring cycle, a heartbeat – is an answer to nature's own rhythms, an echoing of the song of the earth itself.

(2001: 75)

It is unsurprising that John Burnside, the poet Bate claims 'stakes out the ground for a "green poetry" that' will be 'essential to our century', harbours a similar, Heidegger-inflected sense of the relationship between poetic and ecological thought (Bate, 2002). Along with Alice Oswald, Burnside is probably the most popular living British or Irish poet for ecocritical study. His poetry and prose chronicle the local and the numinous, which is not to say that they do not acknowledge environmental issues such as pollution. However, Burnside's own criticism positions what he describes in terms of poetry *as* ecology: an 'attempt to understand and describe a meaningful way of dwelling', with poetry as 'a technique for reclaiming the authentic, a method for reinstating the real, a politics of the actual', where the 'song of the earth is not a metaphor, but an actual sound, one that can be listened to' (2006: 95, 105, 102). The local is privileged, as is that which is immediately available to the senses:

The starlit darkness of the actual night, the salt and physicality and achieved grace of real bodies, the pleasure of walking as opposed to driving. A view of identity that sets terrain and habitat before tribal allegiances, the integrity of place before the idea of nation or state.

(2006: 93)

This notion that the ecological value of poetry lies in the way it might tune the reader's attention into 'actual' or 'authentic' Nature is a recurrent, but problematic, refrain – not least because it raises the question of what, exactly, readers are being attuned to. This is evident in another early theory of ecopoetics, Leonard Scigaj's concept of 'référance'. A purposeful differentiation from Derridean *différance*, 'référance' focuses on the world outside the text, it

turns the reader's gaze toward an apprehension of the cyclic processes of wild nature after a self-reflexive recognition of the limits (the *sous rature*) of language. After this two-stage process, a third moment often occurs, the moment of atonement with nature, when we confide our trust in (*s'en référer*) nature's rhythms and cycles, where reading nature becomes our text.

(1996: 6)

Arguments such as Bate's and Scigaj's present the text as recalibrating the reader's environmental awareness – but they are frequently selective and sometimes mistaken about the qualities of Nature that they read. Their latent Romanticism colours their sense of ecology, suggesting that consciousness comes into harmony with an environment which, as Dana Phillips has emphasised, is seldom as harmonious as is popularly believed and might in fact be typified by sudden, even catastrophic shifts and fluctuations. The values we associate with ecology 'especially balance, harmony, unity and economy – are now seen as more or less unscientific, and hence "utopian" in the pejorative sense of the term' (Phillips, 2003: 42).

Even as literary understandings of ecology have grown more sophisticated, the idea that poetry's primary importance to ecocriticism is the ways it facilitates sensory re-engagement with Nature is not uncommon. In his 2012 study *Ecopoetics: The Language of Nature, the Nature of Language*, Scott Knickerbocker emphasises that 'poetry and our close reading of it demands that we focus our thinking, pay attention with all our senses, and grow in imagination'. And while it is easy to endorse his argument that figurative language 'can help us experience the world as more than inert, unresponsive matter', his focus remains at a certain local scale, with his version of ecopoetics primarily concerned with 'poetic devices which enact, rather than merely represent, the immediate, embodied experience of nonhuman nature' (2012: x, 6, 16).

No matter what climate change denial blogs say, just because it is snowing on Wordsworth's solid ground does not mean that average global temperatures are not rising. An ecological awareness interested in the non-local impacts of pollution (as with DDT or CFCs) or long term climate patterns is not necessarily well served by a poetic focus on sensory immersion or an imaginative at-one-ment always potentially misleading in its claims about 'nature's rhythms and cycles'. Even without the notion that there is potentially no untouched Nature in the Anthropocene, the biosphere was always more dynamic and fluctuating than this phrase implies. This is not to deny that reading Wordsworth or Muir might well prompt a reader to up and leave her books and engage in a practical way with caring (and campaigning) for her environment. Nor does it mean that interrogating the cultural and historical architecture of our notions of Nature is not a valuable project. As the Renaissance ecocritic Robert Watson points out, the 'assumption that our crisis is entirely recent – *pollution ex nihilo* – and addressable only by focusing on our present politics reflects a narrow, anti-ecological view' (2014: 40). And yet, in the Anthropocene, the cumulative force of hydrocarbon-fuelled human activity speaks to a fundamental shift where the effects cannot be considered solely on a local scale any more. Any critical approach which tries to speak to contemporary ecological concerns by going back to the Romantics or out into the landscape has to constantly negotiate the fact that Nature is not what it once was. The biosphere, and our understanding of it, has been terminally modified by advances in science and technology. Critics and poets who fail to acknowledge this risk using 'the aesthetic as an anaesthetic' (Morton, 2007: 10).

The need to highlight this risk is part of the reason why Morton's *Ecology Without Nature*, the most influential critique of early ecocriticism, rejects the privileging of what he calls 'ecomimesis' where writing retunes our senses to the great outdoors: 'While it pretends to rub our noses in the natural world, ecomimesis is caught in the logic of reification' (2007: 137). For Morton, uncritical appraisal of writing about Nature is a form of consumerism, a vicarious armchair enjoyment which ignores the mechanical, the abject and the degraded aspects of the environment which Morton's own project of 'dark ecology' attempts to reintroduce. Morton's challenges to environmental aesthetics provide important criteria for any reading of (eco)poetry. He is particularly interested in asking whether, in its attempt to construct a phenomenology of reengagement and inhabitation, ecocriticism fails to show the complex ways humans are embedded in their environment.

However, one should be wary of straw men in these debates. Garrard has argued that 'ecomimesis already is not what it used (or Morton uses it) to be; while wilderness epiphany no doubt lurks in some corners, nature writing is capable of demonstrating a sophistication (a certain urbanity in both senses?) and self-consciousness' (2010: 14). This is certainly true of some of the so-called 'new' Nature Writing' associated with figures such as Robert MacFarlane and the poet Kathleen Jamie. Such writing is still attentive to the local, but aware of the snares and mores of the pastoral, prepared to locate the local within global networks and acknowledge the technological modification of life and landscape while also being aware of the risks this sort of writing runs both aesthetically and ethically.[2]

First wave ecocriticism's focus on wilderness and the concomitant interest in Nature Writing did not always sit well with what Buell described as a more theoretically aware 'second wave' ecocriticism which moved away from wilderness and deep ecology toward ecological justice and from (natural) place to (constructed) space. He argued that the focus on localised stewardship – which goes hand in hand with notions of dwelling – was potentially counterproductive, leading to 'maladaptive sedentariness, inordinate hankering to recover the world we have lost, xenophobic stigmatization of outsiders and wanderers' (2005: 68). Buell's claim is related to a familiar concern surrounding the relation of National Socialism to Heidegger's philosophy and the perceived misanthropism of deep ecology. More tricky and intractable are emergent problems within environmentalist thinking which increasingly has had to attend to the possibility that one environmentalist goal (like low-carbon energy generation) might stand in the way of another (such as the protection of species and habitats).

While first wave ecocriticism's interest in the relationship between individual and landscape has not gone away, it has become increasingly common to locate it within a wider, sometimes contradictory set of ecological concerns. A decade on, the growth of scientific and environmentalist awareness in and out of the humanities means that Buell's claims about first and second wave ecocriticism no longer apply. The sheer diversity of characteristics that Scott Slovic (2010) argues as typifying the 'third wave' – which he describes as running from 2000 through to the then present – suggests that the wave metaphor has never been entirely felicitous:

> What the 'wave' model fails to take into account, then, is the untidy, uneven character of ecocriticism's development in the U.S. [and even

more so outside it] and the lack of consensus about its proper focus: just what one expects, after all, of a new field, and perhaps a better indicator of its health than the rapid growth and linear progression – or the perfect storm – posited by the 'wave' model.

(Bergthaller et al., 2014: 269)

One cannot speak about ecocriticism (or indeed ecopoetics) in the singular any more, especially when considering approaches which deal with related issues without necessarily identifying them as ecocriticism, such as animal studies, science studies, geocriticism and posthumanism, or the broader transdisciplinary growth of the 'environmental humanities'. The proliferation of approaches indicates, on the one hand, a burgeoning environmental awareness across disciplines which sometimes manifests as a kind of 'greening' of pre-formed critical approaches and sometimes as a radical shift, as with Dipesh Chakrabarty's influential 2009 article 'The Climate of History'. Chakrabarty describes how an awareness of the Anthropocene disrupts the humanities, throwing disciplines, in his case history, 'into a deep contradiction and confusion', not least because a sense of the global scale of environmental crisis challenges both the 'ideas about the human that usually sustain the discipline of history' and also the specific 'analytic strategies' used (2009: 198). After a slow start where, despite honourable exceptions such as Verena Andermatt Conley (1997), some parts of critical theory failed to engage much at all (with some blame laid at the door of Derrida's relative lack of interest on environmental questions), the last decade has seen a massive growth in environmental awareness within critical theory and therefore far more relevant theoretical resources available to literary critics interested in ecology, biology and related issues.

Even as readers and writers of poetry become more scientifically sophisticated, and attuned to some of the critical arguments emerging from within ecocriticism and related fields like cultural geography, the poetics of place remain central to studies of British and Irish poetry that engage with environmental questions. As they strive to find ways of negotiating the relationship between local and non-local, human and non-human, a variety of related and sometimes competing descriptions have emerged for what would previously have been called Nature Poetry.

Critical approaches to dwelling have been challenged by a more dynamic sense of relationships with the landscape and the production of space. In their introduction to a collection of essays on (mostly British) poetry and geography, Neal Alexander and David Cooper describe landscape poetry as 'a way of seeing and a way of doing, transforming its object in the act of apprehension and encounter but also registering the torsions of place in its own language and forms' (2013: 3). They go on to point out the persistence of place even in the face of an awareness of interconnectivity, critiquing Ian Davidson's claim that contemporary poetry 'refuses a fixed location and shifts between places' and Eric Falci's notion that poetry now focuses on 'dissolving landscapes, places that open underfoot into murky indeterminacies, and spaces made and unmade by modernity's alterations, accidents, and disasters' (quoted in Alexander and Cooper, 2013: 5).[3] For Alexander and Cooper such arguments 'underestimate the extent to which the relation of self to landscape continues to be both imagined and experienced in terms of phenomenological embeddedness' (2013: 5). As Heather Yeung puts it in another recent 'geocritical' study of space and poetry that focuses on Jamie and Oswald amongst others, 'However disrupted it may be, attachment to place and the affective and physical development that this brings with it is an important formative factor to the way we subsequently read and engage with poetry' (2015: 2).

The poetics of place, and its relationship to the pastoral tradition, is one driving force behind Gifford's influential work on British and Irish poetry. His theory of the 'post-pastoral' uses a series of poetry and prose writers, including Gillian Clarke, Peter Redgrove, Seamus Heaney and, above all, his doyen Ted Hughes, to attempt to outline six key 'elements' of what he, following Buell, describes as a 'mature environmental aesthetics'.[4] The six characteristics represent an important early attempt to synthesise some of the disparate directions of ecocriticism within the context of British and Irish poetry and there are welcome aspects such as Gifford's acknowledgement of questions of power and justice in element number six ('the exploitation of the planet is of the same mind-set as the exploitation of woman and minorities'). Others are more problematic: the insistence on certain kinds of emotive response (element number one, 'awe in attention to the natural world'), or the too-often disproven notion in the fifth element that 'consciousness' – of the natural world and humanity's relationship to it – necessarily engenders 'conscience' (1999: 164, 152, 163). Gifford's list of post-pastoral elements offers perspectives on ecology which are, if not quite unscientific, then often too vague to be helpful critical guidelines. They are however suggestive in interesting ways.

One related description of poetry and place that often also has an ecological dimension is what Harriet Tarlo has called 'radical landscape poetry', a term which she uses to bring together a range of figures from what is often called 'innovative' or 'experimental' contemporary British poetry. These include figures such as Peter Larkin, Zoë Skoulding, Carol Watts, Barry MacSweeney, Geraldine Monk, Allen Fisher and indeed Prynne, though he is not included in her anthology of radical landscape poetry, *The Ground Aslant* (2011). Tarlo is keen to distinguish radical landscape poetry from both Gifford's 'post-pastoral' and from descriptions of ecopoetry and ecopoetics. While she sees the poems she selects as, like those Gifford calls 'anti-pastoral', offering a 'corrective to the sentimental pastoral tradition' and presenting 'a more realistic view of nature' that 'does not write out agricultural and social issues of significance', Tarlo argues 'that this work moves beyond pastoral to such a degree that much of it is no longer caught up with the pastoral genre as Gifford's anti-pastoral examples are'. Moreover, she rejects the 'post-pastoral' because

> Gifford is seeking out and advocating poetry with an environmental bent here. Unsurprisingly perhaps, given the lack of mention of poetic form,

the poets lauded by Gifford are all definable as more mainstream than innovative.

(2009: 2–3)

As well as a fundamental interest in landscape (any interest in ecology is a secondary if related consideration), it is the issue of 'form', rather than any specific mode of radical politics, that distinguishes Tarlo's writers: 'Above all', she says, 'it is through sound and space on the page that landscape is explored in this work. The relationship between form and space (place) is symbiotic'. For Tarlo,

> landscape writing in particular often challenges the divide between experimental and traditional in all its many guises, a divide which has so painfully haunted British poetry since the 1930s. This is not least because, however innovative, this work retains its link to the local and physical world. It is, to cite Skoulding, 'from here'.

(2009: 198, 195)

While the differences between different schools of British and Irish poetry are often stark it is worth considering Tarlo's argument in the light Alexander and Cooper's claim that

> geography also provides a kind of common ground, as it were, on which the often divisive sundering between so-called 'mainstream' and 'experimental' poetic camps ceases to be quite so pronounced. Although their methods may appear to be very different, post-Romantics and neo-Modernists often turn out to have shared preoccupations with the relations between place and identity, humans and non-humans, nature and culture.

(2013: 2)

There is a danger of overemphasising the important differences between diverse poetic communities. While Gifford does rely on the 'mainstream' as examples for his post-pastoral categories, the idea of the 'post-pastoral' is certainly not necessarily closed to 'innovative' forms – especially as Gifford applies it to drama and fiction too. Alice Oswald's *Dart*, probably the most taught single collection of ecologically orientated contemporary British poetry, is another example of the problematic nature of the division Tarlo paints. This book-length poem's sensitivity to the geographical that sees it move across different spaces, speakers and discourses means that, as Peter Howarth suggests, 'although published in a relatively traditional slim Faber volume', *Dart* also 'has strong affinities with site-specific and performance poetry which try to make both audience and setting formal elements in the poet's happening'; it owes something to Ian Hamilton Finlay (in whose garden, incidentally, Oswald worked) as well as to Ted Hughes (particularly *River*). Oswald takes in the ecological, economic and technological along the Dart's course with a shifting form where, through 'sound and spacing [the poem] is meant to engage our whole sense-making faculty' (Howarth, 2013: 192, 200). Derek Attridge has pointed out that Faber sometimes is taken to stand in as kind of synecdoche for 'mainstream' (2013: 77). Even so, the fact that sections of Oswald's *Dart*, one of the most successful contemporary Faber volumes, would in some important ways sit nicely within Tarlo's anthology is a reminder that, while the divisions between different types of British and Irish poetry are very real and significant (not least in terms of funding, publicity and, too-often, readership) they are not always easily defined, particularly in the case of landscape.

What Tarlo's anthologising does do however (as well as providing an important receptacle for verse not admitted to the mainstream), is highlight how a sense of the ecological, biological and technological has invaded the poetry of landscape. Examples include Colin Simms detailing wolverines' adaption to their changing landscape, Skoulding foregrounding the genetic scale of the 'tangle of DNA' in her 'Through Trees' sequence and Peter Larkin tracking the techniques and technologies which shape forests in 'Open Woods' (all in Tarlo, 2011: 23–27, 137, 25). Tarlo also raises the important question of how form shapes a poem's ecological awareness, organising both its internal elements and its position or framing in relation to any environment. With Tarlo's chosen poets in mind, one might argue that writing which deploys the paratactic shifts associated with a modernist tradition may well be better placed to render the opposing scales and the multiple registers associated with contemporary ecological thought. It is also fair to say that the 'innovative' tradition of British and Irish poetry has a track record of engaging with the sorts of technical and scientific vocabularies that are particularly relevant to ecological crisis. As Mandy Bloomfield (2015) has shown, Allen Fisher's work is a case in point.

There is significant potential common ground, albeit aslant, between the concerns of the innovative tradition and a so-called mainstream that is increasingly interested in questions of ecology as well as landscape. And so it is a critical and imaginative failure that nearly all of the extended list of poets Tarlo groups as writers of 'radical landscape poetry' should have been consciously excluded from the most comprehensive anthology of ecologically orientated British and Irish poetry, Neil Astley's *Earth Shattering: Ecopoems*, as well as the more idio-syncratic anthologies from Oswald (*The Thunder Mutters*), and Burnside and Riordan (*Wild Reckoning*) (see Astley, 2007: 18).[5] Nor does Carol Anne Duffy find room for the innovative tradition amongst the major and minor poets from whom she elicited contributions for *Keep it in the Ground*, the *Guardian*'s fossil-fuel divestment campaign. Which is not to say that the campaign did not bring together some very interesting poems about hydrocarbons and climate change, including the contributions from Sean Borodale, Robert Minhinnick and Imitiaz Dharker (Shabbir et al., 2015).[6]

Tarlo also highlights something important when she says that while

> some landscape poets may be ecopoets and some ecopoets may be landscape poets, the two are by no means interchangeable. Ecopoetics goes beyond

landscape into a wider political and global sphere and landscape poetry goes beyond an exclusive concern with the environment.

(2009: 6)

There are two things to note here. The first is that, justifiably, ecopoetry is normally taken to designate a poetry which deals primarily, if not solely, with ecology and related issues – which begs the question of how we treat poetry in which ecology is a secondary but significant dimension. The second issue is that, as Tarlo's own chosen poets show, it is increasingly difficult to write about landscape without some dimension of ecological engagement; but ecological thinking and environmental concern, particularly the global dimension associated with the Anthropocene, does not necessarily emerge from a consideration of landscape. An insistence on the local might stymie as well as facilitate global environmental awareness. The work may be 'from here' but, as Skoulding says elsewhere in Tarlo's anthology, 'the lines of the landscape | run through me to somewhere else' (2011: 131).

Related tensions emerge in Greg Garrard and Susanna Lidström's recent positing of a critical distinction between what they call 'ecophenomenological' poetry which seeks 'to heighten individual readers' awareness of their natural surroundings' (their example is Ted Hughes) and what they define as '"environmental poetry," that tries to grapple with the changing relationship between human societies and natural environments'. They offer Seamus Heaney as the embodiment of the latter. Given the powerful, albeit diminishing, influence that Hughes exerted on Heaney, and the breadth of ecologically aware British and Irish poetries, it does seem problematic to position these two as exemplars of distinct types of poetry. Also, while it is certainly possible to see the ecophenomenological and environmental(ist) as two broad tendencies within poetry which focuses on ecology and related issues, Garrard and Lidström's notion of '[s]eparating ecophenomenological poetry from environmental poetry' risks forgetting that these two tendencies can exist alongside or in dialogue with each other within the same poem (2014: 37, 50).

Take, for an example from a similar poetic tradition, 'Death of a Field' by Paula Meehan, an Irish poet whose ecology is not only modified by the sorts of postcolonial political awareness Lidström (2015) sees as central to Heaney's ecology, but also by what Kathryn Kirkpatrick (2010) describes as an 'ecofeminist' perspective. As Randolph (2009) has argued, Meehan, like Eavan Boland, positions ecological questions in relation to those of gender, power, urbanisation and globalisation.[7] 'Death of a Field' is a poem about property development, a familiar sight during the Celtic Tiger boom. In it, Meehan (who, interestingly, was taught by Snyder), details threatened bird songs and habitats, as well the embodied experience of a local environment where, in a moment of heightened phenomenological awareness, the speaker imagines walking

Barefoot under the moon to know the field
Through the soles of my feet to hear
The myriad leaf lives green and singing

But alongside her Celan-esque naming of fauna and flora the poem offers various domestic cleaning products: 'The end of dandelion is the start of Flash'. Likewise, the green and white of 'eyebright' is swept away by that of 'Fairy', the livid indigo of 'sloe' is usurped by the more fluorescent pinks and blues of 'Oxyaction' (Meehan, 2009: 13). As commercial chemicals replace the organic, the ecophenomenological moment memorialising a vanishing place becomes vital to the poem's environmentalist concerns.

Awareness of the mutually affecting relationships between phenomenological engagement and environmentalism is also part of Bristow's discussion of the 'Anthropocene lyrics' of Oswald, Burnside and the Australian poet John Kinsella. Bristow's is one of the most sophisticated attempts to date within studies of British and Irish poetry to balance the tension between a poetics of place alongside a global environmental awareness, as we can see from his description of a contemporary '*oikos*':

> Ethically, planetary problems might 'come home' to us if our sense of the household was larger than the dwelling place at which we reside; if our duty of care extended beyond our families to the planet and its inhabitants over the next millennium, we might have a more relevant sense of *Oikos* for the challenges raised by environmental crisis.
>
> (2015: 12)

Bristow blends ecocriticism with a 'geocriticism' that 'incorporates the study of space into literary analysis'. His argument rises to the challenge of reading the *oikos* as both Earth and home/household, refusing to let a fascination with locality obscure ecological awareness. For Bristow, ecopoetics 'is a synonym for contemporary poetry that exhibits a profound sense of selfhood as Worldliness' (2015: 4, 6). He sees ecopoetics as therefore implicitly calling us 'to reflect on how we imagine spaces and formations beyond the purview of the sense horizon'; this means going beyond the human scale to ask

> (i) how we relate to larger and smaller things than ourselves; (ii) how we conceive of biological formations more acute (micro, niche, unseen or present beyond our sense experiences) and obtuse (macro, systems based, unfathomable or present beyond our cognitive timescapes) than that of our own corporeality and its immediate material environment.
>
> (2015: 6, 9)

Bristow's sense of Anthropocene lyricism avoids many of the traps that have haunted ecocriticism focusing on British and Irish poetry, it does not 'not aim at synchronicity, harmony or holism; it is aware of such fallacies as it is acutely informed about its geographical terrain' (2015: 112).

While Bristow's argument certainly suits the 'acutely informed' poetry of Oswald's, Burnside's or Kinsella's specific geographies, it does not necessarily sit well with poetry which is ecologically engaged, but takes on a mythic, or indeed cartoonish, register (like Hughes in *Crow*), nor those which seemingly eschew the particularity of place along with an identifiable lyric subject who might dwell there (like Prynne). Nor indeed does it quite fit with poems primarily concerned with the transnational, interlinked political and economic dimensions of environmentalist consciousness without necessarily grounding themselves in a specific geography. Nor those which focus not on place or space but on one or more of the specific technologies important to the current and future state of the environment whether they be planes, wind farms, automobiles, solar panels or the computer programs which map, model and disseminate climate data. These are modes of Anthropocene lyricism that are not easily tied to geographical terrain, but which are still very much poems of and about the Anthropocene. Nevertheless, it is important to note how Bristow's insistence on the micro and macro scales that exceed human corporeality reflects some major shifts within ecocriticism in the last decade.

Notions of interconnectivity have always been at the heart of ecocriticism. Hence the introduction to Neil Sammells and Richard Kerridge's early ecocritical anthology *Writing the Environment* states that an 'ecological perspective strives to see how all things are interdependent, even those apparently most separate. Nothing may be discarded or buried without consequences' (1998: 8). But some connections are more equal than others. Species extinction rates, environmental justice for indigenous peoples, energy security, so-called 'ecosystem services' and the rights of the unborn to a livable planet are interrelated areas of ecological and economic concern where different focuses might provoke very different courses of action. The danger is that simply emphasising global interdependence leads to a failure to attend to the specificities. As Heise explains, the 'issue isn't so much that all places are connected (one of the great clichés of modern environmental studies), as it is understanding which connections are most important'. Paying attention to regimes of metaphors for connectivity at different scales is central to contemporary ecocriticism, but reading poetry while thinking through the relationship between local and global often requires 'knowledge of scientific principles and processes as well as recourse to metaphor' (Heise, 2008: 39).

Ecological awareness requires not just thinking about a vague interdependence but addressing *how* organisms, species, societies and environments are connected. In the Anthropocene things are increasingly not what they seem:

> Reality as such has been upgraded: phenomena you can see and hear and palpate are suddenly less real than ones you can't [...] This affects our sense of orientation, which traditionally depended on a background of some kind, whether we call it Nature or lifeworld, or biology: whatever seemed to lie beyond our ken, outside of our responsibility, or outside of the social.
>
> (Morton, 2010: 117)

Morton's work has played an important role in developing conceptual schemes for this reality-upgrade. His concept of the ecological 'mesh' problematises the stable closed ecosystem, the bounded organism and the individual subject's agency. Morton reminds us that even our sneeze is not our own but a virus's way of helping us spread its DNA: we are awash with parasites and symbionts from DNA upwards (2010: 34–37). Moreover, Morton asks us to think through ecological embeddedness as both biological enmeshment and as a series of events in which we are entangled. This mesh image usefully describes the imbrication of ecological processes with political and economic ones. It also speaks to the tensions within ecocritical discourse where one limb of the body of environmentalism can pull at cross-purposes against another as both flail around within the ecological mesh. In this way conflicting models and priorities can feed back into the mesh's biotic and metabiotic imbroglio.

Another important conceptualisation of the relations between bodies and environments that has proved useful to reading poetry is Stacey Alaimo's description of 'trans-corporeality' which 'entails a rather disconcerting sense of being immersed within incalculable, interconnected material agencies that erode even our most sophisticated modes of understanding' (2010: 17). Her main poetic example – Muriel Rukeyser's *The Book of the Dead* (1938) – focuses on the migrant miners who develop silicosis thanks to the egregious industrial malpractice by Union Carbide during the Hawk's Nest tunnel disaster.[8] Alaimo's trans-corporeal reading shows how Rukeyser's poem brings together environmental justice (poor communities exposed to toxic substances thanks to avaricious corporate practices), awareness of the specific properties of materials which humans cannot fully control (in this case silica which causes lung fibrosis), and the fact that the impact of these materials on the body is only made available (to legal and media networks as well as to individuals) through the mediating power of certain technologies – here via X-rays. Rukeyser shows the difficulty of mapping 'an ontology in which the body of the worker, the river, the silica, the "natural," and the industrial environment are simultaneously material and social, sites where institutional and material power swirl together'. Significantly, it is through the experimental form of the poem that Rukeyser is able to bring together these competing and contrasting discourses, the 'poem draws heavily from the actual congressional hearings but also includes other reportage, letters, a clip from Union Carbide's stock report, a scientific equation for the energy of falling water, and the symbol for silica, SiO_2, thus mixing languages that are poetic, prosaic, technical, scientific, and colloquial' (Alaimo, 2010: 48, 46).

Alaimo's work, particularly the way it foregrounds not only material enmeshment with bodies and different social systems, but the role of technologies in making this enmeshment visible, is a good example of one of the most significant theoretical developments of the last decade: work which, whether it draws from an engagement with positions such as Morton and others' descriptions of Object-Orientated Ontology (OOO), Jane Bennett's notion of 'vibrant matter' or the work of Bruno Latour or Karen Barad, demonstrates an increasing awareness that the operations of different objects, materials or processes radically challenges our sense of what constitutes agency. Bergthaller has described how this reconfiguration of agency is central to the recent 'new materialist' turn in ecocriticism which is typified by a sense that agency 'is emergent and distributed – that is, it is not the property of concrete, isolable entities, but manifests itself only as distributed throughout the networks in which these entities are embedded' (2014: 38). By distributing agency so that it is not solely the property of the human we might, as Bennett does, start asking questions such as 'Can a hurricane bring down a president? Can HIV mobilize homophobia or an evangelical revival? Can an avian virus jump from birds to humans and create havoc for systems of health care and international trade and travel?' (2010: 107).

On a different but related note we might ask what sorts of object (or indeed network of human and non-human actants), are involved in a given understanding of climate change. In, say, late 2009, a very partial list might include drilled ice-cores, algorithms, (ice)hockey sticks, a Dutch Nobel Prize-winner, the Alberta Tar Sands and the UEA institutional email servers that were hacked on the eve of the Copenhagen IPCC talks. This increased level of awareness about the complex relationships between human and non-human at different scales (including the non-human within the human) suggests, as Bergthaller puts it, 'the patent absurdity of lamenting an abstract alienation from nature when human beings are everywhere and ineluctably enmeshed in material processes that elude human mastery in their irreducible multiplicity, unpredictability and sheer generative excess' (2014: 38).[9]

In the Anthropocene humans become a global geophysical force because of the scale effects of repeating even quotidian actions which seem insignificant in themselves (driving to school, drinking tea, spraying Roundup[TM] weedkiller) by the million and billion.[10] The cumulative effect of these actions may have a planetary impact. Hence, Clark argues, the factors ecocriticism should consider include behaviour patterns, the status of technologies and related societal infrastructures, and the properties of certain materials and biological systems:

A list [of significant environmental issues] might include: day to day assumptions about life style, the voting trends of various countries, the fuel efficiency of modern cars and heating systems, population trends and sexual habits, definitions of the good life, the nature of money and exchange, the aspirations of the poor, the politics of national sovereignty, the impersonal demands of 'advanced' infrastructures that imprison their inhabitants in a kind of 'energy slavery' […] the size of households, the melting threshold of arctic tundra and the exact nature of innumerable other unknown or badly understood biological, meteorological and chemical processes, and so on.

(2010: 136)

Again, this raises the question of whether, in certain instances (for example, Rukeyser's modernist blend of contrasting discourses), particular formal choices are better equipped to address the challenges the Anthropocene poses to individual human agency and what we might think of as its poetic equivalent, the individual lyric subject with its identifiable 'I' and the limited range of its eye. This is an idea central to contemporary discussions of ecopoetics, particularly in North America. From an 'ecological perspective, the self dissolves into the gene pool and the species into the ecosystem' says the poet Evelyn Reilly, meaning that for her, 'ecopoetics requires the abandonment of the idea of center for a position in an infinitely extensive net of relations' (2010: 257). In *Redstart: An Ecological Poetics*, a creative/critical volume co-written with John Kinsella, Forrest Gander points out that the strategies of ecopoetics which make claims to initiating 'a dispersal of ego-centred agency' or 'a reorientation toward intersubjectivity' themselves 'look a lot like innovative poetic strategies championed for the last hundred years' (2012: 11). For Margaret Ronda poets 'affiliated with ecopoetics tend to define their work as strongly committed to the attempt to abandon models of literary authority that would amalgamate anthropogenic power rather than disperse it' (2014: 106).

Tarlo (2008) has argued that the use of the word eco*poetics*, and not merely 'ecopoetry', emphasises form and not just theme. Emphasis on poetics can partly be traced back to a desire to distinguish emergent forms of ecologically engaged poetry from a more conventional sense of Nature Writing which, as Jonathan Skinner indicates in the inaugural introduction to his journal *ecopoetics*, was often marked by 'transparent narratives of self-discovery, or solipsistic, self-expressive displays'; these are, he goes on to say, 'ill-suited to the current crisis' (2001: 6). Reilly too has spoken of her frustration in defining ecopoetics against long-held conceptions of Nature Poetry:

> I'd explain that it's an investigation into how language can be renovated or expanded as part of the effort to change the way we think, write, and this act in regards to the world we share with other living things, and they'd say, 'oh, updated nature poetry'. I'd assert that it has nothing to do with nature poetry, the separation into genre being a symptom of the disease. Still. They would file it under 'species political poetry, subspecies nature,' before turning to other, more urban, social, linguistic, 'literary' concerns, even as I'd insist that all concerns are concerns of our being or doing as nature, that there is nothing more social, urban, post-humanist and po-mo-post-lang-po than 'eco'. Happily, this has begun to change.
>
> (2010: 255–256)

Although most of the poets who feature in the journal *ecopoetics* – figures such as Lisa Robertson or Peter Larkin – would normally be referred to as avant-garde or 'innovative', Skinner himself has offered a fairly ecumenical sense of what ecopoetics can entail:

> ecopoetics can range from the making and study of pastoral and wilderness poetry to the intersection of poetry and animal studies, or from the poetics of urban environments to poets' responses to disasters and matters of

environmental justice. It might mean the study and deployment of formal strategies modelling ecological processes like complexity, nonlinearity, feedback loops, and recycling.

(interview with Hume, 2012: 755)

Skinner had previously grouped ecopoetics into four broad (and not mutually exclusive) categories. Within early ecocriticism, the first of these, the 'topological', often appeared to be the only game in town and is still a powerful presence within studies of British and Irish poetry. For Skinner it is constituted by references to an 'outside' to the poem, to a 'natural topos', meaning that it 'plants at least one foot within the themes and motifs of pastoral tradition' – even if only to counter them. The second category, the 'tropological' is 'seen in the proliferation of exercises in analogy, casting poems as somehow functioning like ecosystems or complex systems, troping on language and ideas from the environmental sciences'. This category is drawn from the work of Jed Rasula, who has pointed out that the Black Mountain Poets, themselves a key influence on the English innovative tradition (Prynne in particular), drew on a notion of the organic understood in the context of cybernetics (Rasula, 2002: 4). Skinner's third category is an 'entropological poetics', a 'practice engaged at the level of materials and processes, where entropy, transformation and decay are part of the creative work'. Amongst other things, this category provides a way of addressing poets such as Maggie O'Sullivan or Ian and Alec (Hamilton) Finlay who work at the intersection of poetry and other arts. Skinner's final category is the 'ethnopoetic' which entails tasks of translation 'outside Western languages and cultures' in its approach to the environment (2005: 128–129).

Skinner's ecopoetic categories are more signposts for future enquiry than strictly delimiting categories and ecopoetics itself is a kind of edge-space 'where different disciplines can meet and complicate one another' (2001: 6). Even so, some environmentally concerned poets have rejected ecopoetics as a limiting category which cannot cope with politics, economics and industry:

> I resist ecopoetics. And definitions of ecopoetics. I resist it as a neat category into which one might insert my own work, like some car slipping into its slot on the freeway. It's important here to mention gas, petrol, 'birth of the crude'.

(Sprague, 2008)

A contemporary attempt to speak to the ecological does not have to (and should not) foreclose on other sorts of critical awareness, and Skinner's version of ecopoetry is very much open to questions of economy, petro-capitalism and global ecological injustice. However, Jane Sprague's fears are a useful reminder that the most interesting theorisations of ecopoetics are in tension not only with each other, but with the differing priorities and issues that have been foregrounded as ecocriticism itself has evolved from the poetics of re-immersion and reengagement into a more politically, theoretically and scientifically aware field.

Ecopoetics and ecocriticism will continue to evolve as more critical and creative approaches emerge to engage with the tensions between organism and environment, localised dwelling and spatial/temporal scales beyond normal experience, human and non-human agency. It remains unclear whether eco-poetics will continue to function as the dominant name for poetry about the Anthropocene as its solid ground becomes increasingly aslant and poets acknowledge a period where the impact of industrial technologies means that any poetic gaze toward an untrammelled outside is problematic. But it is important to realise that humans' relationships to their world have, in some important ways, always been technologically determined.

Anthropos kainos – technology and the posthuman

In their introduction to a 2014 special issue of *The Minnesota Review* dedicated to 'Writing the Anthropocene', the editors highlight one of the key objections to the term 'Anthropocene', the fact that it anthropocentrically asserts human dominance at a time where the centrality of humans, and their capacity to control (as opposed to simply change) their environment, has been undermined. But, 'viewed from a different perspective' the editors go on to say,

> the term seems perfectly appropriate. For the names of the preceding three geologic epochs – the Pliocene, Pleistocene, and Holocene – translate respectively as 'newer time,' 'newest time,' and 'entirely new time' and thus give these seemingly neutral period designators an inexorable orientation toward the present. By contrast, the term Anthropocene derives from the imaginary etonym *anthropos kainos*, which we might translate somewhat awkwardly as the 'time of the new man.' The seeming humanism of the term thus actually reveals its underlying posthumanism.
>
> (Boes and Marshall, 2014: 62)

This question of the posthuman is crucial to questions of (eco)poetry in the Anthropocene.

One problematic feature of poetry-orientated ecocriticism which posits a deep-ecological imaginary as a counterweight to an environment increasingly modified by technology is its (implicit or explicit) positioning of writing as a technology which helps us to imagine the non-technological. Some time ago now, Donna Haraway castigated the ecofeminism of Carolyn Merchant for relying on 'an imagined organic body to integrate our resistance' to the excesses of 'modern technology', but as is evident from the work of figures such as Bate, Scigaj and, as we shall see, Zapf, the positioning of the organic against the technological has persisted (Haraway, 1990: 154). This question of how to approach technology in general subtends any questions of pollution, climate change or environmental justice as it relates to specific technologies. Technology is central to conceptualising human development and the problem of how humans might continue to adapt to an environment they themselves have changed.

Analysing the way technics can determine a consciousness' relation to its environment means turning away from the view of technology which focuses on the inert tool, the status of which is determined by how humans use it to bring about certain ends, a view where '*technē* is a prosthesis (πρόσθεσις: prosthesis, i.e., an addition; what-is-placed-in-front-of) considered "in relation to" nature, humanity or thought' (Bradley and Armand, 2006: 3). One key aspect of Heidegger's importance to ecocriticism, especially in its earlier iterations, rests in his challenging this perspective by addressing both the ontic realm of specific technologies and the ontology of technology. He views *technē* as a mode of revealing rather than constructing. For Heidegger '*Technē* is not "making", or the art of making but, as Michael Inwood helpfully elucidates, the *Wissen*, "knowing", that guides our dealings with *phusis* [nature]' and this sense remains in his version of *Technik* (technology, engineering, technique) (Inwood, 1999: 209). The essence of modern technology is enframing (*Gestell*): 'It [*Gestell*] is nothing technological, nothing on the order of a machine. It is the way in which the real reveals itself as standing-reserve [i.e. a kind of availible resource]' (Heidegger, 1977: 23).

This question of enframing as it relates to ecosystems and organisms is a significant one and particularly visible in the following chapters with Hughes's engagement with animals and Prynne's with energy generation. However, an issue remains with Heidegger's thinking which stymies his philosophy's usefulness in analysing the relationship between the technological and the evolutionary: the spectre of the non-technological 'natural' human. (The same gap persists in Bate and parts of the deep-ecology movement.) Derrida has argued that Heidegger, particularly in his positing of a gap between technology and its non-technological essence, 'maintains the possibility of thought that questions, which is always thought of the essence, protected from any original and essential contamination by technology' (1991: 10). Or, as Bradley and Armand put it, 'an "outside" from which technology itself might be thought' (2006: 7). Instead of pre-technological thought or a pre-technological human, Derrida maintains we are better served by an idea of humanity's originary technicity:

> There is no natural originary body: technology has not simply added itself, from the outside or after the fact, as a foreign body. Or at least this foreign or dangerous supplement is 'originally' at work and in place in the supposedly ideal interiority of 'body and soul'.
>
> (1995: 244)

Bate calls the controlling myth of ecopoetics 'a Rousseauesque story about imagining a state of nature'. Hence it is worth remembering that it is against Rousseau that Derrida deploys the logic of the supplement in *Of Grammatology* – a process continued by his sometime collaborator Bernard Stiegler. *Technics and Time*, Stiegler's examination of the relationship of technology to the formation of the human, skewers Rousseau's vision of pre-technological humans, claiming that the capacity for tool-use has an impact on biological evolution. He affirms

André Leroi-Gourhan's claim that 'the anthropoid apes freed their hand and achieved erect posture long before their brain had reached the level of ours today [...] The development of the nervous system follows in the wake of that of the body structure.' Hence for Stiegler 'cortical evolution might well itself be codetermined by exteriorization, by the nongenetic character of the tool' (1998: 147). The ability to manipulate tools, rather than some solely biological factor (namely a larger brain) may well have been the key factor in the development of the human. Interrogating technology is important to thinking about ecology because technologies not only directly shape environments but also the behaviour, perception and cognition of the human organisms within them, and this problematises any hasty return to organicism or a deep-ecological imaginary.

In showing how our awareness of the biosphere and other animals is itself technologically mediated – and, in the next section, in locating the human within a network of social systems – the theoretical background for this book can be described as 'posthumanist' in Cary Wolfe's sense of the word. Like Lyotard's formulation of the postmodern, Wolfe's posthumanism comes both before and after humanism. Before in the sense that it

> names the embodiment and embeddedness of the human being in not just its biological but also its technological world, the prosthetic coevolution of the human animal with the technicity of tools and external archival mechanisms (such as language and culture).

The human, for Wolfe as for Stiegler, is fundamentally 'a prosthetic creature that has coevolved with various forms of technicity and materiality, forms that are radically "non-human" and yet have nevertheless made the human what it is'. This includes 'the most fundamental prostheticity of all: language in the broadest sense' (2009: xv, xxii).

As well as coming before the 'human', posthumanism also comes after humanism in naming a 'historical moment in which the decentring of the human by its imbrication in technical, medical, informatic, and economic networks cannot be ignored', and which coincides in significant ways with discussions of the Anthropocene (Wolfe, 2009: xv). The 'post-' of posthuman should not be seen as indicating progress or evolutionary fitness. Haraway was anxious that posthumanism risked being co-opted by a kind of techno-fetishism (see Haraway's interview with Gane 2006: 140). Similarly, Wolfe's attacks on the 'the cultural repressions and fantasies, the philosophical protocols and evasions, of humanism as a historically specific phenomenon' include the latent humanism in what he calls 'transhumanism'. For Wolfe, transhumanism emphasises ways the human might be enhanced through emerging technologies – often through biotechnology or through integration with the digital. The danger here is that 'the human' is achieved by 'escaping or repressing not just its animal origins in nature, the biological, and the evolutionary, but more generally by transcending the bonds of materiality and embodiment altogether' (2009: xv–xvi).

Even an awareness of the collective impact of humanity in the Anthropocene does not obvert this sort of extension of humanism. A good example can be found in Michel Serres's description of humans' planetary dependence on Earth and the need to foreground a new 'natural contract' at a time when 'the decisive actions are now, massively, those of enormous and dense tectonic plates of humanity' (1995: 160). Serres's geological metaphor in some ways anticipates the key arguments of the Anthropocene surrounding 'transpersonal agency' but, as Clark makes clear in his recent analysis, Serres's vision of the finite globe for which humanity must take responsibility 'could also represent the hope for a new form of humanism, one tied to a collective self-recognition of the human as "steward" of the planet, envisioning the Earth as a vast garden-city sustained by various geo-engineering schemes', and is therefore 'an exercise in anthropocentric illusion' (2015: 5). For Clark, there is too much of a sense of control and coordination in Serres's vision of collective humanity acting environmentally responsibly, when in fact Anthropocene humanity, if characterised in terms of the psychology of an individual, would be 'a self-destructive and self-deluding figure' rather than any kind of rational agent; a kind of 'tragic environmental leviathan' (2015: 14–15).

It is technology itself, both on a fundamental level and on a complex, emergent level that partially forms the incalculable ramifications of these dense tectonic plates of humanity in the Anthropocene. Clark, drawing on Graden R. Allenby and Daniel Sarewitz's *The Techno-Human Condition*, outlines their three contrasting levels of technology. The first is the traditional one, that of the tool to be used as a predetermined end (a plane or car that takes us from A to B); the second means these technologies 'embedded in higher-level technical networks, systems of social and technical control, with additional complications'. These move beyond simple cause and effect and are less predictable, more liable to unexpected failure (as anyone who has experienced the M25 in a traffic jam, or who saw the pan-European airport chaos caused by the 2010 Eyjafjallajökull volcano eruptions can testify). The third level is marked by a 'proliferation of emergent effects' which has 'long exceeded the possibilities of human foresight' (Clark, 2015: 7). So, automobiles are part of a 'technology constellation' which, in the West,

> co-evolved with significant changes in environmental and resource systems; with mass-market consumer capitalism; with individual credit; with behavioural and aesthetic subcultures and stereotypes; with oil spills; with opportunities for, and a sense of, extraordinary human freedom, especially for women who were otherwise trapped in their houses by social and economic patterns.
>
> (Allenby and Sarewitz, 2013: 39)

These Level III effects speak to those 'complex emergent properties that defy our ability to model, predict or even understand them', something that those scientists attempting to model a future climate are all too familiar with (Clark, 2015: 8).

Situating humans in their biological and technological world as Wolfe does might mean that humans are always already posthuman (or perhaps that 'we have never been human'). This does not mean avoiding an interrogation of shifts in biology and technology due to, say, genetic engineering or new pharmacological technologies. These are ways in which the (late) Anthropocene might indeed be 'the time of the new man'.

However, what makes Clark's approach one of the most significant to questions of literature and the environment is the way that he challenges the anthropocentric focus of the humanities themselves. He argues that, for all their environmentalist concerns, ecocritics have too often drawn on a liberal-humanist sensibility focused on the scale of the individual without fully considering the ramifications and challenges of emergent issues such as climate change.

Posthumanism's destabilisation of the human ruptures liberal-humanist conceptions of the self. Sign systems and technically mediated archival-memory systems partly constitute the human, the beliefs, feelings and perceptions that construct any sense of oneself as a freely choosing rational individual. In spite of this fact, we persist with a language of self-realisation and the way that this language begins

> to resonate with the terms of advertising hints at the deep connection between liberal humanist concepts of subjectivity and the workings of consumerism and late capitalism, with their creation of ever new markers of needs and desires or lifestyle choices and so on.
>
> (Clark, 2011: 125)

This highlights a problem with an approach to environmental crisis that emphasises individual experience and individual choice when, in the Anthropocene, the human race has been morphed 'into a nonhuman geo-physical force – a force with which we can never fully associate ourselves' (Ronda, 2014: 103).

The issue is not so much that some ecocriticism is unaware of the complexities of living in a more sustainable manner, but that it is hampered by a 'methodological liberalism' which 'takes the individual attitude as its starting point and then argues for a change in the choices which that individual makes' and therefore will always struggle with the aporia generated by the global problems of the Anthropocene (Clark, 2010: 144). Lidström and Garrard (2014) have usefully highlighted this tendency in some of the most prominent poetry critics interested in environmental questions. Angus Fletcher states that an art 'like poetry that enhances the presence of the individual is bound to be central in showing how we should understand our environmental rights and obligations. The issue then is this, what is my own response to my surrounding?' (2006: 3–4). Similarly, Felstiner claims that the 'essential choices, ticklish for government and industry, fall to us first as individuals in our eating, housing, clothing, childbearing, transport, recreation, voting' (2009: 13).

Burnside's essay on poetry as ecology provides a useful example of these complexities and contradictions from within British poetry. 'Walking is a political act,' he says, 'If I walk to the beach, I do not drive there' (2006: 105). His words here echo Bate's suggestion that 'Rousseauistic motions of revere, of solitude and of walking are conducive' to what Bate calls 'ecopoetic consciousness' (2001: 42). But this perspective can ignore larger contradictions and ironies that undermine its environmentalist intent. Burnside describes

> attuning of one's art to the song of the earth. To do this, it seems, the contemporary poet in a consumer culture needs to step outside that culture, to step away from the narrowly human realm – as delimited by consumerist mores – and connect with something larger and wider. As walkers, out in the open, we are capable of restoring our ecological accords.
>
> (2006: 105)

The trouble is that this description of ecological accordance comes from a period Burnside spent walking and writing in the Finnmark in the Norwegian arctic, hardly a local landscape. Burnside's perambulatory attunement has its own ecological costs which, given the carbon output of flying, potentially dwarf any benefit. This is ultimately a form of ecotourism which, although it may help the poet 'connect with something larger and wider', does not totally step outside 'consumerist mores'. Burnside should not be singled out as a special case; he is hardly alone in finding himself in this ironic situation where the individual is complicit in the deterioration of the thing he or she wishes to defend. Given their likely social, educational and financial positions, it is all-too-common for poets and critics alike to find themselves compromised (not least because our salaries and funding are still often dependent on universities and charitable trusts with investments in the fossil fuel industry).[11] Ecocritics have to face the fact that

> a critic's being a motorist, flying to conferences, eating beefsteak or even buying a particular kind of banana may ultimately be of more real significance than his or her professed political stance [and this] must destabilise modern criticism in bizarre and uncomfortable ways. Its [ecocriticism's] often vociferous liberalism may come to look like an evasion of that other imponderable 'politics' inherent in undiscussed assumptions about personal affluence and lifestyle, conceptions of professional success and mobility and distinctions between the public and the private.
>
> (Clark, 2008: 52)

Clark sees much ecocriticism, and small scale 'green' behaviour, as wrapped up in what he, following Ingolfur Blühdorn, calls 'simulative politics'. Simulative politics deceives individuals into thinking they are taking meaningful environmentalist action when in fact this action is inadequate, partial or even counterproductive. But it is the belief that the action is meaningful that dis- tinguishes simulative politics from 'symbolic politics'. In situations of symbolic politics there is a pressing call for action – 'a striking consensus between political elites and general electorates that it is time to stop talking about things and take decisive action: Cut through the rhetoric! Get down to the issues!' But, as evidenced at events such as the UN talks on climate change in Copenhagen (the 2009 COP), these changes might be largely cosmetic, merely symbolic. Blühdorn explains that 'lip-service',

> spin doctoring, political show-business are terms commonly used to express dissatisfaction with political and economic elites who are not genuinely committed to the values they are advertising, who always deliver less than they are promising, who are deceiving democratic electorates and credulous consumers.
>
> (2007: 252)

Simulative politics is much more insidious. It posits a politics of 'authenticity' against alienation from the natural world and against mere symbolic politics, but in actuality it conceals a belief in the maintenance of a consumer capitalism:

> To describe ecocriticism as engaged in a simulative politics in this context is not to deny that individual readings – of representations of the nonhuman, environmental racism or of bioregional ideals etc. – are often valuable and desirable, like efforts to preserve ecosystems or reform energy infra- structures, but only to acknowledge the inadequacy of their scope in rela- tion to national and global contexts whose practices so overwhelmingly negate them.
>
> (Clark, 2010: 142)

The danger is that such endeavours, by merely 'simulating' an adequate engagement with ecological questions, become inadvertently complicit in perpetuating environmentally destructive behaviours.

Garrard, although often critical of approaches which emerge from decon- struction, has written approvingly of Clark's challenges to ecocriticism, parti- cularly the limits to individual agency which Garrard pithily frames as 'the unbearable lightness of being green' where 'human population simultaneously magnifies the cumulative impact of our actions and dilutes my individual agency' (2013: 185). He also warns of the danger that deconstruction, for him better at identifying problems then resolving them, might sponsor a kind of paralysing pessimism, a risk not dissimilar to what Clark identifies as 'Anthro- pocene Disorder' – 'the emotional correlate of trying to think the implication of trivial actions in scale effects that make everyday life part of a mocking and incalculable enormity' (Clark, 2015: 140).

While questions of pessimism and cynicism will be discussed in Chapter Three, it is worth noting that some of the most interesting recent poetry about the Anthropocene has tuned in to both the critical hyperawareness about the possibility of complicity even within environmentalist activities and the way that this hyperawareness might lead to a paralysing self-critique. Take, for example, Julianna Spahr and Joshua Clover's #*Misanthropocene: 24 Theses* which rejects both the simulative politics of 'Whole Foods [an upmarket international chain selling organic produce] sustainability' and the 'self-reflexive meta-commentary' of academic critique. Moreover, the poem's Twitter-style aesthetics parodies the feebleness of a clicktivism whose outrage only manifests itself online (2014: 4).

An intriguing example from within British innovative poetry is the prose closing section of Jonty Tiplady's 2015 poem, 'The Death of the Marxist Poetry Scene':

> Since those conditions of life must come first, the idea that we cannot save the world until the issue of wage labour has been addressed is there to be questioned. Dude it's snowing on my iPhone 8. You hold a sheet of screen print out in the rain, and I adopt your voice to turn you off. I don't want to condemn what we're doing, but basically we're killing ourselves. Even if wage labour were to act as metonym of all conditions of life there can be no real change in vital sense as long as we still think on a human-on-human scale. But then what? The disconnect would remain between the species and the life that in an unquestioning way it still seizes by right. And then what? The automatic assumption of more life may be the last thing life now needs. Then what? Man as a striving and labouring animal who knows best how to further his own life is precisely what is questionable given the slide of the species towards its own extinction. Que Celan Celan, whatever won't be won't be! But what may be difficult to accept is that we no longer know how to successfully further our own conditions of life. But do I position you in advance? I lap it up, meditate, release, solicit or go. All without exile. At some point you say, 'it's too much to know,' and, quietly, I agree.
>
> (2015: 201)

The poem foregrounds the fact that new technologies mediate both our relationship with the immediate physical world and with global debates about climate. 'Dude, it's snowing on my i-Phone 8' evokes the potential disjunction between smartphone weather-application and what is going on outside, as well as that old canard that global warming is not happening because of localised (cold) weather events. Tiplady asserts the need for a reappraisal of priorities by avant-garde writers whose politics are, like those they critique, sometimes also hamstrung by anthropocentrism, although it evidences itself in very different ways.

Poetics and poetry do evolve, shifting in response to changes in their environments (though one would resist describing this in terms of 'fitness'). Tiplady has elsewhere suggested that Adorno – one of the preeminent guiding influences of the 'Marxist Poetry Scene' and for whom Celan is a key exemplar – is a kind of 'holocenic thinker' ('Preface', Tiplady, 2015: 9). This does not mean, Tiplady makes clear, that we should dismiss Adorno's relevance to the Anthropocene, but that we have to consider some of the ways it problematises his work and the scales and concerns of particular schools and styles of poetry. The singsong of 'Que Celan Celan' pushes back against some of the shibboleths of the Marxist poetry scene, including Adornian aesthetic theory.[12] Reflections on damaged (human) life are modified by reflections on the damage to life-in-general (or at least to the kinds of flora and fauna that humans associate with their species' period of existence).

The poem highlights some of the challenges arising for an (over-)informed critical or poetic subject looking forward (and backward to Celan) in the age of new humans, not least the lure of despair. The 'whatever won't be won't be' underlines an emergent, unpredictable future that is 'not ours to see' (as the Doris Day song goes). Not only unknown, but no longer necessarily marked by some form of human life. How do we read Tiplady's use of 'won't be' to undermine the 'will be' of the original '*que sera sera*'? 'Whatever will be, will be' might here embody a kind of laissez-faire attitude which excuses itself from responsibility either through the eponymous economic theory (i.e. 'the invisible hand of the markets will sort climate change out'), a more general, misanthropic or even apocalyptic fatalism (as in 'we'll see what happens') or the crippling awareness of the limits, or unbearable lightness, of individual agency ('what I do doesn't matter')? It is this last sense that is hinted at in the poem's final line ('it's too much to know') – though whether the speaker's quiet agreement bespeaks genuine acquiescence or masks a defiance is unclear.

Perhaps it is not too fanciful to see Tiplady's 'Que Celan Celan' as also echoing the words of another text that famously probes how a fatalism, founded on a misconstrued sense of the informed individual's own resistance to self-deception, might itself become the mechanism of one's undoing. *Dr Faustus'* despairing insistence that all is hopeless prevents any mitigating action that might still avert disaster:

> If we say that we have no sin,
> We deceive ourselves, and there is no truth in us.
> Why, then, belike we must sin,
> And so consequently die.
> Ay, we must die an everlasting death.
> What doctrine call you this, *Che serà, serà*,
> What will be, shall be
>   (A-text, Marlowe, 1993: 1.i. 43–48)

After all, Faustus faces a damnation where the (forbidden) knowledge that enables pleasure in the short term is famously described as forming waxen wings which are melted by warming heavens. Fittingly, Icarus' parallel downfall essentially stems from misusing a necessary transport technology for leisure purposes.[13] It is not for nothing that the journalist and environmentalist George Monbiot (2007) used *Dr Faustus* as a metaphor for climate change.

Technologies both enhance and hinder humans, particularly in their attempts to act in less environmentally harmful ways. Ecologically aware poetry, including some of the poems in later chapters, has shown that agricultural, industrial, laboratory and military technologies not only shape our environments but modify our senses of embodiment and materiality and impact upon the way we communicate about and conceptualise our world. While posthumanism would argue that the relationship of humans to their world has always been technological, the current conditions of the Anthropocene mean that interrogating humans' technological adaptation to (and of) their environments takes on new poignancy and poses new issues for both politics and poetics. The question of how individuals and societies might adapt (or not) to their changing environments is one of the key issues for the environmental humanities.

Ecologies of mind: communicating ecosystems and systems of communication

The unpredictability of future climate patterns partially rests in a host of positive and negative feedbacks for which any model has to try and account. Probably the most (in)famous description of how these feedbacks work within the regulation of life on Earth is James Lovelock's Gaia hypothesis which describes the Earth as a self-regulating system maintaining the conditions for life (but not necessarily human life): as he put it in *Nature* 'organisms and their material environment evolve as a single coupled system, from which emerges the sustained self-regulation of climate and chemistry' (2003: 769). Crucially though this regulation is not purposeful, 'Self-regulation emerges as the system evolves. No foresight, planning or teleology are involved' (Lovelock, 1991: 11). While I shall address Lovelock in Chapter Three in relation to Mahon's Gaia poems, my book obviously cannot provide much by way of comment on a highly controversial scientific hypothesis that has itself evolved since it came to light in the 1970s. What the figure of Gaia highlights is how myths and models (such as Lovelock's Daisyworld simulation) play out across different types of communication, and the ways their (mis)interpretation often yields unexpected side-effects.

The question of how the level of greenhouse gas emissions might respond to a shifting awareness of a rise in global temperatures indicates one important way that Earth's feedbacks might be considered as not only geophysical but metabiotic, linked to human behaviours and technologies and therefore, to an extent, beliefs and communication. Even in the late 1970s, Lovelock had suggested that advances in technology and science meant that Gaia was becoming 'self-aware' in a way that might help anticipate and avoid environmental problems (see 2000: 138–142). Latour, who has increasingly used Gaia as a means through which to interrogate conceptions of the various agents and feedbacks which shape our planet, has actually staged this aspect of Lovelock's thinking in his own co-written theatrical project *Gaia: Global Circus*. In one scene the actor playing Lovelock says:

> Why did I call it Gaia if there was no intention? So it would stick in people's minds. But it's not a person, no, not a character, either. Just feedback loops that I've grouped together. I've done a bit of tinkering too. You have to dramatize, as you know very well.
>
> Them, down below? Humph, what do you want me to say? They're sleeping, that's already something; the less they do, the better off we are.
>
> (Latour et al., 2011: 9)

The dramatised Lovelock's words highlight several things, including the often-unacknowledged role of metaphor in scientific communication (Gaia was itself a name suggested by Lovelock's novelist friend, William Golding), metaphor's capacity to distort concepts as well as to make them 'stick' and Lovelock's fears about humanity's planetary impact which, as the play suggests elsewhere, sometimes verges on an almost gleeful apocalypticism about the probable fate of them (us) 'down below'.

Also significant are the stage directions. As the actor speaks, his words are 'shown as extended and enlarged powerpoints', dramatising some of the ways that technologies mediate the data and discourses of the sciences as their models and metaphors circulate through classrooms, courtrooms and newswires.[14] Latour's Lovelock embodies what Bruce Clarke describes as a kind of second (or higher) order observation. Humans observe themselves as an emergent part of the Earth's systems: 'we cannot look at Gaia as a planetary whole without looking, self-referentially, at ourselves, a part of Gaia, looking at Gaia' (2012: 59). These observations of the system from within may themselves partially determine the system's future state. Whether they are influenced by Lovelock's notion of Gaia or, more likely, not, humans' conceptions of their local and global environments form part of humanity's adaptation to its environments. Moreover, through their impact on law, policy, research and the use of technology, these conceptualisations participate in the construction of those environments.

The notion that the perception of ecological relations impacts on ecology echoes Carson's warning that our 'attitude toward nature is now critically important simply because we have now acquired a fateful power to alter and destroy nature' ('The Silent Spring of Rachel Carson', 1963). The linking of mind and ecology found one of its most enduring renderings in the work of Gregory Bateson, an important figure within the history of systems thinking and – due to his interest in the relationships between ideas, perception and environment – an influence on ecocriticism.[15]

In his hugely influential 1969 paper 'Pathologies of Epistemology', Bateson emphasised the importance of thinking of survival not in terms of organismal fitness but in the co-evolutionary terms of 'organism plus environment'. While this still suggested a separation of organism and environment on some level rather than 'trans-corporeal' relation or the imbrication of the 'mesh', it nevertheless emphasised relation and context on multiple scales:

> Formerly we thought of a hierarchy of taxa − individual, family line, sub-species, species, etc. − as units of survival. We now see a different hierarchy of units − gene-in-organism, organism-in-environment, ecosystem, etc.

Bateson, as we shall see Hughes doing in the next chapter, conceives of certain conceptualisations of Nature as poorly adapted to the realities of ecology, and consequently as leading to ecologically destructive behaviours:

> Let us now consider what happens when you make the epistemological error of choosing the wrong unit: you end up with the species versus the other species around it or versus the environment in which it operates. Man against nature. You end up, in fact, with Kaneohe Bay polluted, Lake Erie a slimy green mess.

Bad ideas perpetuate and propagate, ramifying in unpredictable ways. In fact, for Bateson the failure to see the potential for the ramification of these errors across (eco)systems might itself have consequences.

> There is an ecology of bad ideas, just as there is an ecology of weeds, and it is characteristic of the system that basic error propagates itself. It branches out like a rooted parasite through the tissues of life, and everything gets into a rather peculiar mess. When you narrow down your epistemology and act on the premise 'What interests me is me, or my organization, or my species,' you chop off consideration of other loops of the loop structure.
>
> ('Pathologies of Epistemology', 2000: 492)

Bateson's argument here highlights two of my concerns. Firstly, as Peter Harries-Jones puts it in his study of Bateson, the issue that in some ways 'the problem of how to transmit ecological ideas in what seems to be an ecologically "good" direction is, in itself, an ecological problem' (1995: 8). Secondly, that one of the key 'errors' in thinking about ecology is the failure to think in terms of mutually affecting entities or in terms of interrelated systems at multiple scales. Bateson foregrounds the dangers of artificial decontextualisation and reductionism while emphasising the importance of thinking about how the human is always embedded in ecosystems and communication systems. If this embeddedness means that human technologies and culture play a part in ecology then, by inference, the arts too are a potential, if marginal, site for feedback or intervention.

Nevertheless, the notion of an ecological function for art has shown itself to be tricky and susceptible to the lures of a renewed organicism. This can be seen in one of the most developed deployments of systems theory in ecocriticism, Hubert Zapf's 'cultural ecology', which draws on Bateson and other ecological systems analysis to suggest that

> literature and other forms of cultural imagination and cultural creativity are necessary in this view to restore continually the richness, diversity, and complexity of those inner landscapes of the mind, the imagination, the emotions, and interpersonal communication that make up the cultural ecosystems of modern humans.
>
> (2009: 852)

For Zapf, literature is a form of cultural ecology that 'critically balances and symbolically articulates what is marginalized, neglected, repressed or excluded' (2006: 64, 66). Expanding on this thought more recently he says that as

> an increasingly autonomized cultural subsystem in its own right, literature, especially since the romantic period, has provided a discursive space for articulating those dimensions of human life that were marginalized, neglected, or repressed in dominant discourses and forms of civilizational organizations (for example, emotions, eros, the body, non-human nature) [... therefore literature resists] technocratic modernization; it restores diversity.
>
> (2014: 56)

Clark argues that Zapf's conceptualisation of ecology is hampered by its being primarily social and moral rather than biological, 'backing up relatively traditional theories of the social function of literature as an anti-doctrinaire agent of social counterbalancing, inclusion and moderation' (2011: 54). While Clark may be right about the predomination of the social over the biological, the aesthetics implicit in Zapf's theory of cultural ecology are more provocative and interesting than Clark implies. However, Zapf's argument is not helped by the way he fails to supplement his ecological axiom that 'everything is connected to everything else' with an adequate interrogation of the nature of these connections, particularly the way different technologies mediate the relations between humans and their environment (2009: 861).

His reading of *Moby Dick* is a case in point. Here the white whale 'represents the extrahuman, precivilizatory world that resists Ahab's civilizatory will to power over creation', a will to power connected to the processes of whaling, which murders to dissect and sell. Zapf's argument for the power of literature to produce 'regeneration' through the 'symbolic restoration of the broken relationship between humanity and elemental nature' fails to think through the specific role of technology in shaping these relations (2006: 64, 66). Zapf's reading sees 'symbolic restoration' in Ishmael's survival after the Pequod's destruction by an uncontrollable energy which resists domination and sig-nification. However, *Moby Dick* also supports the sort of reading I will show Hughes's work as embodying in the next chapter: that rather than constituting the sheer exploitation of Nature, the particular technologies of the hunt (the harpoon, the small chase boats) necessitate a degree of risk and physical inti-macy that connects the whalers to their cetacean quarry. Seen thus, the hunt engenders an acknowledgement of a creaturely corporeal finitude and the energy expenditure that drives a society that is increasingly economically aware but increasingly unaware of what its food, clothes and power-generation cost in blood and (whale) oil.

As Charles Olson puts it, *Moby Dick* offers 'the technic of an industry analysed, scrupulously described' (1967: 27). Melville's attentiveness to the different sorts of technological engagement with the whales – from the taxonomy-rendering pen to the blubber-rending 'boarding sword' – highlights how technologies determine human interactions with Nature, giving rise to different forms of cognition and different senses of embodiment. Where humans are involved we cannot think about ecology without technology. But even when Zapf does engage more directly with specific technologies – such as nuclear concerns in Don DeLillo – he falls back on a vision of art as forging a vague sense of interconnection. He reads the painted warplanes in *Underworld* as representing the 'transforming power of art that reconnects culture to nature, civilizational structures to vital energies of life' (Zapf, 2009: 863). While it is true that the planes become a kind of land art which foreground an interplay between landscape, military technology and individual humans, there is a question as to how much a contemporary ecological consciousness is offered by Zapf's (re) assertions that art can show that humans channel organic energies and are thereby interdependent with Nature. Of course they are; the question is how.

More problematic, and more interesting, than Zapf's exhortations that literature provides ways of recognising that 'everything is connected to everything else' are the aesthetic questions implied by his argument that literature is a form of 'cultural ecology' which 'acts like an ecological principle or ecological energy within the larger system of cultural discourses' and not just a form of culture about ecology – that literature consolidates these discourses in ways that other forms of communication do not (2006: 55). Zapf criticises 'linear conceptual thought' and positions literature as 'a "reintegrative interdiscourse" in which the dichotomies of mind and body, intellect and emotion, culture and nature are over-come' (2009: 865). This sounds very much like aspects of German Romanticism, particularly the work of Schiller for whom, Rigby explains, the aesthetic provided a space 'unique in stimulating and harmonizing all our faculties (the senses and the intellect, reason and imagination, abstract reflection and practical under-standing) in a way that had become impossible in everyday life' (2004: 98). Hence Zapf's claim that literature can restore the 'richness, diversity and com-plexity' of the cultural ecosystem can be seen as echoing not just Bateson's 'ecology of mind' with its ramifying 'ideas' but also an older aesthetic tradition which has a different sort of organic model at its eighteenth-century roots.

Zapf's cultural ecology becomes more interesting if it is thrown into relief against the aesthetic tradition which it appears to echo. As Robert Kaufman argues in his Marxist formulation of (post)Romantic aesthetics, aesthetic experience shapes our cognitive habits after the aesthetic event. He positions the aesthetic as 'both a boot-up disk for conceptual thought as such' and 'as Adorno and others will stress, the engine for new, experimental – because previously nonexistent (and therefore, free of status quo determined) – concepts' (2000: 711). Similarly, for Zapf, the arts 'constitute a kind of experimental field or innovational space because (using Iser's word) they are depragmatized, unlike other forms of discourse such as economy, law, politics, society' (2014: 56).

For Kaufman the thought-experience enacted by literature, particularly by lyric poetry, means that in the 'post-aesthetic moment' there is a possibility for the 'emergent construction of new concepts themselves, not to mention the new social [or indeed ecological] dispensations that could correspond to them' (2006: 107). Reading Zapf's suggestion that literature introduces 'richness, diversity and complexity' in the light of Kaufman's sense of art as facilitating the emergence of new concepts lets the figure of cultural ecology offer something more than what Clark sees as just another formulation of literature as 'anti-doctrinaire agent of social counterbalancing, inclusion and moderation'. But while literature may in(tro)duce new intensities and conceptual possibilities in Zapf's cultural ecosystems, his description of literature as being a 'reintegrative interdiscourse' for the larger system of cultural discourses is problematic and speaks to a broader question about the sorts of claim that one might make for ecocriticism in general.

Zapf sees literature as having 'special potential for the reintegration of different areas of cultural knowledge that are kept separate in other forms of discourse' (2009: 850). His guiding principle here is that thinking ecologically means thinking about connectivity in society as well as in ecosystems. Literature certainly does sometimes bring different discourses together in the same text or, more commonly, formulates concerns that are normally addressed through political, ethical, scientific, legal or economic discourses which are, by their nature, relatively limited or selective in their focus. Their selectiveness means that aspects of reality are often ignored: whether it's the animal body's capacity for suffering or the ecological processes which operate at spatial and temporal scales outside those normally addressed in societal communication. For Zapf, literature counters the rigid conceptuality of other discourses because it is characterised by 'boundary crossing, dehierarchization, interrelating separated spheres and opening abstract conceptual systems towards the multiformity of concrete life processes' so that the 'basic assumptions of prevailing systems of interpretation are "tested"' (2006: 61). The problem here is not so much with his claims for what literature does, but that this is best described, even metaphorically, as 'ecological'.

Zapf does not offer a satisfactory explanation as to why the play of intellect and affect he sees in literary experience *reintegrates* these discourses. In fact, the opposite seems more accurate. The claim that literature opens out 'abstract conceptual systems' is comparable to the argument we find in Kaufman that literature has the potential to enact 'a thought experience which maintains the form of conceptual thought without being beholden to the status quo concepts and their contents' (2006: 100). In other words, for both Zapf and Kaufman (and, I would add, the poets in this book) literature helps the reader to see, or perhaps experience, the limitations of the 'status quo concepts' determined by society and this can be a source of social, political or ecological possibility. But it is therefore hard to claim that literature has 'special potential for the reinte-gration of different areas of cultural knowledge that are kept separate'. As Beer stresses in her analysis of interdisciplinarity, 'forms of knowledge do not readily merge' (1999: 115). The way Zapf positions literature as helping us think across categories and discourses risks forgetting that literature is not a super-system but one of many discourses that function within society and that it has its own forms of conceptuality and ideological baggage. While it may address other discourses it will always do so in a manner that is itself partial and selective. Aesthetic experience is better described not as reintegrating different forms of cultural knowledge within the social whole, but rather as drawing out their incommensurability with each other and with the subject's experience.

Zapf's aesthetics and his sense of a 'cultural ecosystem' suffer from a similar problem to his ecology in that they are built round an axiom that 'everything is connected to everything else' without properly addressing the nature of these connections – whether it's the technological relation of humans to their environment or the interactions between different parts of society. He asserts that, in the 'cultural ecosystem', the 'different areas of cultural knowledge' are 'interdependent with but cannot be reduced to each other' (2009: 861, 850). However, social systems theory argues that different major communicative systems (such as the law, politics, science, the arts, economy) are not just irre-ducible to each other, they are closed to each other in certain essential ways – though they may still affect each other. Both society and ecosystems can be thought of as containing mutually affecting but organisationally closed sub-systems. Perhaps it is in this respect, rather than because in both everything is connected, that society might, very cautiously and with an awareness of all the attendant dangers of spurious holisms, be described as being like an ecosystem.

Contemporary autopoetic systems theory does not bind the human subject to (capitalised, singular) 'Nature' or 'Environment', but actually asks us to think in terms of the different environments of different autopoetic (self-making) systems, and indeed systems within systems. Developed by the biologists Humberto Maturana and Francisco Varela in the 1970s, theories of autopoiesis describe systems which, while open to the environment, are organisationally closed, meaning that they produce the elements that continue to compose them as systems. Maturana and Varela's original example was living cells which 'pro-duce molecules such that (i) through their interactions [they] generate and participate recursively in the same network of reactions which produced them, and (ii) realize the cell as a material unity' (Varela et al., 1974: 188). The organisms which contain these cells can also be described as autopoetic and operationally closed, as can certain other systems within them. Cary Wolfe explains that such systems are

> both open and closed as the very condition of possibility for their existence (open on the level of structure to energy flows, environmental perturbations, and the like, but closed on the level of self-referential organization [...]).
>
> (2009: xiv–xv)

What this means is that, while autopoetic systems may respond to triggers in their environment they do so by continuing in the same 'network of reactions'. For example, the immune system does not 'function like a military camp', sending out specific antigens to fight pathogens. Rather it seeks to preserve the integrity of its own network of 'antibodies and molecules' so that although it responds to triggers in its environment the triggers do not 'define the system' or its response (Moeller, 2006: 15). They merely irritate the system, causing a shift in antibody levels determined by the system's own internal organisation. Bruce Clarke has pointed out that the operation of autopoetic systems nullifies the notion that Gaia theory (with which Varela saw his work as having points of contact) constitutes some sort of super-regulatory programme: there is no 'holistic totalization and specious unification [...] nothing and no one controls these systems' (2012: 73).

Recent syntheses of systems theory, literature and ecology, such as those of Wolfe, Clarke and Bergthaller have built on the work of the sociologist Niklas Luhmann to show how autopoiesis operates in both biological and metabiotic systems. Luhmann, Bergthaller explains, radicalised autopoiesis, so that

> not only biological organisms, but the individual consciousnesses which some of the latter 'possess' and society as a whole can be described in these [autopoetic] terms, although the operations through which they reproduce themselves do not involve biochemical components.
>
> (2011: 233)

Luhmann does not see society as formed of individuals but of communicative events – it is these events that are the components of the self-reproducing autopoetic subsystems which make up modern society. Some of these systems are major 'function systems' (such as the legal system, the science system, the economic system, the political system). These larger systems 'float on a sea of small-scale subsystems that are continuously newly built and then dissolved' and between these more anarchic, small-scale interactions and the larger systems exist 'organizations' which often have evolved in relation to one of the function systems (e.g. political parties, educational institutions, campaign groups, corporations) (Bergthaller, 2011: 255). It is worth noting that the 'individual human being belongs to each of these functionally differentiated subsystems for only short periods of time with only limited aspects of his person depending on his respective role as a voter, pupil, reader, patient, or litigant' (Dietrich Schwanitz cited in Wolfe, 2009: 115).

In 1986's *Ökologische Kommunikation* (*Ecological Communication*), Luhmann turned his complex theory of social systems to the question of how ecological issues were communicated within society. While his examples have dated somewhat (they are mostly about nuclear power and the German green party), his analysis of why ecological issues often fail to gain traction within society still has significant implications for ecocriticism and for the sort of 'cultural ecology' imagined by Zapf.

As Hans-Georg Moeller explains, each of Luhmann's 'function systems' forms the intrasocial environment of the other system and therefore they 'cannot be supervised or regulated by any social super-system' (2006: 24). Each of the function systems will respond to ecological issues through perpetuating their own operations – the science system might devise new experiments, the legal system might apply planning and conservation laws differently, the economic system might decide to start including ecological costs in its operations. But the function systems will struggle to deal with the pan-social challenges engendered by ecological concerns; their responses will not be coordinated, controllable or proportional. Instead there will be 'unorganized resonance' between systems – 'intentions have unintended results while good intentions have bad side-effects'. Even the political system cannot supervise changes, especially due to 'the lack of an effective international, legal regulation of the transformation of ecological problems into national politics' (Luhmann, 1989: 124, 91). Christian Borch highlights the limits of political environmental control by applying Luhmann's framework to contemporary concerns about industrial emissions. The political system may, say, introduce strict emission regulation, but

> strict emission regulation in Europe may induce corporations to move their production to less regulated regions and countries with negative effects on employment rates in Europe and with no sure net ecological gains [... the system] can communicate about these dangers [e.g. by introducing more legislation], but it is more probable that its communica-tion will have unanticipated effects within society (due to intersystem relations) than it will improve society's relation to its environment.
>
> (2011: 105)

Luhmann's sobering approach asks how the realities of contemporary ecology are registered at a societal level as well as at the level of individual consciousness or, as Luhmann calls it, the level of the individual 'psychic system' (which Luhmann describes as being structurally coupled to social systems through language). Even if, as early ecocriticism asserted, hearts and minds can be won by turning awareness back toward Nature or landscape, ecological consciousness now requires looking at how organisations and function systems communicate about ecological problems. Luhmann asks us to think about how these mutually affecting systems irritate each other in uncoordinated and unpredictable ways across multiple scales which also means thinking about how systems observe their own, and other systems', operations (second order observation). Hence, for Bergthaller, ecocriticism's value does not lie in being 'the academic wing of the environmental movement' nor in 'general consciousness raising or the recruitment of new personnel'. Rather it lies in its capacity to 'observe how environmentalism (or any other organization or social system) observes' and in doing so uncover blind-spots, contradictions and predilections (2011: 227).

At the back of Wolfe's systems theoretical approach to disciplinarity is a 'seemingly simple point', namely that disciplines (which are educational sub-systems) 'do not derive their constitutive protocols from their objects of attention. Quite the contrary, disciplines constitute their objects through their practices, theoretical commitments, and methodological procedures' (2009: 108). In other words, the different disciplines' various approaches to questions of ecology, biology and technology in the Anthropocene are ultimately dictated not by the shifts in their physical or social environments, but by the specific ways those disciplines, each via their own practices and methodologies, will identify and attend to those shifts.[16] The same might be said of poetry. The reason poetry provides interesting ways of interrogating the communication and perception of ecology by individuals and social systems is not just because of some poems' thematic engagement with ecological issues. It is also because the practices, aesthetics, theoretical commitments and methodological procedures of different kinds of poetry produce contrasting perspectives and positions through the ways they encourage us to think and read. Form is not an optional add-on to an ecological awareness: form helps generate and organise a poem's rendering of ecology.

Poetics in the Anthropocene

> I am suspicious of the term 'ecopoetry': either it's redundant, reduplicating the 'eco' already built into the ecology of words that, presumably, is poetry's business, or it instrumentalizes (i.e. pigeonholes) poetry in a way that's distasteful to any poet worth paying attention to. I strongly reject the perverse aim of an ecopoetry that would somehow turn us away from the tasks of poetry, to more important or urgent concerns. (Though I sympathize with the desire to get readers to look up from the page and pay attention to their surroundings.)
>
> – Jonathan Skinner (2005: 127)

Skinner, the founder of the journal *ecopoetics*, flags up some of the ongoing challenges relevant to the varied poetries that want to address ecology in the Anthropocene. In particular, he acknowledges the limiting association with an active environmentalism and its difficult relationship to the 'tasks of poetry', tasks which here imply modes of reading, thinking and concentration rather than the mere purveying of any environmentalist message. Indeed, if we are entering a period where the Anthropocene is a widely acknowledged fact, perhaps the time will arrive when ecopoetics will become, simply, poetics.

At present the situation is closer to Tarlo's suggestion that 'Whichever way the arguments about ecopoetics go, the term does always assume an affiliation with the ecological movement which we cannot assume is held by all the poets who write about landscape and locality' (Tarlo, 2009: 6). What Tarlo does not acknowledge here is the fact that what she calls 'the ecological movement' (by which I take it she means something approximating to 'environmentalism') is itself far from homogenous, and it is probably not best thought of as a cohesive entity. Ecological movements are sometimes more conservative, and indeed sometimes more radical, than contemporary poetry's warring clans (themselves hardly homogenous). The variety of concerns associated with the Anthropocene – species extinction, pollution, environmental justice, climate change and so on – erupt in different ways for different individuals and groups at different moments. As poetry and criticism have evolved in response to these challenges (not always with a sense of agreement on, or even an awareness of, the Anthropocene as a concept) they have faced, as I have suggested, a host of related issues. These include the tension between local and non-local, (post)humans' originary technicity, non-human agency, and the relationship between the different social systems which partially determine societal responses to the hard questions provoked by any sense of the Anthropocene.

Whether used by critics or by the poets themselves, labels like 'post-pastoral', or 'radical landscape poetry' or, most commonly, 'ecopoetics' identify ways of responding to questions of ecology (and normally of biology and technology too) from different although often-overlapping positions. But the various poetic tribes, not to mention parts of the academy, can be thought of in terms of systems theory, observing the important changes in their physical and social environments in the Anthropocene in different ways. Through various communicative events (like chapbooks, poetry readings, conference papers and academic articles) they form autopoetic communicative subsystems which, frustratingly, are sometimes not just organisationally closed to each other (the condition of their possibility), but wilfully neglectful of each other too.

Nevertheless, 'ecopoetics' is a useful signpost, and much of the most informed, exciting and significant contemporary poetry about the Anthropocene coalesces under its banner. But even at its most ecumenical, the term 'ecopoetics' implicitly still bears within it a kind of thematic limit, even if its boundaries remain nebulous. In other words, the term is not always the best way to discuss the many poems that fall outside current schemas of ecopoetics, that initially appear not to be primarily about ecology at all, but which are nevertheless important instances of poetry written about the Anthropocene. While much of what the poets in the rest of this study write is, by Skinner's reckoning, 'ecopoetics' (and by Gifford's 'post-pastoral' or by Tarlo's 'radical landscape poetry'), I do not think that it is ultimately helpful to label it as such. Those terms do not encompass these poets' complex, various and sometimes tangential engagements with ecology, technology and biology, nor the way their ecologically orientated poems are related to other parts of their work which are not easily subsumed by Skinner's broad description of ecopoetics, let alone the more limiting, if also interesting, definitions offered by Bristow, Bate and others. Although important, ecopoetics is only one of multiple critical/creative systems for exploring and engaging with the Anthropocene. Perhaps this is why Skinner desires his journal *ecopoetics* to be a 'site for poetic attention and exchange, where many different kinds of making (not just poetry, or not even just writing, and certainly not just "ecopoetry") can come to inform and be informed' (2005: 128).

So, what do we talk about when we talk about 'poetry and the Anthropocene'? Systems theory, although not known for its aesthetic sensibility, has a special interest in the density and complexity of poetic communication, particularly the way poetry uses the relationship between the sensual/perceptual and the semantic/denotational to exploit self-referentiality and engender particular reading strategies. As Luhmann puts it, poetry 'appeals to perception, not to thinking'; 'sounds, meanings and rhythms conspire' to generate 'contextual dependencies, ironic references and paradoxes, all of which refer back to the text that produces these effects'. Author and reader 'must leave behind the linearity of the text and apprehend its structure in a circular manner; they must be able to take apart the network of multiple circles that makes up a text' (2000: 124).

Of course we do not need systems theory to tell us that poetry's formal qualities mean that our (re)readings of poems are often non-linear. However, I am not primarily concerned with whether systems theory offers a fertile approach to poetry, but rather why poetry might be particularly useful in thinking about the biological, ecological and social systems important to the Anthropocene – not least in its capacity to foreground, interrogate and mutate what Kaufman calls the 'status-quo concepts' determined by different social systems.[17] If Bergthaller is right that ecocriticism can usefully 'observe how environmentalism (or any other organization or social system) observes', then on a comparable note it is worth thinking about how poetry demands a focused and circular thinking. In a more concentrated manner than other types of text, poetry is constantly interrogating and playing with its own ways and means, the proclivities and patterns associated with different forms, dictions, modes of address, sets of imagery, metaphors and thematic traditions, particularly the ways we conceptualise and perceive what is still normally called Nature. More broadly, poetry can explore the differences between the ways individuals and social systems communicate, observe and communicate about observation. Poetry makes (self-)awareness of (self-)perception part of its processes. The most interesting British and Irish poetry engaging with the Anthropocene embodies the fact that, just as good ecocriticism is not agitprop, ecologically orientated art does not simply consist of ornamenting an environmentalist message; it helps explore why and how communication about ecology, biology and technology might be affecting or (in)effective.

Ecologically orientated systems theory is not about arguing how, in a facile sense, literature and other sorts of communication have an ecological force because everything is connected. Instead it highlights how biological, psychic and communicative systems register and respond to changes in their environment, and how some systems may observe their own (or other systems') operations. Poetry can explore how, in the Anthropocene, the ways we speak, write think and act are part of the (unpredictable) interrelated processes that constitute local and global ecosystems. It provides ways of conceiving the relations between (human) organisms and their environments at the level of communication and cognition as well as emissions.

Notes

1 Another reading, of Earth as an almost Winnicottian holding environment is available, but this is problematised by the notion of 'housekeeping'.
2 For a discussion of Jamie and also Burnside's poetry in an ecological context, see Louisa Gairn's enlightening *Ecology and Modern Scottish Literature* (2008). Discussions on the practices and personalities of the 'new' Nature Writing can be found in the special issue of *Green Letters*, 17 (1) (2013).
3 Of the poets covered in *Poetry and Geography*, Jo Shapcott should be of particular interest to readers interested in poetry and climate change. Shapcott is one of the writers and artists – others include Lemn Sissay, Ian McEwan, Rachel Whiteread and Jarvis Cocker – who have been on one of the Cape Farewell Project's voyages to the arctic that are designed to bring together scientists and artists interested in climate change.
4 For an interesting analysis of Gillian Clarke's ecology in relation to the Welsh landscape and Welsh poetry more generally see Matthew Jarvis (2008). In addition, Jarvis's book addresses the work of Robert Minhinnick, another contemporary Welsh poet who, as John Redmond (2013) has also shown, offers an intriguing way of thinking about environmentalist questions.
5 In response to Tarlo's complaints about the marginalisation of the 'innovative', Astley brusquely states that 'I wasn't persuaded to correct this imbalance in *Earth Shattering*' (2007: 18). Interestingly it is Gifford, whose position Tarlo has criticised as favouring the 'mainstream', who rightly criticises Astley for the unjustified exclusion (2011: 9).
6 There is room for the inclusion of actor, green(ish) goblin and writer James Franco's underwhelming poem 'I was Born', though this can hopefully be put down to reasons of publicity rather than editorial taste.
7 For an extended discussion of Boland in the light of Irish writing and ecocriticism see Wenzell (2009).
8 Union Carbide would also be implicated in the Bhopal chemical leak, an event which has been covered by critics interested in postcolonialism and ecocriticism such as Rob Nixon, in particular in relation to Indra Sinha's novel *Animal's People*. See Nixon (2011: 44–59).
9 Indeed, the idea of alienation is itself problematic. As the philosopher Simon Hailwood puts it: 'The common assumption that alienation is always negative should be abandoned: alienation can play a positive critical role in environmental contexts by expressing, through the ideas of estrangement and relinquishing possession, the negation of domination' (2012: 898).
10 John Kinsella has written some of the more interesting poetry and criticism about herbicides and pesticides (2008: 215–220).
11 It should be noted that The University of St Andrews, where Burnside is based at the time of writing, has a sustainable investment policy.
12 See Tiplady (2012) for a more detailed discussion of his approach to Marxist poetic thought.
13 Compare Marlowe (1993: Prologue, lines 21–22): 'His waxen wings did mount above his reach, | And melting heaven conspired his overthrow'. Icarus is the central model for another contemporary British poet who fuses prose and poetry in her writing about climate change, Lucy Burnett (2015).

14 Richard Grusin has suggested that the communicative systems operate in such a way that not only are events associated with climate change (say, Hurricane Katrina) remediated by different technologies, but 'potentialities, future events or occurrences which may or may not ever happen' might be said to be premediated (2010: 59).

15 See, for example, Conley (1997), Iovino (2010) and Sussman (2012). Bateson has also been a key influence on biosemiotics, an increasingly significant field for ecocriticism, particularly the work of Wendy Wheeler who, in a manner not too dissimilar to Hughes, positions ideas as cultural organisms, which 'exert evolutionary pressures' (2009: 21).

16 Wolfe points out that one interesting ramification of seeing disciplines in terms of systems is that it is people, rather than disciplines, that participate in interdisciplinarity (see Wolfe, 2009: 115).

17 For an interesting example of how systems theory can be used to explore questions of perception and self-reference see the discussion of Wallace Stevens in Chapter 10 of Wolfe (2009).

References

Alaimo, Stacy. 2010. *Bodily Natures: Science, Environment, and the Material Self.* Bloomington: Indiana University Press.

Alexander, Neal, and David Cooper. 2013. 'Introduction'. In *Poetry and Geography: Space and Place in Post-War Poetry*, edited by Neal Alexander and David Cooper. Liverpool: Liverpool University Press. 1–19.

Allenby, Braden R., and Daniel Sarewitz. 2013. *The Techno-Human Condition.* Cambridge, MA: MIT Press.

Astley, Neil, ed. 2007. *Earth Shattering: Ecopoems.* Tarset, Northumberland: Bloodaxe.

Attridge, Derek. 2013. *Moving Words: Forms of English Poetry.* Oxford: Oxford University Press.

Bate, Jonathan. 1991. *Romantic Ecology.* London: Routledge.

Bate, Jonathan. 2001. *The Song of the Earth.* London: Picador.

Bate, Jonathan. 2002. 'Eco Laurels'. *The Guardian*, 23 November. Available at: http://www.theguardian.com/books/2002/nov/23/featuresreviews.guardianreview8 [accessed 25 June 2015].

Bateson, Gregory. 2000. *Steps to an Ecology of Mind: Collected Essays in Anthropology, Psychiatry, Evolution, and Epistemology.* Chicago: University of Chicago Press.

Beer, Gillian. 1999. *Open Fields: Science in Cultural Encounter.* New York: Oxford University Press.

Bennett, Jane. 2010. *Vibrant Matter: A Political Ecology of Things.* Durham, NC: Duke University Press.

Bergthaller, Hannes. 2011. 'Cybernetics and Social Systems Theory'. In *Ecocritical Theory: New European Approaches*, edited by Axel Goodbody and Kate Rigby. Charlottesville: University of Virginia Press. 217–229.

Bergthaller, Hannes. 2014. 'Limits of Agency: Notes on the Material Turn from a Systems-Theoretical Perspective'. In *Material Ecocriticism*, edited by Serenella Iovino and Serpil Oppermann. Bloomington: Indiana University Press. 37–50.

Bergthaller, Hannes, Robert Emmett, Adeline Johns-Putra, Agnes Kneitz, Susanna Lidström, Shane McCorristine, Isabel Ramos, Dana Phillips, Kate Rigby, and Lily Robin. 2014. 'Mapping Common Ground: Ecocriticism, Environmental History, and the Environmental Humanities'. *Environmental Humanities* 5: 261–276.

Bloomfield, Mandy. 2015. 'Unsettling Sustainability: The Poetics of Discomfort'. *Green Letters* 19(1): 21–35.

Blühdorn, Ingolfur. 2007. 'Sustaining the Unsustainable: Symbolic Politics and the Politics of Simulation'. *Environmental Politics* 16(2): 251–275.

Boes, Tobias, and Kate Marshall. 2014. 'Writing the Anthropocene: An Introduction'. *The Minnesota Review* 83: 60–72.

Borch, Christian. 2011. *Niklas Luhmann*. London: Taylor & Francis.

Bradley, Arthur, and Louis Armand. 2006. 'Thinking Technicity'. In *Technicity*, edited by Louis Armand and Arthur Bradley. Prague: Litteraria Pragensia. 1–14.

Bristow, Tom. 2015. *The Anthropocene Lyric: An Affective Geography of Poetry, Person, Place*. Basingstoke: Palgrave Macmillan.

Bryson, J. Scott. 2002. 'Introduction'. In *Ecopoetry: A Critical Introduction*, edited by J. Scott Bryson. Salt Lake City: University of Utah Press. 1–13.

Buell, Lawrence. 2005. *The Future of Environmental Criticism*. Oxford: Blackwell.

Burnett, Lucy. 2015. *Through the Weather Glass: & What Icarus Found There*. Merseyside: Knives Forks and Spoons Press.

Burnside, John. 2006. 'A Science of Belonging: Poetry as Ecology'. In *Contemporary Poetry and Contemporary Science*, edited by Robert Crawford. Oxford: Oxford University Press. 91–106.

Burnside, John, and Maurice Riordan, eds. 2004. *Wild Reckoning: An Anthology Provoked by Rachel Carson's Silent Spring*. London: Calouste Gulbenkian Foundation.

Chakrabarty, Dipesh. 2009. 'The Climate of History: Four Theses'. *Critical Inquiry* 35(2): 197–222.

Clark, Timothy. 2008. 'Towards A Deconstructive Environmental Criticism'. *Oxford Literary Review* 30(1): 45–68.

Clark, Timothy. 2010. 'Some Climate Change Ironies: Deconstruction, Environmental Politics and the Closure of Ecocriticism'. *Oxford Literary Review* 32(1): 131–149.

Clark, Timothy. 2011. *The Cambridge Introduction to Literature and the Environment*. Cambridge: Cambridge University Press.

Clark, Timothy. 2015. *Ecocriticism on the Edge: The Anthropocene as a Threshold Concept*. London: Bloomsbury Academic.

Clarke, Bruce. 2012. 'Autopoiesis and the Planet'. In *Impasses of the Post-Global*, edited by Henry Sussman. Ann Arbor, MI: Open Humanities Press. 58–76.

Clover, Joshua, and Juliana Spahr. 2014. *#Misanthropocene: 24 Theses*. Oakland: Commune Editions. Also available at: https://communeeditions.files.wordpress.com/2014/08/misanthropocene_web_v2_final.pdf [accessed 21 May 2015].

Conley, Verena A. 1997. *Ecopolitics: The Environment in Poststructuralist Thought*. London: Taylor & Francis.

Derrida, Jacques. 1991. *Of Spirit: Heidegger and the Question*. Chicago: University of Chicago Press.

Derrida, Jacques. 1995. *Points …: Interviews, 1974–1994*. Stanford, CA: Stanford University Press.

Felstiner, John. 2009. *Can Poetry Save the Earth?* New Haven, CT: Yale University Press.

Fletcher, Angus. 2006. *A New Theory for American Poetry*. Cambridge, MA: Harvard University Press.

Gairn, Louisa. 2008. *Ecology and Modern Scottish Literature*. Edinburgh: Edinburgh University Press.

Gander, Forrest, and John Kinsella. 2012. *Redstart: An Ecological Poetics*, Iowa City: University of Iowa Press.

Gane, Nicholas. 2006. 'When We Have Never Been Human, What Is to Be Done? Interview with Donna Haraway'. *Theory, Culture & Society* 23 (7–8): 135–158.

Garrard, Greg. 2010. 'Ecocriticism'. *The Year's Work in Critical and Cultural Theory* 18(1): 1–35.

Garrard, Greg. 2013. 'The Unbearable Lightness of Green: Air Travel, Climate Change and Literature'. *Green Letters* 17(2): 175–188.

Gifford, Terry. 1995. *Green Voices: Understanding Contemporary Nature Poetry*. Manchester: Manchester University Press.

Gifford, Terry. 1999. *Pastoral*. London: Routledge.

Gifford, Terry. 2011. *Green Voices: Understanding Contemporary Nature Poetry*. Second edition. Nottingham: Critical, Cultural and Communications Press.

Glotfelty, Cheryll. 1996. 'Introduction'. In *The Ecocriticism Reader*, edited by Harold Fromm and Cheryl Glotfelty. Athens, GA: University of Georgia Press.

Grusin, Richard A. 2010. *Premediation: Affect and Mediality after 9/11*. Basingstoke: Palgrave Macmillan.

Hailwood, Simon. 2012. 'Alienations and Natures'. *Environmental Politics* 21(6): 882–900.

Haraway, Donna J. 1990. *Simians, Cyborgs, and Women: The Reinvention of Nature*. New York: Routledge.

Heidegger, Martin. 1977. *The Question Concerning Technology, and Other Essays*. Translated by William Lovitt. New York: Harper and Row.

Heise, Ursula K. 2006. 'The Hitchhiker's Guide to Ecocriticism'. *PMLA* 121(2): 503–516.

Heise, Ursula K. 2008. *Sense of Place and Sense of Planet*. New York: Oxford University Press.

Howarth, Peter. 2013. '"Water's Soliloquy": Soundscape and Environment in Alice Oswald's Dart'. In *Poetry and Geography: Space and Place in Post-War Poetry*, edited by Neal Alexander and David Cooper. Liverpool: Liverpool University Press. 190–203.

Hume, Angela. 2012. 'Imagining Ecopoetics: An Interview with Robert Hass, Brenda Hillman, Evelyn Reilly, and Jonathan Skinner'. *Interdisciplinary Studies in Literature and Environment* 19(4): 751–766.

Inwood, Michael. 1999. *A Heidegger Dictionary*. Oxford: Blackwell.

Iovino, Serenella. 2010. 'Ecocriticism, Ecology of Mind, and Narrative Ethics: A Theoretical Ground of Ecocriticism as Educational Practice'. *ISLE* 14(4): 759–762.

Jarvis, Matthew. 2008. *Welsh Environments in Contemporary Poetry*. Cardiff: University of Wales Press.

Kaufman, Robert. 2000. 'Red Kant, or the Persistence of the Third "Critique" in Adorno and Jameson'. *Critical Inquiry* 26(4): 682–724.

Kaufman, Robert 2006. 'Lyric's Expression: Musicality, Conceptuality, Critical Agency'. In *Adorno and Literature*, edited by David Cunningham and Nigel Mapp. New York; London: Continuum. 99–116

Kerridge, Richard. 2012. 'Contemporary Ecocriticism between Red and Green'. In *Ecology and the Literature of the British Left: The Red and the Green*, edited by John Rignall and H. Gustav Klaus. Farnham: Ashgate Publishing. 17–32.

Kinsella, John. 2008. *Disclosed Poetics: Beyond Landscape and Lyricism*. Manchester: Manchester University Press.

Kirkpatrick, Kathryn. 2010. 'Between Country and City: Paula Meehan's Ecofeminist Poetics'. In *Out of the Earth: Ecocritical Readings of Irish Texts*, edited by Christine Cusick. Cork: Cork University Press. 108–126.

Knickerbocker, Scott. 2012. *Ecopoetics: The Language of Nature, the Nature of Language*. Amhurst, MA: University of Massachusetts Press.

Latour, Bruno, Chloé Latour, and Frédérique Ait-Touati. 2011. '*Cosmocoloss: Global Climate Tragi-Comedy*'. Translated by Julie Rose. Availible at http://www.bruno-latour.fr/sites/default/files/downloads/KOSMOKOLOS-TRANSLATION-GB.pdf [accessed 20 September 2015].

Lidström, Susanna. 2015. *Nature, Environment and Poetry: Ecocriticism and the Poetics of Seamus Heaney and Ted Hughes*. Abingdon; New York: Routledge.

Lidström, Susanna, and Greg Garrard. 2014. '"Images Adequate to Our Predicament": Ecology, Environment and Ecopoetics'. *Environmental Humanities* 5: 35–53.

Lovelock, James. 1991. *Gaia: The Practical Science of Planetary Medicine*. Oxford: Oxford University Press.

Lovelock, James 2000. *Gaia: A New Look at Life on Earth*. Reissued and corrected edition. Oxford: Oxford University Press.

Lovelock, James 2003. 'Gaia: The Living Earth'. *Nature* 426(6968): 769–770.

Luhmann, Niklas. 1989. *Ecological Communication*. Translated by John Bednarz. Cambridge: Polity.

Luhmann, Niklas. 2000. *Art as a Social System*. Translated by Eva M. Knodt. Stanford, CA: Stanford University Press.

Marlowe, Christopher. 1993. *Doctor Faustus*. Edited by David Bevington and Eric Rasmussen. Manchester: Manchester University Press.

McKusick, James. 2000. *Green Writing: Romanticism and Ecology*. New York: Palgrave Macmillan.

Meehan, Paula. 2009. *Painting Rain*. Manchester: Carcanet.

Moeller, Hans-Georg. 2006. *Luhmann Explained: From Souls to Systems*. Chicago: Open Court.

Monbiot, George. 2007. *Heat: How We Can Stop the Planet Burning*. London: Penguin.

Morton, Timothy. 2007. *Ecology without Nature*. Cambridge, MA: Harvard University Press.

Morton, Timothy. 2010. *The Ecological Thought*. Cambridge, MA: Harvard University Press.

Nixon, Rob. 2011. *Slow Violence and the Environmentalism of the Poor*. Cambridge, MA: Harvard University Press.

Olson, Charles. 1967. *Call Me Ishmael: A Study of Melville*. London: Jonathan Cape.

Oswald, Alice, ed. 2005. *The Thunder Mutters: 101 Poems for the Planet*. London: Faber & Faber.

Harries-Jones, Peter. 1995. *A Recursive Vision: Ecological Understanding and Gregory Bateson*. Toronto: University of Toronto Press.

Phillips, Dana. 2003. *The Truth of Ecology*. New York: Oxford University Press.

Randolph, Jody Allen. 2009. 'New Ireland Poetics: The Ecocritical Turn in Contemporary Irish Women's Poetry'. *Nordic Irish Studies* 8: 57–70.

Rasula, Jed. 2002. *This Compost: Ecological Imperatives in American Poetry*. Athens, GA: University of Georgia Press.

Redmond, John. 2013. *Poetry and Privacy: Questioning Public Interpretations of Contemporary British and Irish Poetry*. Bridgend: Seren.

Reilly, Evelyn. 2010. 'Eco-Noise and the Flux of Lux'. In *((eco(lang)(uage(reader))*, edited by Brenda Iijima. Brooklyn, NY; Callicoon, NY; Lebanon, NH: Portable Press at Yo-Yo Labs; Nightboat Books. 255–274.

Rigby, Kate. 2004. *Topographies of the Sacred: The Poetics of Place in European Romanticism*. Charlottesville, VA: University of Virginia Press.

Ronda, Margaret. 2014. 'Anthropogenic Poetics'. *The Minnesota Review* (83): 102–111.

Sammells, Neil, and Richard Kerridge. 1998. 'Introduction'. In *Writing the Environment: Ecocriticism and Literature*, edited by Neil Sammells and Richard Kerridge. London: Zed Books. 1–9.

Scigaj, L.M. 1996. 'Contemporary Ecological and Environmental Poetry Différance or Référance?' *Interdisciplinary Studies in Literature and Environment* 3(2): 1–25.

Serres, Michel. 1995. *The Natural Contract*. Translated by Elizabeth MacArthur and William Paulson. Ann Arbor, MI: University of Michigan Press.

Shabbir, Nabeelah, Eva Krysiak, Alex Breuer, Jason Phipps, Xaquín GV. 2015. '"Our Melting, Shifting, Liquid World": Celebrities Read Poems on Climate Change'. *The Guardian*, 20 November. Available at: http://www.theguardian.com/environment/ng-interactive/2015/nov/20/our-melting-shifting-liquid-world-celebrities-read-poems-on-climate-change [accessed 30 December 2015].

Skinner, Jonathan. 2001. 'Editor's Statement'. *ecopoetics* 1: 5–8.

Skinner, Jonathan 2005. 'Statement for "New Nature Writing" Panel at 2005 AWP (Vancouver)'. *ecopoetics* 4/5: 127–129.

Slovic, Scott. 2010. 'The Third Wave of Ecocriticism: North American Reflections of the Current Phase of the Discipline'. *Ecozon@* 1(1): 4–10.

Snyder, Gary. 1969. *Earth House Hold: Technical Notes & Queries to Fellow Dharma Revolutionaries*. New York: New Directions.

Sprague, Jane. 2008. 'Ecopoetics: Drawing on Calfskin Vellum'. *How2* 3(2). Available at: https://www.asu.edu/pipercwcenter/how2journal/vol_3_no_2/ecopoetics/essays/sprague.html [accessed 22 July 2014].

Stiegler, Bernard. 1998. *Technics and Time, 1: The Fault of Epimetheus*. Translated by Richard Beardworth and George Collins. Stanford, CA: Stanford University Press.

Sussman, Henry. 2012. 'Auto-Immunity'. In *Impasses of the Post-Global*, edited by Henry Sussman. Ann Arbor, MI: Open Humanities Press. 251–274.

Tarlo, Harriet. 2007. 'Radical Landscapes: Experiment and Environment in Contemporary Poetry'. *Jacket* 32. Availible at: http://jacketmagazine.com/32/p-tarlo.shtml [acessed 22 May 2015].

Tarlo, Harriet. 2008. 'Women and Ecopoetics: An Introduction in Context'. *How2* 3(2). Availible at: https://www.asu.edu/pipercwcenter/how2journal/vol_3_no_2/ecopoetics/introstatements/tarlo_intro.html [accessed 22 June 2015].

Tarlo, Harriet. 2009. 'A Preview of The Ground Aslant: Radical Landscape Poetry (Forthcoming, Shearsman Books, 2010)'. *English* 58(222): 192–198.

Tarlo, Harriet, ed. 2011. *The Ground Aslant: An Anthology of Radical Landscape Poetry*. Bristol: Shearsman Books.

'The Silent Spring of Rachel Carson'. 1963. *CBS Reports*. 3 April.

Tiplady, Jonty. 2012. 'OK Kosmos'. The Claudius App 2. Available at: http://thecla udiusapp.com/2-tiplady-ok-kosmos.html [accessed 2 January 2016].

Tiplady, Jonty, ed. 2015. 'Confuse Your Hunger'. Available at: http://www.con fuseyourhunger.com/Confuse%20Your%20Hunger.pdf [accessed 22 September 2015). Print version forthcoming in 2016.

Varela, F.G., H.R. Maturana and R. Uribe. 1974. 'Autopoiesis: The Organization of Living Systems, its Characterization and a Model'. *Biosystems* 5(4): 187–196.

Watson, Robert. 2014. 'Shadows of the Renaissance'. In *The Oxford Handbook of Ecocriticism*, edited by Greg Garrard. New York: Oxford University Press. 40–59.

Wenzell, Tim. 2009. *Emerald Green: An Ecocritical Study of Irish Literature*. Newcastle upon Tyne: Cambridge Scholars Publishing.

Wheeler, Wendy. 2009. 'Creative Evolution: A Theory of Cultural Sustainability'. *Communication, Politics & Culture* 42(1): 19–41.

Wolfe, Cary. 2009. *What Is Posthumanism?* Minneapolis: University of Minnesota Press.

Yeung, Heather H. 2015. *Spatial Engagement with Poetry*. New York: Palgrave.

Zapf, Hubert. 2006. *Nature in Literary and Cultural Studies*, edited by Catrin Gersdorf and Sylvia Mayer. Amsterdam: Rodopi. 49–70.

Zapf, Hubert. 2009. 'Literary Ecology and the Ethics of Texts'. *New Literary History* 39(4): 847–868.

Zapf, Hubert. 2014. 'Creative Matter and Creative Mind: Cultural Ecology and Literary Creativity'. In *Material Ecocriticism*, edited by Serenella Iovino and Serpil Oppermann. Bloomington: Indiana University Press. 51–66.

2 'Life subdued to its instrument'

Hughes, mutation and technology

pronaque cum spectent animalia cetera terram,
os homini sublime dedit caelumque videre
iussit et erectos ad sidera tollere vultus:
sic, modo quae fuerat rudis et sine imagine, tellus
induit ignotas hominum conversa figuras.

[Other animals, prone, look at the ground, he gave men a sublime countenance
to see the sky, forcing them to raise erected view to the stars: Thus, just now
rude and without shape, the world was changed and put on the unknown shapes
of men].

– Ovid (2004: bk 1, lines 84–88, my translation)

Though all the beasts
Hang their heads from horizontal backbones
And study the earth
Beneath their feet, Prometheus
Upended man into the vertical—
So to comprehend balance.
Then tipped his chin
So to widen his outlook on heaven.

In this way the heap of disorder
Earth
Was altered.
It was adorned with the godlike novelty
Of man.

– Hughes ('Creation; Four Ages; Flood; Lycaon', 2003: 868–869)

Like the Latin original, Hughes's 1997 volume *Tales from Ovid* marks the entry
of humans into creation with both a change in what the world contains and
how it is conceived. Hughes however also hints at the concomitant birth of
technology. Prometheus' 'novel' creations view the Earth in a new manner;
this myth speaks to both the posthuman and the Anthropocene. Humans are
a telluric force. Upended – and therefore implicitly destabilised – their

upturned gaze orders 'disorder' and 'comprehends balance'. They both are a 'novelty' – a new form of technological animal – and have the capacity for 'godlike novelty', the power of invention, meaning that they can develop technologies that will shape Earth in new and increasingly alarming ways as the poem continues through The Golden Age to the conflict and ecological mismanagement that typify The Age of Iron. My chapter has a similar backbone.

Beginning with Hughes's presentation of the human as simultaneously technologically imbricated and animal, I address the co-development of humans and their environment through technology, particularly the relation of technology to questions of abstract thinking and embodiment, and ask how this impacts upon ecology. I then examine *Crow* (published 1970) as a project which approaches myth in terms of evolutionary adaptation before finally showing why, in Hughes's clearest literary statement of his underlying ecological mythology, the world has to be saved by giant robots.

Jonathan Bate's reading of the above *Tales from Ovid* passage is indicative of how critics have failed to deal with Hughes's radical approach to technology and evolution. For Bate, Hughes offers a mythologisation of a failure to attend to the Earth: 'Once man looked away from where he walked, the earth became vulnerable. The desire for transcendence, the aspiration to higher realms, was predicated upon a denial of biological origin' (2001: 26). While this may chime with Hughes's distrust of philosophies that privilege the spirit at the expense of the animal body, the denial of biological origin here is Bate's. Hughes does not, here at least, show man turning away from earth or the deep-ecological dreams that Bate sees as corresponding to it, such as Schiller's naïve or Rousseau's state of Nature. Instead he locates different forms of cognition and technicity at the origin of the human – an emergent technological departure from the non-human animal that is itself biologically predicated.

Hughes's poem is better thought of as an instance of what David Wills calls *dorsality*: 'the name for that which, from behind, from the back of the human, turns (it) into something technological'. 'In standing upright' – the Promethean upending – 'the simian turns anthropoid and, in so doing, immediately turns technological […] a fundamental realignment of the human in its relation to technology occurs with the upright stance'. Dorsality usefully describes not only how the technological turn comes through a physical mutation but how the technological capacity announces itself in unpredictable ways. Standing upright allows for different sorts of tool to be manipulated but it also widens the cortical pan, giving more room for the brain and more capacity for (technological) invention and abstract thought. For Wills, technology 'defines and redefines the human, and does so downstream from the point at which a given technological creation was brought into effect'; it takes the human from behind (2008: 1, 8, 7).

Although they do not emerge until after the idyllic Golden Age, the technological usurpations of the organic that mark the descent of man through Hughes's poem's four ages are already immanent and imminent with the inception of the human. The prelapsarian trees have 'no premonition of the axe | Hurtling towards them on its parabola' (Hughes, 2003: 869). Here, despite the axe not having been fashioned yet, the suggestion is that the technological re-shaping of the Earth exists in potential. As the four ages progress, the humans develop instruments and techniques in different spheres: domestic (shelter, fires), agricultural (ploughs, husbandry) and martial (axes, longships). In this way 'Earth | Was altered' by the 'novelty | Of man'.

Hughes often speaks about art and culture in technological terms. He posits the ritual origins of religion as a 'technology to regain' an animal '*samhadi*' (bliss) lost at the last instance of hominid brain-evolution ('Letter to Merchant – 29 June 1990', 2007: 581). Notably, despite its 'biological origins', such bliss is not an escape from originary technicity but rather attained via the technological. In Hughes's descriptions of his work, myths are 'factories of understanding'. Myths are ways of externalising and sharing knowledge and their function changes across time, new 'revelations open out of their images and patterns continually, stirred into reach by our own growth and changing circumstances' ('Myth and Education', 1994a: 141). Any appeal to a simple, non-technological humanity is problematised from the outset as Hughes asks his readers to consider aspects of the ritual, mythic and poetic in terms of technology.

At the same time Hughes never forgets that the animal affects the technological. While keen to assert that 'language is an artificial human invention' he gives it an evolutionary edge:

> Its [language's] credentials for stating the case are seized on by the animal need to manipulate, outwit, circumvent and gain power over its evolutionary (social) competitors or potential mates. The (dumb) animal in us understands this perfectly well.
>
> ('Letter to Gamage – 29 November 1989', 2007: 572–573)

Hughes, as so often, overstates the case here but the point that the emergence of a new technology does not separate it from the influence of more primordial but still-operational evolutionary inheritances is an important one for him. Hughes's approach to the relationship between humanity's own animality and its use of language and other technologies to give it a competitive edge is evident in one of his most famous poems, 'Pike', in which the fisherman speaker ponders on the monsters that lurk below the surfaces of his surroundings and his own consciousness.

Fishing: adaptation and contact

Like some of the other animal descriptions in the 1960 collection *Lupercal* – particularly the stabbing beaks in 'Thrushes' or the jaws in 'Relic' – pike, 'Killers from the egg', connote predation, the violence of a world red in tooth and probably claw. But they are also symbols which organise the poem's meanings as it casts its lines into unplumbed depths. The final stanza brings this experience of fishing alongside a 'dream' which 'Darkness beneath night's darkness had freed, | That rose slowly towards me, watching' (2003: 86). What dream has risen to the surface here that the speaker feels has fixed him with its gaze? Not just the 'iron' eye of a pike but a vision of predation that implicates the speaker in its processes. The darkness beneath night's darkness is both the murky depths of the pond and the depths of the unconscious. Hughes sees fishing as a process where he sinks himself 'up to the fontanel in evolution's mutual predation system within which every animal cell has been fashioned' ('Letter to Gifford – 16 January 1994', 2007: 659).

The poem positions the speaker within the food chain; he is both the pike's predator and a more developed evolutionary adaptation – not necessarily the same thing, as the extinct monsters in 'Relic' suggest. Though its bite is terrifying, the phrase 'The jaws' hooked clamp' indicates that the clamp of the pike's bite has been hooked, has been superseded by a superior instrument. The pike's 'jaws' are 'Not to be changed at this date'; the pike is 'A life subdued to its instrument' (2003: 85). Pike cannot change, their evolved predatory instincts and instruments for biting dictate their existence. Conversely (fisher)men's tools have evolved in response to the specific needs of their environment; they can develop technologies – in this case the rod – that increase their capacity for predation, they can adapt without a biophysical change.

But pike embody more than predation on the level of individual humans. The rod and hook are not the only instances of human technology; the poem introduces the implicit link between animal predation and human technology early on when the pike cast a 'silhouette, | Of submarine delicacy and horror'. Hughes, writing towards the start of the Cold War, describes his predator-fish in terms of military technology so that when the fish come to reflect the speaker's position as carnivore they bring with them the earlier militaristic hue. The significance of this move is only revealed later when, in a typical Hughesian movement between individual and social scales, the poem reveals that the darkness of the pond signifies more than the individual unconscious and the animal drives and motivations therein; this 'legendary depth' is 'as deep as England'. The pikes' killer-instinct implicitly maps onto England's own modes of survival – the submarines it has developed to defend itself which, like the animal drives Hughes sees in the unconscious, may remain hidden for sustained time periods only to emerge with destructive consequences. We might even read the image of two pike, 'One jammed past its gills down the other's gullet' as a vision of Mutually Assured Destruction (2003: 84–85).

I believe Richard Kerridge is right that the stripes 'tigering' the pike recall Blake's Tyger. It is a revealing link. Blake's Tyger is

> at once real animal and symbol of the ruthless energy of creation. Both senses of creation are involved: the created world itself, and the act or process of making and changing that world. 'In what furnace was thy brain?', asks Blake's speaker.

As I discuss in Chapter Four, Prynne has argued for some of the ways that Blake's poem is very much engaged with the particular technological transformations – the metal-smelting of blast furnaces – central to the industrial revolution (and therefore, by some reckonings, with the start of the Anthropocene). Kerridge springboards off Prynne's claim to remind us that the

> aligning of the fearsome 'burning' of the tiger and the actual controlled burning of the blast-furnace suggests that the creative violence of industrial production is an extension of primal, generative natural energy not different in kind from natural processes. Natural life and the industrial manipulation of that life are not contrasted, but seen as different manifestations of the same creative power, though a power in which the divine and the demonic are hard to separate.

This sense of technology as emerging-from but still impacted-on by more fundamental forces is very much at play in Hughes's poem – he aligns 'natural and technological processes'. However, Kerridge also reminds us that critics should also be wary of such 'analogies since it is possible to read in them a fatalistic perception that technological warfare and ruthless industrial exploitation are primarily determined by evolved natural instinct, and therefore not susceptible to conscience' (2014: 181–182).

The comparison with Blake provides some indications of why fishing, as much as the predatory fish, is so important to this poem, and to Hughes's work in general. It constitutes an act of hunting, a technologically mediated engagement with the animal and a recognition of his own animality. Moreover he saw it as a time for meditative thinking and, most significantly for our purposes here, used it as one of the core descriptions of his *ars poetica*:

> There is the inner life, which is the world of final reality, the world of memory, emotion, imagination, intelligence, and natural common sense, and which goes on all the time, consciously or unconsciously [...] the thinking process by which we break into that inner life and capture answers and evidence to support answers out of it. That process of raid, or persuasion, or ambush, or dogged hunting, or surrender, is the kind of thinking we have to learn and if we do not somehow learn it, then our minds lie in us like fish in the pond of a man who cannot fish.
>
> (1967: 7)

In using the pike to reveal the primal animal-evolutionary survival drive within his own mind, Hughes presents himself as a man who can fish. Fishing becomes a metaphor for the act of writing, an attunement to both the real pike in the outer world and the pike in the inner world which embody his understanding of himself as animal – the psyche's 'darkness beneath night's darkness'.

The technology that enables both catches, the rod so to speak, is of course poetic language – exemplified by that guttural /k/ in 'hook' which precedes and supersedes the /c/ of the pike's 'clamp' in 'The jaws' hooked clamp'. By inserting 'hooked' between jaws and clamp Hughes prevents the pike's bite coming together, the suffix '-ed' snagging amongst the muscular monosyllables while the /k/ rasps in the throat of the pike and the reader. Moreover, the fisherman-poet knows that casting his lines may drag up more than writer or reader initially expected. Here that military 'submarine' both captures his sense of the pike's evolved weapons of survival and brings out the 'horror' that this predatory survival instinct still operates in the human and the tools they develop (including the hunter-killer submarine of the 1950s which takes its name from a fish resembling a pike, the barracuda). Language becomes the instance of technicity that separates the speaker from the creature whose defining characteristics are determined further back on the evolutionary timeline.

Living form and posthuman adaptation

Carey Wolfe suggests that language, while it should be considered a form of technicity, arises from 'fundamentally ahuman evolutionary processes', in this case stemming from

> recursive co-ontogenies [the mutual development of organisms] linked in complex forms of social behaviour and communication among so-called higher animals, which have themselves emerged from specific forms of embodiment and neurophysiological organization.
>
> (Wolfe, 2009: xxii)

Contemporary human languages – with their semiotic units and syntax – may be specific to our species, but our capacity for language is linked to inherent biological capacities which may not initially, Haraway explains, have had a communicative function. Rather these capacities were probably used in 'territory mapping, spatial navigation and foraging' (2008: 373). Such biological conditions of possibility mean that technology should not be artificially separated from embodiment. The way language, especially poetic language, brings forth our world is tied up with our embodiment – a notion Hughes explored most fully in his creation of a non-semantic Ur-language for his *Orghast* play which he developed in collaboration with Peter Brook. However, as this section makes clear, Hughes not only saw language in evolutionary terms but saw the myths and images that it carries as having an evolutionary function.

Fishing is Hughes's key example of a technology that foregrounds embodiment because the need that fishing attends to is no longer hunger but a different sort of appetite – those desires which palpitate in the 'inner life' or 'inner nature' from which Hughes sees modern humans as too often alienated. As several critics such as Ann Skea (1994), Nick Bishop (1991) and Leonard Scigaj (1986) have explained in detail, one of Hughes's core influences is Jung. What has been less well established is that Hughes's description of ecological crisis as a manifestation of humans' being alienated from 'inner and outer nature' reflects Jung's use of an evolutionary lexicon to describe his psychology.

In the January 1994 letter to Gifford, Hughes points to Jung's description of his therapy as a 'way of putting the human being back in contact with the primitive human animal', an important process as Hughes feels that 'most neuroses, of individuals and of cultures – result from the loss of that contact'. Hughes lists fishing as one activity (others include attending raves, adultery and farming) that 'put the individual back in contact with the primitive being [...] contact that satisfies and *contains* its requirements' (2007: 658, 660, Hughes's emphasis). The word 'contains' plays into Hughes's belief in poetry's immunising or adaptive function that mediates energies which, if repressed, become destructive.

In 1970's 'The Environmental Revolution' Hughes criticises the 'fanatic rejection of Nature' and the exile 'from inner and outer nature' and six years later in his second 'Myth and Education' essay lamented, in the strongest terms, the abjection of the 'inner world' and its drives: 'It has become a place of demons [...] we recognize it with horror – it is an animal crawling and decomposing in hell. We refuse to own it' (1994a: 129, 151). His vision of the stymied energies which cause ecological and psychological crises draws heavily on Jung's writings on (libidinal) 'psychic energy' which describe a constant 'process of psychological adaptation [...] a continual satisfaction of the demands of environmental conditions'. Jung claims that if something blocks the libido from adapting then without the regulatory flow we have 'tension', 'conflict' and the 'stage is then set for neurosis'. Neurosis itself 'can be formulated as an act of adaptation that has failed'.

> The symptoms of a neurosis are not simply the effects of long past causes [...] they are also attempts at a new synthesis of life – unsuccessful attempts [...] They are seeds that fail to sprout owing to the inclement *conditions of inner and outer nature*.
>
> (1971: 46, emphasis added)

Hughes repurposes Jung's model. For Hughes, civilisation's current neuroses, its ecologically destructive behaviours, are 'syntheses of life' at odds with the 'conditions of inner and outer nature'. There is maladaptation, evolutionary error which stems from foundational mythologies no longer being appropriate to the 'growth and changing circumstances' of their environment. To put it in more straightforward terms, Hughes argues that the ideologies and behaviours of the twentieth century, and the myths and images which both describe and condition them, are no longer conducive to the health of the biosphere, partly because they often prevent humans from acknowledging the demands of their own libidinal energies. But this same logic means Hughes presents the operation of myth as dynamic, shifting in response to environmental conditions. Hence Hughes sees his heavily symbolic poetry as offering something more than a smash and grab on what Larkin disparagingly called the 'myth kitty' ('Statement', 1983: 79). Instead, never one for half measures, Hughes positions the poet's work as a shamanistic intervention into a neurotic civilisation's modes of cognition and communication because, for him, myths and symbols are not just descriptions or stories but rather circulate on psychic and communicative circuits, shaping our cognition and behaviour as they do so.

For Hughes

> Mythologies are dodgy things [...] the picture languages we invent to embody and make accessible to casual reference the deeper shared understandings which keep us intact as a group – so far as we are intact as a group.
>
> ('Myths, Metres, Rhythms', 1994a: 310)

What Hughes is suggesting here is akin to what Stiegler describes as a process of externalisation that typifies the human as a prosthetic creature. For Stiegler humans have a third type of memory as well as the 'species level' memory (located in the genome) and the individual-somatic memory which is 'rooted in experience and located in the central nervous system'. This third memory transmits

> individually acquired knowledge in a nonbiological way. This technical memory is epiphylogenetic; in it, individual epigenetic experience provides phylogenetic [species or population level] support for the intergenerational cultural phylum.

Epiphylogenetic memory is 'supported and constituted by technics' – changing technologies are central in determining how populations think and recall (2010: 74). Stiegler's formulation is useful because it shows how, in a version of cultural memory like Hughes's, myths can be thought of in evolutionary terms as providing 'support' which is 'intergenerational'. Moreover it suggests that, like the operation of humans' biological inheritance, their relationship toward the non-biological transmission of cultural memory (their 'shared understandings') will be affected by the emergence of new technologies.

This extension of the evolutionary adaptive into the cultural and technological is crucial to Hughes's thinking, particularly his idiosyncratic, Jungian-inflected approach to the adaptive force of the myths which archive and carry cultural memory. In 'Myth and Education' he asserts that every 'story [...] contains two separable elements: its patterns and its images. Together they make that story and no other. Separately they set out on new lives of their own' (1994a: 152). The pattern of a story can have a symbolic function as well: for example the shamanistic journey into the underworld of the self that forms the structure of *Cave Birds* or the quest structure of *Crow*. It is the fluidity of these patterns and images that makes them 'dodgy', their capacity to circulate while carrying the emotional charges and associations of their previous contexts: 'revelations open out of their images and patterns continually, stirred into reach by our own growth and changing circumstances'.

The description of outer and inner world in 'Myth and Education' resonates with aspects of systems theory's description of mutually affecting psychic and social systems. For Hughes the subject always exists at a nexus of psyche and its environment: 'outer world and inner world are interdependent at every moment. We are simply the locus of their collision.' The culturally communicated mythological descriptions of lived experience obtain in the psyche and, through that process, feed back into individual behaviour. For Hughes,

> these dramatis personae [myths in the psyche] are really striving to live, in some way or other, in the outer world. That is the world for which they have been created. That is the world which created them.
>
> (1994a: 145)

So, for Hughes, the myths that describe and inform social behaviour are part of the way individuals and societies adapt to their various environments. However, as shall become clearer, their effects in different contexts and on different consciousnesses are unpredictable. Hughes's suggestion that myths may be of ecological import builds on Jungian psychology's use of the symbol where symbols cannot be reduced to coded meaning; they arise as adaptive psychological responses to environmental pressures. For Jung the symbol

> is always a creation of an extremely complex nature, since data proceeding from every psychic function have entered into its composition [...] not only the data of reason, but also the irrational data of pure inner and outer perception, have entered into its nature.
>
> ('Definitions', 1971: 478)

In Jung symbols cannot ever be fully decoded because their functions are transcendent – psychological consequences (and thereby 'real world' effects) arise from the interaction of consciousness with the symbol.

Paul Bishop (2008) has detailed the way Jung's conception of the symbol (which he sometimes referred to as 'living form') reworks Friedrich Schiller's *lebende Gestalt* (living form).[1] Like the *lebende Gestalt* described in Letter 15 of *Über die ästhetische Erziehung des Menschen*, Jung's notion of the symbol marries the sensory with the intellectual:

> the prospective meaning and pregnant significance of the symbol appeals just as strongly to thinking as to feeling, while its peculiar plastic imagery, when shaped into sensuous form, stimulates sensation just as much as intuition.
>
> (Jung, 1971: 478)

Hughes's evolutionary-adaptive dynamics separate him from Schiller's notion of redemption through living form which is, for Schiller, necessarily beautiful and therefore beneficial (Schiller's example is the sculpture of Juno Ludovisi). However Hughes – who is certainly aware of Schiller's 'Letter 15', quoting it in a draft review for *The Sunday Times* – does display something similar to

Schiller's sense that living form entails a kind of play between the viewer and the artwork.[2] Comparably Hughes, rather than emphasising any inherent meaning, suggests that the importance of the symbol rests in the way it operates on an individual consciousness. This means that the symbol functions in unpredictable ways:

> The roads they [myths] travel are determined by the brain's fundamental genius for metaphor. Automatically, it uses the pattern of one set of images to organize a quite different set. It uses one image, with slight variations, as an image for related yet different and otherwise imageless meanings.
>
> ('Myth and Education', 1994a: 152)

In an unpublished letter to his daughter Frieda offering advice on how to write, Hughes indicates how this sense of the power of the symbol to organise thinking permeated his analysis of his own practice:

> A feeling is always looking for a metaphor of itself in which it can reveal itself as unrecognized. When you find yourself writing directly about something that preoccupies you with rage etc. just remember that a metaphor provides an escape route.
>
> (Hughes, 1994b)

The way Hughes credits a single moment of aesthetic experience with the power to carry on shifting perception, replicating like a virus, has significant implications for the work he sees poetry as doing:

> The operations of the inner life are more analogous to microbiology than to the building of a motorway. Inevitably our lives are shaped by our daily work, but what transforms our innermost self – when it is transformed – are those momentary confrontations, either with some experience that somehow opens internal connections between unexplored parts of ourselves, [...] or with some few seconds of spontaneous vision that does the same. The analogy is with contracting an infection – the single touch of the virus is enough, only in this case what spreads through the cells is illumination, a new richness of life, a deeper grip on ourselves.
>
> ('draft foreword to The Way to Write – MS', n.d.)

By implication, Hughes's emphasis on intense experience suggests that it is not just the information contained in any mythology that is important, but the way the individual encounters it. Myths become bound up in our cognitive and emotional habits in complex ways. Hughes's belief in the transformative power of the myth reflects Jung for whom 'by being charged with emotion, the image gains numinosity (or psychic energy); it becomes dynamic and consequences of some kind must flow from it' ('Approaching the Unconscious', 1964: 96). Normally this 'energy must be artificially [*kunstlich*] supplied to the unconscious symbol in order to increase its value and bring it to consciousness' ('On Psychic Energy', 1971: 114). The adverb '*kunstlich*', Bishop explains, can be 'translated as "artificially" but, significantly, it also implies an artificial technique or aesthetic aspect' (2008: 133).

This charging of the symbol sits at the centre of Hughes's heavily symbolic poetics: 'the more concrete and electrically charged and fully operational the symbol, the more powerfully it works on any mind that meets it'. Crucially, the effects of the symbol are not predictable, but interactive and generative:

> The way it works depends on that mind [...] on the nature of that mind. I'm not at all sure how much direction, how much of a desirable aim and moral trajectory you can fix on to a symbol by associated paraphernalia.
>
> (interview with Faas, 1980: 199)

Under various names – myths, symbols, factories for understanding – these images and patterns circulate in psychic and social systems, shaping behaviour and communication, impacting on ecology. The function(s) of a myth depends upon the conditions of its environment(s): its prevalence and role within a discourse, the ways it is taken up by individuals, the accretions and associations it gathers across time, the behaviours it might lead to which themselves take place within shifting social and ecological contexts. In the current ecological moment the notion that a myth might ossify, becoming a maladaptation with potentially disastrous consequences, is actually quite common. The now almost clichéd commentary on how the classic image of the American West as a space of untrammelled freedom has been repurposed for SUV advertisements is a case in point; the myth of the great outdoors ironically becomes a cause of ecological degradation.[3] In the face of this conceptual crisis Hughes tries to generate new symbols or rather, with one eye on Darwin, tries to induce a mutation in the old ones so that they better adapt societies to their environments.

Hughes sees part of the ecological crisis as a failure to think in symbolic terms, the loss of mythological thinking itself. 'The Environmental Revolution' argues for the need to view Nature as sacred rather than as a collection of 'raw materials' for our 'exclusive profit and use' (1994a: 129). Again this echoes Jung:

> We talk of 'matter'. We describe its physical properties. We conduct laboratory experiments to demonstrate some of its aspects. But the word matter remains a dry, inhuman and purely intellectual concept, without any psychic significance for us. How different was the former image of matter – the Great Mother – that could encompass and express the profound emotional meaning of mother Earth.

Hughes predicates his mythic environmentalism on this argument from Jung that essentially post-Enlightenment Western civilisation 'places emphasis on pure actuality, and subordinates meanings to facts' (1964: 85). But Hughes also claims that this de-sacralising instrumentalisation of inner and outer Nature has its roots in mythology. Hence it is the roots of this drive toward enlightenment that he confronts and attempts to mutate in *Crow*, a project which not only attempts to evolve new mythologies but to reinvigorate society's capacity to interrogate their myths.

Crow is Hughes's poetic response to the fears he detailed in 'The Environmental Revolution' which was also published in 1970. The poems, which were originally 'songs' in a long and never-published prose narrative, tell an alternative creation story. The eponymous Crow, so the legend goes, is created by an unnamed demiurge in response to a challenge from a recognisably Judeo-Christian God to make a better go of things than God's creation 'man' has.[4] Crow (and *Crow*) flies in and out of myth and history, sometimes dying, sometimes adapting, sometimes changing his environment – this is a narrative of mutation and (co)evolution.

The rest of this chapter examines why the intertwining of myth and evolution is such a striking aesthetic response to what Hughes perceives as an ecological and conceptual crisis. In 'The Environmental Revolution' Hughes contends that both scientism and a biblically derived attitude to the world as resource, have engendered a tendency toward a pernicious abstraction that is ecologically disastrous on a global scale. Reading this claim alongside his poetry's exploration of the relation between technology and embodiment I will address how Hughes uses violence as a means of reasserting a lost sense of corporeality. This discussion segues into an examination of *Crow*'s treatments of the St George myth as an example of how he sees evolutionary maladaptation functioning on a mythic level. Finally I will address the question of form and self-reference to show why *Crow*'s mythologisation of evolution is self-consciously playing with the idea of myth *as* evolution.

Science, religion and the environmental revolution

'The Environmental Revolution' claims that Western Civilisation's constitutive mythologies have forced the moment into ecological crisis, because they lead us to conceive of the Earth as a series of inert resources rather than a finite, interconnected system:

> The fundamental guiding ideas of our Western Civilisation are against Conservation. They derive from Reformed Christianity and from Old Testament Puritanism. This is generally accepted. They are based on the assumption that the earth is a heap of raw materials given to man by God for his exclusive profit and use.
>
> (1994a: 133)

Seldom one to give references, it is unclear from the essay to what Hughes is referring when he says that these ideas are 'generally accepted'. However, Susanna Lidström (2013) has argued that Hughes was very much tuned in to the environmentalist debates that followed the publication of *Silent Spring* and, later, Lynn White's seminal 1967 article 'The Historical Roots of our Ecologic

Crisis'. Given the similarities between White's article and 'The Environmental Revolution', it is certainly credible that Hughes came across White's ideas either first or second hand. At the very least Lidström is right that Hughes's article demonstrates the 'contemporaneity' of his and White's ecological ideas. For White, the behaviour which has led to environmental crisis 'is rooted in, and is indefensible apart from, Judeo-Christian theology' and, in a passage which Hughes's article echoes, he goes on to claim that:

> Man named all the animals, thus establishing his dominance over them. God planned all of this explicitly for man's benefit and rule: no item in the physical creation had any purpose save to serve man's purposes. And, although man's body is made of clay, he is not simply part of nature: he is made in God's image.
>
> (1967: 1204, 1205)

Hughes's work also takes issue with what he sees as the assertion in *Genesis* of human dominion (or domination) 'over the fish of the sea, and over the fowl of the air, and over the cattle, and over all the earth, and over every creeping thing that creepeth upon the earth' (1:26). As well as resisting the desacralisation and exploitation of the Earth and its 'raw materials', Hughes, in his essay and in *Crow* itself, mirrors White in challenging the theological origins of human exceptionalism. In its place he mythologises an evolutionary-ecological narrative that firmly emphasises the human as emerging from, and dependent on, the more fundamental processes of life on Earth. It seems to me that one reason Hughes positions an awareness of evolution as supporting environmentalism is because such an awareness disrupts what he calls our 'amnesia against the fears of extinction' thereby cautioning against the misconceived exploitation of finite resources (or indeed endless growth).[5]

While 'The Environmental Revolution' supports certain work within the sciences, Hughes's essay, like White's, moves from a criticism of Christianity into a critique of the way the sciences have become yoked to industry. Hughes's own rhetoric here clumsily elides the methods of the sciences with the ecological exploitation facilitated by innovations in technology and science. What confuses the article's argument is Hughes's harbouring a slightly different, although related, anxiety about what he sees as a tendency toward abstraction and reductionism. While abstraction might be appropriate to experimentation, Hughes believes that it could engender a dangerous emphasis on objectivity when scientific discourses seep outside the laboratory. He also suggests that it can support a reductionism which stymies the development of the sciences themselves. 'The Environmental Revolution' laments the balkanisation of the sciences,

> the over-specialization of its experts so that Geophysics, Physiography, Hydrology, Botany, Zoology, Genetics, Biometrics, Ecology, Meteorology and the rest work in nearly complete insulation from each other.
>
> (1994a: 133)

This is almost a plea for interdisciplinarity; not for less science but for a different sort of approach to communication and research. It is clear from his career-long interest in scientific developments that Hughes does not reject the work of the sciences but rather the scientism which only accepts certain types of knowledge as valid, and which leads to a reductive perspective, meaning that externalities are ignored and connections fail to get drawn. Hughes also resists the notion that science should become the only court of appeal and that we must foreclose on intuition or other forms of non-quantifiable response. As Hughes puts it in a particularly exasperated unpublished 1962 manuscript:

> The scientific spirit has bitten so many of us on the nape, and pumped us so full of eggs, the ferocious virus of abstraction [...] The scientific spirit, we say, is hard headed, it fears nothing, it faces the facts, and how it has improved our comforts!

For Hughes the trouble stems from over-privileging abstraction, destroying our sensitivity towards our own, and others', corporeality and shifting the way we conceptualise our lifeworld:

> losing eyes, ears, smell, taste, touch, nerves and blood, adapting to the sensibility of electronic gadgets and the argument of numbers, to become a machine of senility, a pseudo-automaton in the House of the Mathematical Absolute.
>
> ('Engravings of Leonard Baskin – TS', 1962)

Crow emphasises that this may have disastrous consequences for contemporary thought and for ecology. In one of the many unpublished manuscripts for 'A Bedtime Story' poems contained in the files of *Crow* drafts Hughes, as he does several times over the project, plays with a proto-Anthropocene mythology of the global influence of technoscience. Here he imagines a man driving faster and faster around the earth. 'Here Birds and insects' (possibly a reference to Carson) 'interfere'

> With his speed
> So they had to cease
> He words the mountains flat
> He wore the seas dry
> [...]
> For convenience he converted all the people
> Into numerals
> Between one
> And whatever they amounted to
> So they were safe in his memory
> He called this game – God
> ('Bedtime Story III – MS', n.d.)

Crow sets itself against such destructive metaphysics of abstraction. A draft note on his published works reminds us that the

> crow is another word of course for the entrails, lungs, heart etc. – everything extracted from a beast when it is gutted [...] the vital organism of the creature [...] The crow of a man, in other words, is the essential man – only minus his human looking vehicle.
>
> (Hughes, 1992a)

Hughes is slightly wrong here; the crow is in fact the mesentery, the membrane which envelops these organs in the abdominal cavity. Nevertheless, his point affirms the collection's interest in what is ignored (or eviscerated) from our ideas of the human, the vital processes (like our purportedly selfish genes) that still operate behind the surface of the 'human vehicle'.

Crow's violent renderings of the human crow work to counteract the deadening effects of modern technology and artificial objectivity on human sensibility. The way the violence of the collection works against the violating of ecosystems and organisms is a rhetorical strategy Hughes uses throughout his work. Alarmed by the destructive capacity of modern technology Hughes asserts the importance of recognising that the technological capacity that has led to humans' evolutionary success now risks becoming an evolutionary error if it prevents them from acknowledging the finite and dynamic nature of the organic. As I shall show, this is one of the reasons why *Crow* suggests that art can have an evolutionary impact. Before that though it is necessary to elucidate *Crow*'s resistance toward the depredations of modern technology.

Violence and technology

In an attempt to answer two questions posed to him by Ekbert Faas 1971 (eventually published in *Winter Pollen* as 'Poetry and Violence'), Hughes presents us with the gap between violence and violation. Partly by way of a response to the charge from critics such as W.I. Carr that his poetry was the 'poetry of violence' – 'violent, combative gesturing without moral commitment' – Hughes argues that it is, in fact, our 'customary social and humanitarian [or indeed humanist] values' that lead to the worse sorts of violence (Carr, 1958: 26; Hughes 1994a: 260). That is, violence where a desensitised sensibility allows for instances of mechanised slaughter or environmental destruction because technological distancing has separated the human from its corporeal being and its capacity to acknowledge pain and death. He calls these instances of industrialised slaughter 'violations'. Hughes goes on to suggest that, in fact, a certain kind of violence works to counteract the violation done to our sensibility by the false-consciousness of humanist thought, our 'customary social and humanitarian values' (1994a: 260).

For Hughes our moral awareness rests on an ability to acknowledge the violence of corporeal reality. As Cora Diamond (2008) argues in an essay on animals and ethics which takes Hughes as a central example, acknowledging this reality, and its ramification for the treatment of other human and non-human embodied beings, is always difficult. However, the inability to bear the reality of corporeality results in that worse violence, the violation that stems from an anaesthetised sensibility. As should be clear from my argument so far, technology itself cannot be seen as that which necessarily alienates the human from the realities of its lifeworld. There are tools – the poem, the rod – which help us acknowledge violence as well as repress it.

In Hughes's work the way that humans have become estranged from their own animal finitude is one of the central questions concerning technology, or rather concerning modern technology. A certain correlation exists here between Hughes and Heidegger's supposition that the modern condition of anxiety stems from an inability to 'own' death and, since pain is an intimation of death, an inability to own pain as well.

Rather than acknowledging the embodied finitude of animal life, the irreducible complexity of the living being is reduced to an object. The phenomenon of death is tucked out of sight, or as Heidegger puts it, 'self-assertion of technological objectification is the constant negation of death' (1971: 125). In relation to environmentalism, meat-eating and war, technology's capacity to transform living flesh into an object is a constant concern in the poetry. This sentiment plays out in 'Crow Tyrannosaurus', a procession poem where Hughes registers each animal's engagement with those lower in the food chain: the swift pulsates with insects, the cat's body writhes with 'incoming death struggles'

> And the dog was a bulging filterbag
> Of all the deaths it had gulped for the flesh and the bones
> It could not digest their screeching finales.

Non-human animals feel their victims' creatureliness, their resistance to being forcibly incorporated into a different part of the food chain, but things are different for the proverbial top carnivore. 'Crow Tyrannosaurus' tracks the lack of human engagement with either death or pain; technological abstraction supersedes animal immediacy. Man, when he makes an entrance, appears as

> [...] a walking
> Abattoir
> Of innocents—
> His brain incinerating their outcry.
>   (2003: 214–215)

The technological combines with the human who becomes an abattoir, a site of techniques and technologies for facilitating meat eating. The poem's linking of the capacity for physical distancing (in the abattoir) and ontological distance (in 'His brain') melds the human with its ur-technology, fire. Unlike Hughes's canine carnivore, humans do not suffer from the problems of partial digestion where they have to acknowledge other animals' pain. Hughes's extended interest in the Prometheus myth soon after the time of the *Crow* project means that this reference to incineration glows with a certain light in its distinguishing of the raw from the cooked.

For Diamond, acknowledging shared animal embodiment is itself a challenge to our perspective, not least because to do so would be to open ourselves to what we do to this living flesh: 'horror at the conceptualization of animals as putting nothing in the way of their use as mere stuff' resides alongside 'a comparable horror at human relentlessness and pitilessness in the exercise of power' towards human-animals (2001: 136). This echoes Hughes's attack on the biblically derived assumption that 'the earth is a heap of raw materials given to man for his exclusive profit and use' and his insistence that technologised meat-eating and an ethical failure towards the human are inextricably linked.

> For all who are horrified by the predation on the screen, our own internal involvement in the killing and eating of animals can only exist as an equally horrifying crime. And beneath it but inseparable from it, moves our extraordinary readiness to exploit, oppress, torture and kill our own kind.
>
> (1994a: 256)

The bombast of the second sentence masks an important issue in the first which demands unpacking. Hughes claims that those horrified by televised predation are horrified by their own carnivore identity and its link to violent behaviour towards other humans. But because of the wounding nature of this admission, the essay suggests, we repress our own capacity for violence and our own animality and instead view animal-violence with a phobic distaste and distance. Hughes champions the importance of not turning away from the screen in horror. Rather, in a risking of our 'customary social and humanitarian values', his thinking works toward acknowledging the difficulty of our reality. This is the same process we saw at work in 'Pike' where humans and fish are compared in order to show how humans have mechanised their defence mechanisms, the predatory drive is displaced, becoming devastatingly efficient in the poem's 'submarine horror'.

All this raises the question of how, given that Hughes positions himself as able to face up to animal violence and acknowledge its relation to certain human proclivities and behaviours, we negotiate the ethical import he ascribes to violence, especially as Hughes was certainly no vegetarian. It is important not to reduce Hughes's argument about the barbarism of modern food production to Kant's famous argument from the *Metaphysics of Morals* (used more recently in the Luc Ferry's (1995) influential critique of Deep Ecology) which argues that

> violent and cruel treatment to animals is far more intimately opposed to a human being's duty to himself [than destruction of inanimate Nature], and

he has a duty to refrain from this; for it dulls his shared feeling of their suffering and so weakens and gradually uproots a natural predisposition that is very serviceable to morality in one's relations with other men.

(Kant, 1996, '§17': 192–193)

As shall become clearer, Hughes's concern is for life in general and not just human life – which is not to say he supports a deep-ecological sense of species equality.[6] I would suggest that Hughes sees the ethical force of his writing as stemming from its radical unsettling of our familiar ways of being; it does violence to 'customary social and humanitarian values'. These values would include any enlightenment sense of rationality as a crowning human virtue and the bulwark against violation. Hughes's thinking is similar to that of his favourite philosopher Schopenhauer, who criticised Kant's perspective on animal cruelty and also argued that 'reasonable and vicious are quite consistent with each other, in fact, only through their union are great and far-reaching crimes possible' (1998: 86) The poem 'Thrushes', claims Hughes's essay, challenges 'values' which 'protect the familiar human condition', a condition which, in its apartness from its own animality, cannot give credence to a 'lucid acceptance of the true nature of the activities by which it survives' (1994a: 261).

Hughes's examination of how, to a degree that we refuse to acknowledge, the interconnectivity of ecosystems and a shared evolutionary heritage means that we are what we eat, places him in line with Wolfe (2009) and David Wood's (1999) argument that

the specific practice of eating animals becomes simply one more version of the larger symbolic structure by which 'man' in the western philosophical tradition secures its transcendence through mastery of nature, repression of the body – everything that Derrida associates with the term 'carnophallogocentricism'.

(Wolfe, 2009: 95)

Hughes challenges those conceptual and technological structures that Derrida sees as encouraging a notion of human exceptionalism:

The attitude that recoils from animals eating animals on the screen – with a disapproval that masks the speaker's implication in the process which among other things constructs the unspoken abattoir between the bullock in the field and the steak on his plate. The attitude that effectually denies its own guilt and openly condemns what it colludes with and profits from.

Hughes tries to speak the unspoken abattoir, the out-of-sight technologised space enclosing 'animals that have been killed by methods and in circumstances that make any predator's kill seem by comparison merciful and blameless' (1994a: 259, 256). Rather than the fishing rod which tunes the speaker of 'Pike' into his own carnivorous depths, these technologies allow cerebral being to flourish at the expense of corporeal awareness. Hughes echoes Lawrence's 'Touch' in claiming that this might engender viciousness:

> For if, cerebrally, we force ourselves into touch,
> into contact
> physical and fleshly,
> we violate ourselves,
> we become vicious.
>
> (Lawrence, 2002: 384)

In the abattoir, and presumably in the 'abattoir of innocents' of 'Crow Tyrannosaurus', Hughes sees 'whirling knives, zapping power saws [... lamb] electrocuted through clamps [...] on the eyeballs (for better contact)' (1994a: 259). Mechanistic processes portion out the living animal into its commercially manageable and exchangeable fleshy substrates. This animal's destruction comes via a mechanically mediated human desire which inscribes itself on the body of the destroyed animal and connects, like a Kafkaesque torture machine, to institutions and legislation (commercial, industrial, agricultural, educational) outside its immediate space. In fact, one might consider what remains unspoken in the word 'abattoir' itself. It derives from the French *abattre*, meaning 'to knock down' (presumably with a sledge hammer), an indication of violence that, in English, is lost in translation. But abattoir also carries behind it, via its relation to the older 'abate', a sense of diminishing, and of being brought down in value. The animal (and frequently in Hughes's work, the ecosystem) is physically and conceptually brought down to the level of lifeless material.

The susurrus of the concentration camp that haunts the incinerating 'abattoir of innocents' (in the draft, man is a 'walking death camp') serves as a reminder that the violation of our sense of other animals' corporeality flows into our capacity to harm each other – 'our extraordinary readiness to exploit, oppress, torture and kill our own kind'.[7] Hughes uses the next poem in the *Crow* sequence, 'Crow's Account of the Battle' to slide from the war of Nature to the nature of war and in doing so develops a continuum between instances of mechanised slaughter and advanced technology's capacity to harm.

> Shooting somebody through the midriff
> Was too like striking a match
> Too like tearing up a bill
> Blasting the whole world to bits
> Was too like slamming a door

The domestic, everyday similes, with their air of childish petulance and insouciance, are purposefully inappropriate to the horror they describe. 'Reality' is said to be 'giving its lesson'; the discourses of war – and as corollaries we might think of the newspeak of 'collateral damage' or the Cold War 'button' – prove irreconcilable with its actual happenings. The poem debunks those romanticised battlefield-myths in which 'pocket books' stop bullets from pursuing their course. Here they push on through 'intestines [...] brains, hair, teeth'. Military technology violates the human body both physically and conceptually. Bodies are reduced, described as unfeeling tools and materials, foregrounding the loss of perspective and the painful finitude of living flesh – blood 'Squander[s] as from a drain pipe', 'Bones were too like lath and twigs' (Hughes, 2003: 222–223). These serve as pertinent reminders of Heidegger's (1977) argument that technological objectification is the constant negation of death.[8]

The poem's 'Reality' is a 'mishmash of scripture and physics'. It not only foregrounds the disjunctions between the human body and modern technology but also presents the repression of the suffering body as bound up with a set of discourses inappropriate to the human. When revealing the physicality behind technical language – 'From sudden traps of calculus, | Theorems wrenched men in two' – the comic disjunction between representation and actuality is both absurd and tragic (2003: 222). On the one hand it bespeaks a cartoonish violence, on the other hand it elucidates the fleshy nature of the signified that the technical signifier denotes. Political, economic and scientific theorems, because they cannot adequately disclose the complexity of the reality they describe, provide all-too-real, all-too-human and all-too-final solutions to theoretical problems. What we have here is what Heidegger, who also railed against the 'mechanized food industry', laments as the modern tendency of *Gestell* (enframing) 'holding sway' as the mode of world-disclosure. *Gestell* is the way in which the living or the 'real reveals itself as standing-reserve' (1977: 23) The animal becomes a head of cattle, the soldier reduced to a number on a casualty list or a marker on a military map. '*Gestell* makes violation inevitable' says Julian Young, 'because, fundamentally it takes away the concept of violation' (2002: 53).

'Crow's Account of a Battle' does not only extend the technologisation of meat-eating into contemporary warfare, but it also feeds into Hughes's argument that our response to environmental crisis might be compared to anti-war discourses. Not least in terms of the need for the human species to come to terms with its relation to its own technologies and practices and the tragic disjunction between these features and an acknowledgement of the suffering, living-body. All are part of a wider 'carnophallologocentric' repression of the body and (perceived) mastery of Nature. But the embodied awareness that stems from recognising violence is not alone enough to provide an ethical or practical corrective; there must be a paradigmatic shift in our conceptual apparatus. This is why *Crow* works on the reader by violating the sanctity of the human by presenting it as object, as animal, as machine and by cross-breeding the poems' violent imagery with the patterns and symbols of Christian and classical mythology.

The cartoonish mode of *Crow*'s universe, where meteorites crash with 'extraordinary ill-luck' on prams, makes its violence seem absurd, but the same question of how technology and language obscure brute corporeal reality also operates when Hughes adopts a more elegiac voice in 'Six Young Men' ('In Laughter', 2003: 233). Through looking at the photo of the six men soon to die in the trenches the speaker gains an intimation of mortality: the figures 'smile from the single exposure and shoulder out | One's own body from its instance and heat' (2003: 45–46). Surprisingly, given their focus on animals, what Wolfe and Diamond miss in their analysis of the poem is Hughes's own subtle engagement with meat-eating. These men are described as 'trimmed for a Sunday jaunt'. The association of 'trimmed' with roast-dinner trimmings and the phonic closeness of 'jaunt' to joint is more than suggestive that, as elsewhere, Hughes is using the image of the abattoir to organise our perception of the battlefield. (A notebook version reads 'they sit on their Sunday jaunt' indicating that Hughes altered his draft to emphasise this link ('Notebook', n.d.).) But if he knows that his 'Six Young Men' are soon to 'die as cattle' then the simile is, of course, Wilfred Owen's, and his relationship to war is already mediated by the images and discourses that precede the immediacy of a visceral reaction to death and loss.

Hughes calls up quintessential images of Englishness (the Sunday stroll before Sunday dinner) but knows we cannot see jaunt or joint unmediated by the imagery of the First World War's definitive anthem. Access to the war is provided by the camera's (selective) mechanical eye along with an external archive of historical fact and poetic discourse that precedes and exceeds both the speaker and the men's presence. Hence the 'contradictory permanent horrors' of the photograph, that moment during which the speaker acknowledges both the feeling of the men's absent presence and their bloody passing: 'That man's not more alive whom you confront [...] Nor prehistoric or fabulous beast more dead; no thought so vivid as their smoking blood' (2003: 46). Technicity is central to human perception and instead of trying to find a way round it to a chimeric position free from mediation, any literary attempt to capture a primordial sense of corporeality must negotiate the technical.

Hughes later drew together the desire to present the shock of war and the need to portray the environmental crisis. In a 1990 open letter to Margaret Thatcher and Neil Kinnock (the candidates for the general election) he asked the next Prime Minister to consider the environmental crisis as they would a war, 'on all its fronts. In other words, as an Emergency, displacing every other concern that stands in its way' (printed in Astley, 1990: 96). Writing to Michael Hamburger in 1987 he claims 'Margaret [Thatcher] can't be frightened [about pollution]. She's like that general who says "We can afford 25% casualties"' (2007: 538). Hughes's disquiet at this gap between statistical language and horrific actuality connects to his discussions of the difficulty of expressing war. As he says in an *Observer* review on environmental photography:

> His [Owen's] feeling for the totally new calamity of the trenches and his inexpressible raging need to communicate it to what he saw as domestic England's old fashioned inability to imagine it, was not that far from the environmentalist's position between the injured Earth on one hand and Government, industry and certain fixed ways of life on the other.
>
> (1992d: 39)

What is notable here is the sense of the failure of representational technologies to perforate society's imaginative failure. In fact as Zoe Jaques has pointed out, Hughes has written of cameras (and binoculars) as an alienating as well as connecting technology (2015: 177). In a 1965 piece on Owen, Hughes says that Owen's poems 'are partially substitutes or verbal parallels for those photographs. The main thing was that they could never be terrible or vivid enough' ('National Ghost', 1994a: 71). Behind the full-bloodedness of Hughes's verse sits the determination to be 'vivid enough' to make his mark and force humans to relocate themselves in a finite and connected ecosystem, to 'correct the regime of our "customary social and humanitarian values"', as it advertises itself, and rescue not only mankind from it, but all other living creatures, to rescue life itself' (1994a: 267). But the vividness of Hughes's martial imagery itself operates in tandem with his desire to find metaphors and myths which will give shape to environmental issues which, because not immediately visible, are not properly acknowledged.

Wolfe argues that the failure in communicating mortality (and with it morality) partly occurs because

> our relation to flesh and blood is fatefully constituted by a technicity with which it is prosthetically entwined, a diacritical, semiotic machine of language in the broadest sense that exceeds any and all presence, including our own.
>
> (2009: 92)

Moreover, the capacity to abstract, to render bodies and ecosystems into quantifiable information, plays a key role amongst the tools and techniques which distance humans from the material conditions of their lifeworld. Poetic language is a type of technicity which may reveal violence, corporeality, the embodied existence of ourselves and other animals. Thus it works to restore our awareness, to correct our 'customary' perspectives which have been alienated from corporeal existence by those technologies which instrumentalise the living. But, as well as a renewed attention to embodiment, *Crow*'s violence against our customary ways of knowing attempts to challenge the mythology of abstraction on a symbolic level, nowhere more so than in its engagements with the myth of St. George.

Crow: evolving myth/mythologising evolution

In 'Crow's Account of St. George', Hughes replaces the Christian hero with a scientist who 'sees everything in the Universe | Is a track of numbers racing towards an answer'. And so, in an attempt to take things back to first principles he 'Decreates all to outer space, | Then unpicks numbers'. To de-create, seemingly in this case to the Big Bang and the 'numbers' of physics and chemistry, risks failing to attend to emergent phenomena, like nervous systems. It enables the St. George scientist, like Descartes, to view animals as incapable of genuinely experiencing pain and so he 'melts cephalopods' without any sense of moral anxiety (2003: 226). Hughes has probably chosen these creatures for their appearance but given his penchant for biology he may have had some awareness of the research which, from the 1920s onwards, had suggested that cephalopods have far more developed brains and nervous systems than had been imagined; they also use tools.[9]

Hughes has his scientist reduced to murderous madness by the scientific method. Driven by the quest to pick out the 'gluey heart' of the mystery he kills a series of 'demons' who invade his laboratory. Realising too late the identity of the demons (or dragons) he has slain, he 'Drops his sword and runs dumb-faced from the house | Where his wife and children lie in their blood' (2003: 226). He butchers them just as he butchers his laboratory creatures with his 'tweezers of number'; the poem amalgamates the numeric with martial and laboratory technology, working to facilitate a brutal de-creation of animals, lover and descendants.

In a draft letter to *The Spectator* Hughes defended the poem against the criticism of 'nihilistic violence', explaining the similarity the poem bore to a Japanese folktale and Seneca's *Hercules Furens* as well as spelling out its central conflict:

> The hero's dilemma, in this plot, is that the dragon of chaos, the destruc-
> tive demon or whatever to which he finds himself opposed, is also the vital
> life. In the earliest myths, it is specifically the mother of all things, womb
> of creation etc. In Christianity it is the female, sexuality, the serpent of the
> out, and in general the demonic life of the body. In St. George (as in
> many parallel legends) it is everything that threatens the ascetic moral ideal,
> Christian inevitably puritan ideal, and in particular it is the maiden herself,
> as she focuses the physical nature of the Knight.

Crucially Hughes associates the ascetic rejection of the corporeal with a later reductive paradigm which 'aspires to the "rationalism" of mathematical order and to that kind of scientific objectivity which regards the human colouring of the observing eye as the worst error' ('Letter to the Spectator, 5 March – MS', 1971). To corrupt our value systems and perception by hiving off facts from values, concept from emotion, information from affect leads toward the societal neurosis that Hughes sees as ecologically destructive. This is an extension of the repression of the body and sexuality Hughes reads into the St. George myth which, in his 1970 'Myth and Education' essay, he describes as a 'symbolic story of creating a neurosis', 'the key symbolic story of Christianity', and 'key to the neurotic-making dynamics of Christianity' (1970b: 66).

The poem links the St. George scientist's horror at his wife to a horror at the sexual which threatens to engulf him:

> An object four times bigger than the others –
> A belly ball of hair, with crab-legs, eyeless,

Jabs its pincers into his face,
Its belly opens – a horrible oven of fangs,
The claws are clawing to drag him towards it

That the final defeat where he 'bifurcates it' and 'Steps out of the blood wallow' appears to be a kind of horrendous auto-caesarean takes on added significance within the collection's overarching framework (2003: 226). Not only does this action anticipate Oedipus' matricidal emergence in 'Song for a Phallus' but, as Hughes reminds us in his explanatory essay 'Crow on the Beach', the womb is one of *Crow*'s key images. Both the womb 'that bore him [Crow], and the womb of his Beloved' furnish Crow with an unconscious lack that drives him on his evolutionary quest (1994a: 133). The creator/bride/ goddess figure in *Crow*, as so often in Hughes's work, is associated with desire, fecundity, creativity and the living Earth. Finding a way of thinking about the organic world without either reducing it to a series of algorithms or abjecting it in horror becomes a central part of *Crow*'s ecological project of virally infecting myth's patterns and images.

The character of God in *Crow* embodies 'the man-created, broken down, corrupt despot of a ramshackle religion', but the collection does not try to dissolve all symbolic resonances, rather it repurposes them (Hughes, 1973). In 'Crow Communes', Crow finds that God has fallen asleep – 'God lay, agape, a great carcase'. The internal rhyme of 'God lay' suggests that the carcase is not just a slack-jawed deity but *agape* (ἀγάπη). In allowing the 'hierophant' Crow to bite 'off a mouthful' of *agape*/God – a meal which makes him feel 'much stronger' – Hughes tells us how he nourishes his mythopoeia with old myths, digesting Christian love and putting whatever nutrients it has into something that Hughes sees as more vital and fundamental (2003: 224).

In *Crow*'s universe the serpent displaces God in the causality of creation and becomes associated with something more like *eros* than *agape*. In 'Apple Tragedy' the serpent has created the world ('on the seventh day | The serpent rested') and also manages to have congress with Eve (2003: 250). More tellingly, in 'Snake Hymn':

The snake in the garden
If it was not God
It was the gliding
And push of Adam's blood.

The blood in Adam's body
That slid into Eve
Was the everlasting thing
Adam swore was love
          (2003: 254)

In the Faas interview Hughes remarks that 'the only philosophy I ever really read was Schopenhauer's. He impressed me all right' (1980: 205). 'Snake

Hymn' reconfigures Schopenhauer's pre-Darwinian thought for evolution. The 'everlasting thing' bears the hallmarks of Schopenhauer's *Wille zum Leben*, appearing as an ahuman force which lies behind human motivation, and which appears to maintain across time, individuals and species as a 'love that cannot die' which 'sheds a million faces'.[10]

The notion of life in general which operates behind division into individuals and species is a central feature of *Crow*'s ecology, having implications for both Hughes's sense of the biosphere and a shared genetic history. Hughes borrows Schopenhauer's concepts rather than adhering to his conclusions. While he might have sympathy with the view that in human behaviour, the sex-drive is the most complete manifestation of the will to life's cross-species operations, Hughes, of all people, is hardly one to reduce recreation to procreation or to propose Schopenhaurean asceticism. Instead, his locating human sexuality in its origins as an evolutionary mechanism, while sanctifying it as a 'hymn', creates a more robust mythology of creation and of the creator's 'love'. This new mythology is predicated on an awareness of a shared animal-embodiment that does not supress *eros* in favour of what Hughes sees as the more abstract *agape* and thereby, in the words of the Faas interview, gestures towards a 'new Holy Ground [...] one that won't be under the rubble when the churches collapse' (1980: 207).

A similar mixing of Christian love and animal reproduction occurs in 'Crow's First Lesson' where God tries to force Crow to say 'LOVE'. When he does speak, Hughes's upstart Crow, who is not a parrot and therefore resistant to learning by rote, coughs out man and woman locked in a coital death-struggle where 'woman's vulva dropped over man's neck and tightened' (2003: 211). In *Crow*, as in the myth of The Fall where Adam and Eve are denied immortality and expelled from the garden but give birth to humanity, sex comes hand in hand with death as a necessary condition for an Earth-bound existence based on reproduction, mutation and adaptation.

Crow turns the refusal to acknowledge the animality implicit within sexual desire into a rejection, or perhaps an abjection, of the animal body tied to the alienation from Nature. This is part of Hughes's broader intention to help readers re-examine myths in terms of the way that they codify attitudes towards body and organic life in general. The relations between sexuality, reproduction and evolution hold the key to the tangled symbols of the most complex of *Crow*'s St. George poems, 'A Horrible Religious Error' which blends The Fall, Oedipus and St. George together with a dash of D.H. Lawrence in an attempt to undo what Hughes sees as an alienation from the processes of organic life. It begins:

When the serpent emerged, earth-bowel brown,
From the hatched atom
With its alibi-self twisted around it

Lifting a long neck
And balancing that deaf and mineral stare
The sphinx of the final fact

And flexing on that double flameflicker tongue
A syllable like the rustling of the spheres

God's grimace writhed, a leaf in the furnace

Hughes infects the biblical mythology of the snake with *Crow's* awareness of the abject and the bodily. Linked to the earth in its faecal bowel-brownness – like the 'ordure' dripping from the demon in 'Crow's Account of St. George' – and hissing with a sibilance that ties it to the cosmic energy of the 'spheres', the serpent shows up as more vital than God, who can only grimace in displeasure while man and woman prostrate themselves to it.

The 'alibi-self' anticipates the skin-shedding evolutionary rebirths of 'Snake Hymn'. These births are *alibi* in its etymological sense, they will show up *elsewhere*, in other poems, forms and organisms, like Hardy's 'place to place'.[11] The *Crow* drafts show Hughes playing with this association. Elsewhere in his *Crow* notes Hughes tests the lines 'alias the serpent of begetting', the etymon of alias being 'at another time, otherwise, in another place, elsewhere' ('Untitled Draft [Snakes in Crow] – MS', n.d.). The continual generation of the serpentine rebirth speaks to the proliferating operation of myths in cognition and communication, the way they arise elsewhere. It also has a more direct evolutionary aspect. In 'A Horrible Religious Error' the reptile-snake is an incarnation of the nameless generative force that made Crow (and the world in 'Apple Tragedy'), as well as being his evolutionary ancestor. As another unpublished *Crow* poem reminds us, birds have reptilian (dinosaur) roots: 'And you see that the bluetits and budgies are also vile reptiles, | Or lovely reptiles' ('Crow is About the Cleverest Bird – MS', n.d.). However, in 'A Horrible Religious Error' Crow, still at an early stage of his development, fails to recognise this avatar of his creator and eats the serpent.

Behind Hughes's serpent stands Lawrence's poem 'Snake', where the serpent is 'earth brown' and 'from the burning bowels of the earth'. Lawrence's snake similarly challenges the order of things; it stands 'before' the speaker at the 'water trough', an evolutionary predecessor as opposed to the human 'second comer'. Lawrence's speaker's 'Accursed human | education', which overcomes his natural affinity for the snake causing him to hurl a log at it, stems from a phobic reaction to the sexual aura which surrounds the animal – 'A sort of horror, a sort of protest against his withdrawing | into that horrid black hole' (1972: 138). 'A Horrible Religious Error' keeps Lawrence's rejection of the animal but in contrast to 'Snake' and 'Apple Tragedy' there is a reason that it is not given the male pronoun. In fact, on a mythological level, Hughes here associates the serpent with female entities, compounding the question of what (or who) this horrible religious error is.

In their worshipping of the abject snake, man and woman commit a religious error which, from the Christian perspective at least, is horrible. But the real error is Crow's. He mistakenly destroys the skin-shedding, self-recreating, sexualised serpent associated with the artistic and creative energy of 'the spheres'.

This parallels the 'evolutionary error' of 'Western Civilization' in its 'neurotic' rejection of Nature – as with the horror at the sexualised animal in Lawrence's 'Snake'. But this complex rejection also ramifies at a symbolic level; the poem brings into focus a series of interrelated myths, forcing the reader to actively move between different resonances.

The description of the serpent as the 'Sphinx of the final fact' brings the snake into the orbit of another (female) monster destroyed by human knowledge, and we might even read Oedipus' answer to the Sphinx ('man') as the 'final fact' which forces her to kill herself. Excavating further reveals other links. Oedipus' hubris stems from knowledge about 'man' but his tragic reversal in fortunes directly follows on from the partialness of his self-knowledge and knowledge of his ancestry. This parallels the anthropocentric arrogance of the St. George scientist and other matricidal figures in *Crow* who forget their evolutionary ancestry and thereby their dependence on the rest of organic world – not least the man in 'Revenge Fable' who kills his mother with 'numbers', 'equations', 'bulldozers' and 'detergents' after which his own head falls off (2003: 244). Oedipus' actions, like those of the St. George scientist, will inadvertently end up killing his wife/mother (Jocasta) and eventually three of his children (Polynices, Eteocles and Antigone).

Hughes's syncretic attunement between different myth systems organises itself both around and against Jung's reading of dragon slaying as itself a type of oedipal myth. Jung sees the killing of the dragon as the archetypal rite of passage from childhood to manhood, the final separation from the maternal space which provides sustenance, the space which in *Crow*'s universe is always associated with Nature. In *Crow* the slaying of the snake, dragon or demon, by force or science, shows up as primarily negative, and this in turn suggests something about the 'error' of the title.

By choosing the word 'error' Hughes turns his serpent monster into an avatar of *The Faerie Queen*'s 'errour' – Spenser's serpentine embodiment of Catholicism's religious errors – and so the snake itself is the 'horrible religious erro[u]r'.[12] This casts Crow in the role of 'Red Cross', St. George himself. Hughes holds a particular loathing for the Reformation, crediting the iconoclasm as central to the loss of the contemporary ability to think symbolically.[13] Red Cross's battle with Errour displays the sort of horrified sensibility that overcomes Hughes's (and indeed Lawrence's) St. George figures. The knight cannot abide the thought of the female dragon in her 'darksom hole' lying on the 'durtie ground' in 'filthie sin'. She cannot abide the light or knight of (totalising) truth and tries to engulf him in her 'wreathed' snake coils. An additional disgust surrounds the little 'errours' she begets, 'deformed monstors' of 'sundrie shapes' (*The Faerie Queen*, bk 1, canto 1: xiv–xxiv).

Recasting St. George in *Crow*'s evolutionary inversions, Hughes makes the zealot's religious or rational 'truth' destructive while error's mutative nature makes it potentially generative, opening up possibilities for new ecological futures. After all, genetic mutations are copying errors. And so it is a horrible error to see error (or Errour) as horrible. Hughes's re-workings show that the

St. George myth is not a stable, decodable literary object, but rather a dynamic living form that manifests itself in different ways – Spenser's Red Cross as destroyer of misleading Catholic mystification in his quest to secure the 'true' church's female (Una) becomes the St. George scientist's destructive quest to unpick the 'mystery' of the universe. Myths combine and coalesce and, because they both describe understanding and are embodied in behaviour, they sometimes resemble or even breed with other discourses and concepts. For Hughes the continual operation of these myths means that imaginative literatures may be positive 'hospitals where we heal, where our imaginations are healed', or dangerous 'battlefields where we get injured' (Hughes, 1970b: 67).

Hatching a crow: mutation and poetry

For all their syncretic coherence, the real power of the *Crow* poems does not stem from the way they encourage the sort of comparative mythology I've shown at play behind the St. George poems – although paralleling myths is often Hughes's approach in his own critical writing. The impact of the work is more direct:

> I wanted to free my image from the intellectual entanglement with my reader's response to specific meanings. I wanted to liberate it into imaginative freedom behind the reader's defences, where the real meaning could operate at leisure, in the nature of a radiation.
>
> ('Untitled Crow Notes – MS', n.d.)

Radiation here refers to a kind of mutative power, the operation of the charged symbol on the reader's psyche. The relationship between life, mutation and form underpins Hughes's idea of what the *Crow* project does. The project's various nods to an unspecified creative energy – the force that creates Crow – point toward a sense of life in general. As previously suggested this bears some of the hallmarks of Schopenhauer's will to life which has implications for the project's ecology and aesthetics.

While it is hard to establish direct parameters of influence, Hughes's admiration for Schopenhauer either prepares him for, or at least supports, perspectives on evolution and ecology which emphasise the interconnectivity of life and its operation below the level of species. As Laurence Wright puts it in a different context:

> Well before Richard Dawkins started talking about the gene machine, Schopenhauer had understood that the meanings our intellects and imaginations construct from experience are only incidentally necessary to the physical forces that shape us.
>
> (2008: 38)

The ecological picture, if it can be called that, found in Schopenhauer interrelates all life, though it is wrong to argue as Julian Young does that Schopenhauer essentially 'subscribes' to the 'Gaia Hypothesis'. Young argues that in Schopenhauer we see a Gaian homeostasis where 'world will [the whole of Nature] has no goal whatsoever beyond realising, in perpetuity, its system of ideas [gradations of the will, in this case species]' (2005: 77). Writing before Darwin, Schopenhauer describes Earth's current state, or 'system of ideas', as being stable and perpetual. Young's argument is misleading. In contrast to Schopenhauer, the Gaia hypothesis refers to the conditions for life in general, not life in its present form and distribution. Even so, Schopenhauer's pre-Darwinian holism resonates with Hughes's evolutionary-adaptive and proto-Gaian perspective evident in 'The Environmental Revolution'.

Hughes's article links organic and inorganic, noting the biosphere's 'extreme intricacy and precision of its interconnected working parts – winds, currents, rocks, plants, animals, weathers' across micro and macro scales where the 'tiny area of usable land, the fragility of the living cell' are, in their finitude, a challenge to our world view. He embeds the human-animal within the rest of life, highlighting life's fragile interdependence and its biochemical makeup – the Earth 'has our stomach, our blood, our precarious vital chemistry [DNA], and our future'. For Hughes, what another reader of Schopenhauer, Nietzsche, 'mistook for Dionysus', 'the vital, somewhat terrible spirit of natural life' challenges the stable category of the human in its capacity to generate, mutate and develop even in the face of being modified by human technologies: 'new in every second. Even when it [life] is poisoned to the point of death, its efforts to be itself are new in every second.' Here we see the drive to reproduction – that energy that typifies *Crow* and drives Crow on his quest. 'Nature's obsession [...] is to survive'; an obsession which, crucially, sees a shift in focus from the individual organism to the eco-system ('The Environmental Revolution', 1994a: 130–134). Hughes sees life on Earth, as with genes or the will to life, as more fundamental than individuals or even species, even though its fate is intertwined with their behaviours. And so, in 'A Crow Hymn', 'Life works at life using men and women' and all are parts of the same 'strange engine' (2003: 201).

Arguably Hughes would have come to these ecological perspectives anyway. More striking is the way that Schopenhauer also influences Hughes's aesthetics because he informs Jung's view of psychic/libidinal energy. Jung's concept of libidinal energy is based on the will – 'To Schopenhauer I owe the dynamic view of the psyche; the will is the libido that is back of everything' (1977: 204). In *Crow* we see a kind of coming together of Hughes's version of the generative and mutational striving of (the will to) life with Jung's model of psychic regulation. The adaptive failure which creates neuroses, like those of the scientist St. George, causes what Jung calls regression. The process of regression 'raises the value of contents that were previously excluded from the conscious process of adaptation, and hence are totally unconscious or only "dimly conscious"'. The Knight-scientist's mechanical universe, a dream of reason, breeds monsters of the mind and he, like Crow in the garden, commits a horrible religious (and evolutionary) error, shutting down the possibility of mutation and vitality. This error of judgement stems from a harmful preconception founded in myth. What Jung's notion of regression brings to the surface certainly seems at first sight to be slime from the depths; but if one does not stop short at a superficial evaluation and refrains from passing judgment on the basis of a preconceived dogma, it will be found that this 'slime' contains not merely incompatible and rejected remnants of everyday life, or inconvenient and objectionable animal tendencies, but also germs of new life and vital possibilities for the future.

(Jung, 1971: 34)

Not only does this chime with the ways that the mutative and abject in *Crow* actually constitute new vital possibilities in the face of a destructive techno-capitalist culture but it reflects Hughes's broader view on poetry:

Poetry, in every unstable or revolutionary situation, is on the side of eruption. It speaks for what is suppressed, or rejected, or denied; it speaks for whatever in a society is alive but undervalued, for whatever is shit in the dark and made to suffer. It speaks for everything, finally which the status quo deems irrelevant or undesirable or, perhaps, unmanageable, and so it speaks for the future, the time when those undesirables shall have broken up the status quo and come into the open as an accepted part of life.

('Why even bad poetry is good – MS', n.d.)

The collection's drive toward mutation and transformation make *Crow* an instance of Romantic monstrosity as described by Gigante, where monstrosity is typified 'by its capacity to turn aside unexpectedly from "normal" developmental processes and perpetuate its own brand of productivity' (2009: 227).[14] *Crow* is a narrative in which a new being (Crow) is created in order, Hughes hopes, to create new, ecologically sounder, ways of being. The opening poem purports to 'hatch a crow' and this hatching also takes place inside the reader ('Two Legends', 2003: 217). In this frame-breaking *Crow*/Crow develops inside us, breeding with our own myths and changing them; crow-ifying our consciousness as it were through its symbols' 'radiation'. The essay 'Crow on the Beach' explains that the key figure behind *Crow* is the myth of the trickster – that being who disobeys normal developmental processes, boundaries and categorisation, and perpetuates its own brand of productivity by creating new states of affairs as it does so 'in the evolutionary way [...] an all-out commitment to salvaging life against the odds'. Hughes argues that the collection is not a 'Black Comedy' which draws its effects from the 'suicidal nihilism' that afflicts 'a society or an individual where the supportive metaphysical beliefs disintegrate', but rather an instance of 'Trickster literature' sustained by the 'unkillable, biological optimism that supports a society or individual whose world is not yet fully created' (1994a: 241, 239).

Hughes's version of the trickster connects it to libidinal energy and lends it an interspecies quality: 'Trickster and sexuality are connected by a hotline [...] the optimism of the sperm still battling along after 150 million years' (1994a: 240). As Leonard Baskin's drawings for the project suggest, Crow himself is neither quite avian nor human and timescale here long pre-dates modern humans (c. 200,000 years) or even corvids (c. 20 million years). In Hughes the trickster embodies the capacity of life to respond to (evolutionary) pressure: 'life energy compressed under misery, the real value, recoiling and gathering itself, ransacking its roots for new directives, searching for a new way forward into new beginnings and new growth' ('Crow on the Beach – MS', n.d.).

Hughes's mixing of evolution with ideas from Jung, and behind him Schopenhauer, positions the libidinal 'psychic energy' which is central to art's affective power as an emergent property of a more general 'life energy'. Moreover, the notion of generating new patterns and images from old myths – 'ransacking' roots for new growth – not only addresses biological mutation and adaptation but asks us to consider the cultural under the auspices of the evolutionary. Passing on genetic mutations means that an individual talent might change the direction of a (species') tradition. While superficially Hughes's rhetoric risks turning Nature into the sort of static whole criticised by Morton, his emphasis on a tricksterish, mercurial and dynamic energy fundamentally challenges our sense of organic life and its emergent, metabiotic properties including the evolution of human technologies (Hughes's 'nearly autonomous technosphere') which, in the Anthropocene, have a global impact. Hughes's vision for *Crow* is comparable to the way Clarke's evolutionary-orientated systems theory has approached narratology.

Transformation stories challenge the stability of the human. Technicity supplements genetic mutation so that now, Clarke explains, '[a]mplified by emergent complexities induced by verbal languages and subsequent technologies of communication, social developments outpace biological evolution'. Clarke's systems-theoretical approach to narratology joins up biological and technological adaptation. The possibility of error plays an important role in both: 'the variations necessary to [biological] evolutionary processes are driven by the increment of noise within the channel of genetic transmission.' For Clarke, '[p]remodern tales of metamorphosis anticipate and overlap modern and contemporary stories of posthuman transformation' (2002: 170–171). In such stories the human is recombined with communicative technologies which, in their transmission of a message across a channel, always risk interference, changing the human's relation with its environment. Clarke's key example is David Cronenberg's 1986 film *The Fly*, where the protagonist's monstrous mutation stems from the error in technologically communicating (teleporting) biological material. However, as I shall show, the cybernetic human-techno metamorph fits very well with Hughes's Iron Man and Iron Woman.

Clarke links biological mutation and epiphylogenetic adaptation to the interrelated operation of metamorphic tales and metadiagetic tales (stories within stories). He argues that as well as describing the mutation and (mis) adaptation in relation to the environment, transformation stories can frequently be read as allegories of writing: 'the turns of metamorphic stories in any medium are also narratives of narrative – self-referential structures, typically stories within stories [like Arachne in Ovid, and his *Metamorphoses* more generally], that embed the transformations of events within the transformations of characters' (2008: 47).

Clarke compares metadiagesis, where we are aware of the story and its teller simultaneously, to second order observation in systems theory – where a system observes its own operations. Though not strictly metadiagetic, the way Hughes constantly plays on the reader's metatextual awareness of Crow as *Crow* means the collection operates in a comparable manner as the text depends on self-referentiality for rhetorical effect. The way Crow's actions cause his own, and others', metamorphosis are mirrored by *Crow*'s metamorphosing of myths. Thereby the book mythologises the operation of art alongside its evolutionary patterns. The short poem 'Crowego' reflects this process:

> Crow followed Ulysses till he turned
> As a worm, which Crow ate.
>
> Grappling with Hercules' two puff-adders
> He strangled in error Dejanira.
>
> The gold melted out of Hercules' ashes
> Is an electrode in Crow's brain,
>
> Drinking Beowulf's blood, and wrapped in his hide,
> Crow communes with poltergeists out of old ponds.
>
> His wings are the stiff back of his only book.
> Himself the only page – of solid ink.
>
> So he gazes into the quag of the past
> Like a gypsy into the crystal of the future,
>
> Like a leopard into a fat land.
>
> (2003: 240)

In this litany of mythic (mal)adaptation Hughes gives us his method for *Crow* via its self-aware 'Crow ego', the way it self-consciously feeds off the form and content of old myths; 'Beowulf's blood' fires the collection's alliterative lines as well as its dragon slaying. With its 'ink' and its 'stiff' cover Hughes draws attention to *Crow* as text and here, like the book that bears his name, Crow gets the myths wrong, not just strangling the wife when he should strangle the snakes but strangling the wrong wife (Dejanira instead of Megara). This mistake replays the nightmare in 'Crow's Account of St. George' – *Hercules Furens* becomes one of the mythic channels, or 'electrodes', that organise *Crow*'s brain, and also impacts upon the conceptual apparatus of *Crow*'s readers. As Crow gazes on the 'quag' of the past's myths, *Crow* grazes on them, re-tooling them for *Crow*'s future-orientated ecological project. This process is intriguingly similar to that described by Clarke:

The narrative depiction of fantastic bodily metamorphoses sets into further play the formal possibilities of linguistic and conceptual combinations. Moreover, the narrative drive toward images of bodily transformation tests and contests the boundaries of 'identities' and their psychic and social regimes. Transformation stories are a kind of social-systemic program tool for tweaking the cultural hard drive.

(2008: 46)

In other words, Clark argues that narratives about the way that stories can change how we perceive and conceive things encourage further transformations of our concepts, perception and cognition. Hughes's own tweaking of the cultural hard drive – what he would call the myths of our inner world – revolves around a mythologisation of evolution, one which includes the role of art and other imbrications of the organic and technical. This mythologisation itself is intended to set into play the possibility of new 'linguistic and conceptual combinations' which might in turn engender behaviours and technologies better suited to an environment in crisis.

Such fluctuating relations between evolutionary adaptation, embodiment, communicative technology and epiphylogenetic cultural memory confounds the model of Nature reconciling with Culture offered by the Hughesean ecocritics Gifford, Sagar and Scigaj. Instead it forces a powerful rethink of what evolution means for contemporary ecological thought. Hughes, perhaps more clearly in his creative work than his criticism, encourages a sense that art does not just revivify our senses in the manner that early ecocriticism proposed but becomes an engine for mutating new concepts, and thereby new possibilities. This intertwined process of perceptual sensitivity and conceptual possibility means that, for Hughes, art might play a significant role in adapting humans to the environmental crisis, and this seems most apparent in his two children's stories *The Iron Man* and *The Iron Woman*.

Testing his metal

a cyborg world might be about lived social and bodily realities in which people are not afraid of their joint kinship with animals and machines, not afraid of permanently partial identities and contradictory standpoints
– Donna Haraway (1990: 154)

In 1968 Hughes published *The Iron Man*, a children's parable about technology and biological energy in which a metal giant becomes the world's defender. The Iron Man's arrival on the first page positions technology as not under human control but always already on the scene: 'Where had he come from? Nobody knows. How was he made? Nobody Knows' (1989: 11). As with the Promethean upendings of *Tales from Ovid*, Deep Ecology's dream of the pre-technological human (and going back to a pre-technological Earth) appears untenable; Earth is 'altered' by humanity's 'godlike novelty'. Hughes tells us of the failure of those misguided characters who, terrified of the Iron Man, try to bury him underground because they 'want to restore the earth to the status quo', but the repressed Iron Man simply returns ('Draft of Myth and Education – TS', n.d.). Luckily for humans, the intervention of a plucky young boy called Hogarth means that the Iron Man becomes their friend because he later defends them against the Space-bat-angel-dragon, a monster which, Hughes has explained, embodies the energies of the 'biological world, with its mysterious, subconscious vitality, which rises out of the chemistry of our organism, which in turn emerges from the chemical elements themselves – the stuff of creation' (1992d: 149).

We can see Hughes's background in anthropology come into play in the way the Iron Man defeats the Space-bat-angel-dragon by besting it in a series of trials of fortitude which are quite clearly rituals of self-sacrifice or self-mutilation. Explaining his parable Hughes argues that in many ways the modern 'world of technology' is

> incompatible with the other, instinctive, inner world of overwhelming nameless forces. At one time, religion named these forces, and set them in a kind of technological frame, a constructed mythology, and gave the growing child a manageable relationship to them. That has now largely gone.

Like Jung's 'slime from the depths',

> The forces are once more nameless, mythologies have evaporated, and all negotiation between these forces and the growing child has ceased. Many things in education and culture discourage, or even prohibit any sponta- neous attempt to negotiate between the child and the shadowy inhabitants of that inner world. In fact, that mysterious internal being is generally presented as hostile, destructive, to be shunned and if possible annihilated.
>
> (Hughes, 1992d: 149)

The Iron Man's sacrifice creates a new ritual, one with the technological human at its centre: 'I deliberately designed the plot in the faith that my younger readers (my own children) would internalize it as a map for real life' (1992d: 149). It is striking that the book, written while Hughes was working on *Crow*, offers us the knight and dragon of the St. George myth in a configuration that asserts negotiation and canniness rather than domination. In the end the Space-bat-angel-dragon, as with the Iron Man, becomes a friend of Earth and, like the snake in 'A Horrible Religious Error', harmonises with the music of the spheres.

Hughes explained in an interview with Blake Morrison that

> In *The Iron Man* you have the whole mysterious world of technology, the mechanical world, and the boy is brought into relation with it in a friendly way [...] so he feels he can control it.
>
> (Morrison, 1998: 159)

'Control it' supposes the dangerous alternative of it controlling him, which is what has happened in the more complex and more overtly environmentalist sequel, *The Iron Woman* in which the discourses of industry prevent a waste processing plant from accepting the harm of its actions. Instead the book's polluters insist that 'We follow good industrial practice. We stick to the rules'; but the failures of self-regulation encourage bad behaviour, allowing for a steady polluting of the countryside (1993: 44).

Laurence Buell, partially in response to what he saw as first wave ecocriticism's naivety, proposed the literary category 'toxic discourse', where concern with human pollution ruptures early ecocriticism's model of (deep) 'ecological holism' and consequently the belief that 'acts of imagination' have the capacity to enact an unmediated reconnection with Nature (1998: 656). Buell dates modern toxic discourse back to *Silent Spring* which in many ways is itself the source-text for *The Iron Woman*'s narrative of water pollution. The Iron Woman, as Zoe Jaques puts it, 'operates for Hughes as a posthuman antidote to the posthumane condition of mankind – she is a redemptive and punitive answer to a humanity that has cut itself off both from "being human" and from being part of a wider world' (2015: 194).

Hughes has said that *The Iron Woman* 'began by my thinking: how does nature feel about being destroyed? Presumably it's enraged, and the obvious response is an aggressive one, to remove the destroyer' (interview with Morrison, 1998: 166). To that extent it would be tempting to read the Iron Women as a kind of avenging Gaia when she says she will tear down the factory and 'DESTROY THE POISONERS. | THE IGNORANT ONES' (1993: 24). With her technological form, she cannot just be a metal manifestation of (Mother) Nature. As Jaques points out, 'she transcends the boundary division between the artificial and the natural', but in a manner that Jaques tells us Haraway would align 'with Gaia: "itself a a cyborg, a complex auto-poetic system that terminally blurred the boundaries among the geological, the organic and the technological"' (Jaques, 2015: 197).

Hughes, returning to his notion of evolutionary error which leads to extinction, offers a vision of technology becoming the agent of human destruction. But the Iron Woman does not tear down the factory; she realises that they 'have to be changed [...] not just stopped' (1993: 36). When characters touch the Iron Woman they are overcome by a terrible scream, 'the cry of the rivers and the lakes. Of all the creatures under the water, on top of the water, and all that go between.' Crucially this scream can travel, in a quasi-viral fashion, from person to person; its power is contagious and its effects worsen when infected people touch each other. The first person to realise the significance of the scream is the book's heroine, Lucy, who, along with Hogarth and the Iron Man, tries to curb the destructive potential of the Iron Woman. Lucy sees that the humans' and the other animals' fates are intertwined when she dreams of a human baby crying 'as if the world had ended' amidst the poisoned rivers, birds and amphibians (1993: 20, 22).

But for the rest of the humans the new awareness of animal suffering fails to change their behaviour. They remain bound by economic necessity. Lucy's father, like most of the locals, works for the polluters and the population know the risks and some worry about 'how the Waste Factory poisons everything'. But, like those who refuse to acknowledge the abattoir, they cannot face up to 'the true nature of the activities by which [they] survive'. Perhaps most importantly the townspeople are hamstrung by the inability to conceive of an ecological constraint. The factory's 'unspoken motto is "Impossible is not a word"' (1993: 24, 40).

Change only comes when the Iron Woman takes on the powers of the Space-bat-angel-dragon, whom the Iron Man has called for help. Galvanised by the dragon's bio-energy the Iron Woman transforms the men into giant water creatures; they literally become-animal.[15] This transformative event, caused by technology's channeling of biological energy, is inarticulable and untranslatable: while they are animals, and even after, the characters cannot unfold the tale of what has harrowed them, but on their return they are changed. Here technology engenders an engagement with otherness, thereby transforming behaviour toward industrial technologies and improving the ways humans adapt to, and adapt, the ecosystem.

The Morrison interview and *The Iron Woman* see Hughes suggesting an approach to modern technology that resonates with Heidegger's notion that, while the technological world cannot be abolished, it might be assimilated and transformed – you 'can't turn back the technology of the world, but you can learn to handle it' (Morrison, 1998: 166). *The Iron Woman* shows the characters becoming aware of their material environment (Hughes's outer Nature) and their own animality (inner Nature) via technology which is always already modifying both their environment and their subjectivity. Technology does not just come from the outside, it is not a controllable prosthesis, but a supplement now inextricable from the human's adaptation of and to its world. The Iron Woman knows this foolishness of separating the technical from the human: 'I am not a robot' she reminds us mysteriously, 'I am the real thing' (1993: 18).

The technologically induced transformative event encourages 'listening and thinking'; the population begin to try and focus on their organic and cultural environments (1993: 82). The humans' inability to articulate their experience corresponds to the fact that, as Heidegger puts it in his famous *Spiegel* interview, 'one can no more translate thought than one can translate a poem' (2010: 63). Hughes is suggesting that the (aesthetic) event does not just make things more vivid (the scream of the animals), or help the polluters see things from a different angle (the transformation into animals) but it also opens up the potential for changes in the way the world is perceived and conceived in the future, highlighting the possibility that the story's pattern and images might function in new, and unpredictable, ways. *The Iron Woman* is not just an ecoparable: 'in the end,' Hughes explains to Morrison, perhaps '*The Iron Women* is an image of the creative act? The whole story is a myth about writing a poem' (1998: 166).[16]

Notes

1 Hughes read *Psychological Types*, the book that engages most directly with Schiller and the symbol as living form, aged 19. He claims that *Psychological Types* 'was the one book [he] knew backwards' by the time he went to university. See his ' Letter to Gammage' (2007: 679).

2 'Schiller said people are only truly human when they play' (Hughes, 1970a).

3 Allan Stoekl offers an interesting discussion of the way the acknowledged excessiveness of the SUV makes it desirable (2007: 122–125). For an excellent and still-relevant critique of the use of the American landscape in SUV advertising, see the Canyonro song from *The Simpsons* (Anderson, 1998).

4 Keith Sagar (2000) has helpfully pieced together Hughes's various comments about *Crow* into a rough narrative and published them as an appendix to his study.

5 Despite his evolutionary thinking, Hughes resists any misapprehended social Darwinism. In a striking passage in Hughes's notes he alludes to Shakespeare to attack the way that the 'survival of the fittest' is conceptualised, particularly the way it has destroyed any sense of cooperation and coadaptation: the 'prevailing law is competiveness with no limits' where each 'thing meets in sheer oppugnancy' and 'appetite makes a universal prey and last eats itself' ('Oppugnancy – MS', n.d.).

6 For an extended engagement with Hughes's meat eating see Gifford (1995: 133–140).

7 In the draft 'Crow's Fast' man appears as 'a walking death camp | Cattle wallowed in their slaughter terror' ('Crow's Fast', n.d.).

8 In the draft Hughes fuses the mechanical and the linguistic by describing the blood as 'unravelling from a tap | into bits of etymology' ('Crow's Account of a Battle – MS', n.d.).

9 Octopus behaviour featured in Jacques Cousteau's popular books, TV shows and films in the 1950s and 1960s. Emory library records show that Hughes owned a 1970 edition of Cousteau's *The Shark* so it is possible that he was aware of cephalopod behaviour from Cousteau's other writings and broadcasts.

10 It is worth noting the purposeful similarity with another poem about evolution, the (Schopenhauerean) Thomas Hardy's 'Heredity' where 'Flesh perishes, I live on | Projecting trait and trace […] The eternal thing in man, | That heeds no call to die' (2001: 96).

11 The snake remained an important animal for Hughes. His last major critical piece in *Winter Pollen*, 'The Snake in the Oak', finds him tracing the figure of the serpent throughout Coleridge's work.

12 The allusion to Spenser has also been noted by Hirschberg (1980).

13 Hughes's zealous criticisms of Renaissance Protestantism are developed at length in *Shakespeare and the Goddess of Complete Being* (1992c).

14 Gigante's key example is Keats's 'Lamia'. The way Keats shows rational philosophy as unweaving the rainbow and thwarting a snake-female chimes interestingly with *Crow*.

15 The fact that only men are transformed is not quite as baffling as it may first seem. Hughes is not saying that woman are not polluters too. As Jaques puts it, 'Although the men of the story quite clearly represent male-dominated capitalism, the transformation of them alone creates an unsettling gender divide' (2015: 197).

16 This chapter is derived, in part, from an article published in *The Ted Hughes Society Journal* 2 (2011): 4–16.

References

Anderson, Mike B. 1998. 'The Last Temptation of Krust'. *The Simpsons*. 20th Century Fox.

Astley, Neil. 1990. *Dear Next Prime Minister: Open Letters to Margaret Thatcher & Neil Kinnock*. Newcastle: Bloodaxe Books.

Bate, Jonathan. 2001. *The Song of the Earth*. First paperback edition. London: Picador.

Bishop, Nick. 1991. *Re-Making Poetry: Ted Hughes and a New Critical Psychology*. London: Harvester Wheatsheaf.

Bishop, Paul. 2008. *Analytical Psychology and German Classical Aesthetics: Goethe, Schiller, and Jung*. Vol. 1. London: Routledge.

Buell, Laurence. 1998. 'Toxic Discourse'. *Critical Inquiry* 24(3): 639–665.

Carr, W.I. 1958. 'Review of *The Hawk in the Rain*'. *Delta* 14: 25–27.

Carroll, Robert, and Stephen Prickett. 2008. *The Bible: Authorized King James Version*. Oxford: Oxford University Press.

Clarke, Bruce. 2002. 'Mediating The Fly: Posthuman Metamorphosis in the 1950s'. *Configurations* 10(1): 169–191.

Clarke, Bruce. 2008. *Posthuman Metamorphosis: Narrative and Systems*. New York: Fordham University Press.

Diamond, Cora. 2001. 'Injustice and Animals'. In *Slow Cures and Bad Philosophers: Essays on Wittgenstein, Medicine and Bioethics*, edited by Carl Elliott. Durham, NC: Duke University Press. 118–149.

Diamond, Cora. 2008. 'The Difficulty of Reality and the Difficulty of Philosophy'. In *Philosophy and Animal Life*, by Stanley Cavell, John McDowell, Ian Hacking, Cary Wolfe, and Cora Diamond. New York: Columbia University Press. 46–91.

Faas, Ekbert. 1980. *Ted Hughes*. Santa Barbara: Black Sparrow Press.

Ferry, Luc. 1995. *The New Ecological Order*. Translated by Carol Volk. Chicago: University of Chicago Press.

Gifford, Terry. 1995. *Green Voices: Understanding Contemporary Nature Poetry*. Manchester: Manchester University Press.

Gigante, Denise. 2009. *Life: Organic Form and Romanticism*. New Haven, CT: Yale University Press.

Haraway, Donna J. 1990. *Simians, Cyborgs, and Women: The Reinvention of Nature*. New York: Routledge.

Haraway, Donna J. 2008. *When Species Meet*. Minneapolis: University of Minnesota Press.

Hardy, Thomas. 2001. *Thomas Hardy: Poems Selected by Tom Paulin*. Edited by Tom Paulin. London: Faber and Faber.

Heidegger, Martin. 1971. *Poetry, Language, Thought*. Translated by Albert Hofstadter. New York: Harper and Row Publishers.

Heidegger, Martin. 1977. *The Question Concerning Technology, and Other Essays*. Translated by William Lovitt. New York: Harper and Row.

Heidegger, Martin. 2010. '"Only a God Can Save Us": The Spiegel Interview (1966)'. In *Heidegger the Man and the Thinker*, edited by Thomas Sheehan, translated by William Richardson. New Brunswick: Transaction publishers.

Hirschberg, Stuart. 1980. *Myth in the Poetry of Ted Hughes*. Portmarnock: Wolfhound Press.

Hughes, Ted. 1962. 'Engravings of Leonard Baskin [TS]'. Box 112, Folder 18. Ted Hughes papers, Stuart A. Rose Manuscript, Archives, and Rare Book Library, Emory University.

Hughes, Ted. 1967. *Poetry in the Making: An Anthology of Poems and Programmes from Listening and Writing*. London: Faber & Faber.

Hughes, Ted. 1970a. 'Draft of Play the Game [TS]'. Box 114, Folder 23. Ted Hughes papers, Stuart A. Rose Manuscript, Archives, and Rare Book Library, Emory University.

Hughes, Ted. 1970b. 'Myth and Education'. *Children's Literature in Education* 1(1): 55–70.

Hughes, Ted. 1971. 'Letter to the Spectator, 5 March [MS]'. Box 114 Folder 10. Ted Hughes papers, Stuart A. Rose Manuscript, Archives, and Rare Book Library, Emory University.

Hughes, Ted. 1973. *Crow*. [Record Sleeve Notes]. Claddagh Records.

Hughes, Ted. 1989. *The Iron Man: A Story in Five Nights*. Illustrated by Andrew Davidson. 3rd Reprint. London: Faber & Faber.

Hughes, Ted. 1992a. 'Notes on Published Words [TS]'. Box 115, Folder 24. Ted Hughes papers, Stuart A. Rose Manuscript, Archives, and Rare Book Library, Emory University.

Hughes, Ted. 1992b. 'The Interpretation of Parables'. *Signal* 69: 147–152.

Hughes, Ted. 1992c. *Shakespeare and the Goddess of Complete Being*. London: Faber & Faber.

Hughes, Ted. 1992d. 'Your World'. *Observer Magazine*, November 29.

Hughes, Ted. 1993. *The Iron Woman*. Illustrated by Andrew Davidson. London: Faber & Faber.

Hughes, Ted. 1994a. *Winter Pollen: Occasional Prose*. London: Faber & Faber,.

Hughes, Ted. 1994b. '"Letter to Freida Hughes". October 31'. Box 1, Folder 76. Ted Hughes papers, Stuart A. Rose Manuscript, Archives, and Rare Book Library, Emory University.

Hughes, Ted. 2003. *Collected Poems*. Edited by Paul Keegan. New York: Farrar, Straus and Giroux.

Hughes, Ted. 2007. *Letters of Ted Hughes*. Edited by Christopher Reid. London: Faber & Faber.

Hughes, Ted. n.d. 'Bedtime Story III [MS]'. Box 85, Folder 53. Ted Hughes papers, Stuart A. Rose Manuscript, Archives, and Rare Book Library, Emory University.

Hughes, Ted. n.d. 'Crow Fast [MS]'. Box 57, Folder 5. Ted Hughes papers, Stuart A. Rose Manuscript, Archives, and Rare Book Library, Emory University.

Hughes, Ted. n.d. 'Crow Is About the Cleverest Bird [MS]'. Box 85, Folder 6. Ted Hughes papers, Stuart A. Rose Manuscript, Archives, and Rare Book Library, Emory University.

Hughes, Ted. n.d. 'Crow on the Beach [MS]'. Box 106, Folder 13. Ted Hughes papers, Stuart A. Rose Manuscript, Archives, and Rare Book Library, Emory University.

Hughes, Ted. n.d. 'Crow's Account of a Battle [MS]'. Box 61, Folder 1. Ted Hughes papers, Stuart A. Rose Manuscript, Archives, and Rare Book Library, Emory University.

Hughes, Ted. n.d. 'Draft foreword to The Way to Write [by John Fairfax and John Moat] [MS]'. Box 113, Folder 5. Ted Hughes papers, Stuart A. Rose Manuscript, Archives, and Rare Book Library, Emory University.

Hughes, Ted. n.d. 'Draft of Myth and Education [TS]'. Box 114, Folder 16. Ted Hughes papers, Stuart A. Rose Manuscript, Archives, and Rare Book Library, Emory University.

Hughes, Ted. n.d. Notebook. Box 57, Folder 1. Ted Hughes papers, Stuart A. Rose Manuscript, Archives, and Rare Book Library, Emory University.

Hughes, Ted. n.d. 'Oppugnancy [rev. of Dröscher, Mysterious Senses] [MS]'. Box 114, Folder 19. Ted Hughes papers, Stuart A. Rose Manuscript, Archives, and Rare Book Library, Emory University.

Hughes, Ted. n.d. 'Untitled Crow Notes [MS]'. Box 106, Folder 13. Ted Hughes papers, Stuart A. Rose Manuscript, Archives, and Rare Book Library, Emory University.

Hughes, Ted. n.d. 'Untitled Draft [Snakes in Crow] [MS]'. Box 85, Folder 72. Ted Hughes papers, Stuart A. Rose Manuscript, Archives, and Rare Book Library, Emory University.

Hughes, Ted. n.d. 'Why Even Bad Poetry Is Good [MS]'. Box 115, Folder 3. Ted Hughes papers, Stuart A. Rose Manuscript, Archives, and Rare Book Library, Emory University.

Jaques, Zoe. 2015. *Children's Literature and the Posthuman: Animal, Environment, Cyborg.* New York; London: Routledge.

Jung, Carl Gustav. 1964. *Man and His Symbols.* Edited by Marie-Luise von Franz and Carl Gustav Jung. London: Aldus Books.

Jung, Carl Gustav. *The Collected Works of C.G. Jung.* 1971. Edited by Herbert Read, Michael Fordham, and Gerald Adler. Translated by Helton Godwin Baynes. Revised editon. Vol. VI. London: Routledge and Kegan Paul.

Jung, Carl Gustav. 1977. *C.G. Jung Speaking: Interviews and Encounters.* Edited by William McGuire and R.F.C. Hull. Princeton: Princeton University Press.

Kant, Immanuel. 1996. *The Metaphysics of Morals.* Translated by Mary J. Gregor. Cambridge: Cambridge University Press.

Kerridge, Richard. 2014. 'Ecocritical Readings'. In *Ted Hughes,* edited by Terry Gifford. Basingstoke: Palgrave Macmillan: 176–190.

Larkin, Philip. 1983. *Required Writing: Miscellaneous Pieces 1955–1982.* London: Faber and Faber.

Lawrence, David Herbert. 1972. *Selected Poems.* Edited by Keith M. Sagar. London: Penguin.

Lawrence, David Herbert. 2002. *The Complete Poems of D.H. Lawrence: With an Introduction and Bibliography.* Edited by David Ellis. Ware: Wordsworth Editions.

Lidström, Susanna. 2013. 'Different Shades of Green: A Dark Green Counterculture in Ted Hughes's "Crow"'. *Ecozon@: European Journal of Literature, Culture and Environment* 4: 12–29.

Morrison, Blake. 1998. *Too True.* London: Granta Books.

Ovid. 2004. *P. Ovidi Nasonis Metamorphoses.* Edited by R.J. Tarrant. Oxford: Clarendon Press.

Sagar, Keith. 2000. *The Laughter of Foxes.* Liverpool: Liverpool University Press.

Schopenhauer, Arthur. 1998. *On The Basis Of Morality.* Revised edition. Translated by E.F.J. Payne. Indianapolis: Hackett.

Scigaj, Leonard M. 1986. *The Poetry of Ted Hughes: Form and Imagination.* Iowa City: University of Iowa Press.

Skea, Ann. 1994. *Ted Hughes, the Poetic Quest.* Armidale, NSW: University of New England Press.

Solnick, Sam. 2011. '"Life Subdued to its Instrument": Ted Hughes and Technology'. *The Ted Hughes Society Journal* 2: 4–16.

Spenser, Edmund. 1978. *The Faerie Queene.* Edited by Thomas P. Roche. London: Penguin.

Stiegler. 2010. 'Memory'. In *Critical Terms for Media Studies,* edited by W.J.T. Mitchell and Mark B.N. Hansen. Chicago: University of Chicago Press. 64–87.

Stoekl, Allan. 2007. *Bataille's Peak.* Minneapolis; London: University of Minnesota Press.

White, Lynn. 1967. 'The Historical Roots of Our Ecologic Crisis'. *Science* 155(3767): 1203–1207.

Wills, David. 2008. *Dorsality: Thinking Back through Technology and Politics.* Minneapolis: University of Minnesota Press.

Wolfe, Cary. 2009. *What is Posthumanism?* Minneapolis: University of Minnesota Press.

Wood, David. 1999. 'Comment Ne Pas Manger – Deconstruction and Humanism'. In *Animal Others: On Ethics, Ontology, and Animal Life*, edited by H. Peter Steeves. Albany, NY: SUNY Press. 12–35.

Wright, Laurence. 2008. 'Ecological Thinking: Schopenhauer, J.M. Coetzee and Who We Are in the World'. In *Toxic Belonging?: Identity and Ecology in Southern Africa*, edited by Dan Wylie. Newcastle: Cambridge Scholars Publishing. 24–42.

Young, Julian. 2002. *Heidegger's Later Philosophy*. Cambridge: Cambridge University Press.

Young, Julian. 2005. *Schopenhauer*. New York: Routledge.

3 'Germinal ironies'

Changing climates in the poetry of Derek Mahon

One part of my mind must learn to know its place

                 – 'Spring in Belfast'

'Spring in Belfast' opens Mahon's *New Collected Poems*, situating him in his home ground, describing both the city that nurtured him and the perennial effort of his poetry to (re)discover from where and what it emerges. Walking among his 'own' the speaker addresses his 'conspiracy with the wet | stone', the internal rhyme highlighting the bedrock he is hewn from, the material, religious and social environs – the 'things that happen' in 'kitchen houses' under the 'cold gaze of a sanctimonious God'. The poem's closing financial metaphor indicates his lack of investment in these happenings which 'Should engage more than my casual interest, | Exact more interest than my casual pity' (2011: 15). This early piece – originally called 'Poem in Belfast' when it appeared in 1965 – contains many of the features recognised as hallmarks of Mahon's work: dextrous use of rhyme; his imbrication of the spatial, social and economic; an ironical or detached view from the margins; a refusal to fully invest himself and a concomitant guilty conscience at this failure to do or feel what he 'should'.

An awareness of roots is not automatic, it must, at least in part, be learned – 'Once more, as before, I remember not to forget' (2011: 15). The rhyme of more/before indicates the repetition inherent in not forgetting, of the mind learning to 'know its place'. Mahon is anxious about his own possible miseducation; his poetry's 'ground note', claims Neil Corcoran, 'is always misgiving' (1983: 160). Hence the process of knowing one's *place* comes bound up with an awareness of the power structures within any locality or community that shape subjectivity and perspective (knowing *one's* place). While still an undergraduate, he wrote an editorial for Trinity College Dublin's student magazine proclaiming the importance of poetry addressing 'the economic and psychological conditions in which people live', conditions which are 'as much a part of the natural landscape as a thunderstorm, a full moon, or the seasonal habits of trees and birds' (1962: 3).

It is this foundational concern with linking the economic and psychological alongside the spatial and ecological that, for me, makes Mahon the most interesting contemporary Irish poet for exploring the Anthropocene – though strong cases might be made for Eavan Boland and Paula Meehan for similar reasons. Mahon offers a more challenging ecological vision than his friend Seamus Heaney who, partly due to his stature, remains the favoured contemporary Irish poet for critics interested in ecocriticism. Yet even Garrard and Lidström, who position Heaney as the embodiment of 'environmental' (as opposed to what they see as a Hughesean 'ecophenomenological') poetics, acknowledge that the Nobel Laureate's later environmentalist 'internationalism' emerges out of an earlier 'bioregionalism' (2014: 45). In contrast, Mahon is a poet whose modernity, urbanity and self-deracination has made him more famous as a chronicler of the city (Belfast, Dublin, London, New York, Paris) than the country; he is less tied to specific geographies and bioregions.

Mahon's formative internationalism has fed into what is arguably the first sustained, direct engagement with climate change from a major British or Irish poet. Yet a 2010 anthology on Irish writing and ecocriticism, the first of its kind, omits his pressing contemporary concerns, choosing instead to focus on what John Elder calls 'the deep history of the Irish land' (2010: 1). The volume advertised itself as focusing on 'what cultural representations of nonhuman nature reveal about how humans care for and dwell in place' (*Out of the Earth*, 2010). Tellingly, of the famous generation of poets who began publishing in the 1960s, the one given a chapter here is Mahon's college companion Michael Longley, a poet whose ecological concerns are primarily orientated around the local, refracted through his close observations of the flora and fauna in the Mayo landscape of Carrigskeewaun. While certainly not wanting to castigate any single publication for a particular omission, always a dangerous game, I nevertheless believe that it is fair to say that the balance of essays in *Out of the Earth* represents a still-common tendency within British and Irish ecocriticism to privilege what Clark calls the 'tradition of romantic humanism' as a way of addressing 'local and easily identifiable [environmental] outrages and injustices'. But climate change, he goes on to say,

> challenges some green critics with the fact that while they have been inventing ways to think and act in relation to their national cultures and histories, they seem – like almost everyone else – still a long way short of thinking in the way and on the scale demanded by an issue both so global and multiplicitous.
>
> (2010: 142)

These are exactly the sorts of tensions that Mahon's work negotiates. His is partly, as Haughton puts it, 'a poetry of place and critical resistance, responding to and resisting the tyranny of modernity', which often displays a kind of 'romantic humanism or metaphysical ecology' (2007: 6). But, particularly in the collections published after Haughton's landmark 2007 study, Mahon's sense of 'place and critical resistance' has been increasingly problematised by the awareness of climate change. If Mahon 'started out as a poet in resistance to his home place, he went on to become a uniquely compelling poet of other places without abandoning the notion of poetry as a form of resistance'. There is 'always an edge of political anger, and cultural critique in his work, born of a sense of damage that has become increasingly ecological' (Haughton, 2007: 18). Mahon's ironic tone and his awareness of global relations rupture any Romantic ecology which posits poem or landscape as a space which positively alters consciousness and conscience – Bate's 'imaginary parks' which teach readers how to dwell. These imaginary parks are the sort of poetic spaces that Clark, Morton and other challengers of early ecocriticism have lambasted for de-coupling the potential for an alteration of consciousness from a detailed socio-political attention and critique.

In the first section of this chapter I show how Mahon's uneasy relationship with place and history gives rise to an awareness of the marginalised and ignored, and how irony and style combine in a form of poetic thinking which challenges nationalist violence and then post-national cultural imperialism. The second section tracks Mahon's emergent ecological sensibility, in particular how he imagines global interconnection and the relationship between economic and ecological systems. In the next section I return to irony in an ecological context, arguing that what makes Mahon's work so interesting is that the same ironic consciousness that subverted simplistic atavisms in his early work comes up against the pieties and contradictions of contemporary green thinking. I read his work in the light of recent (eco)critical approaches which focus on the anxieties of an inadequate ecological consciousness in the era of climate change – particularly those of Szerszynski, Clark, Blühdorn and Morton. The final third of the chapter explores how Mahon's treatment of some of the most recognisable phenomena of climate change – from wind farms and rising sea levels to Lovelock's Gaia – offer a series of powerful challenges to readers interested in ecology and poetry.

Mahon's poetry makes a fascinating arena in which to explore the difficulties faced by the contemporary, ecologically aware, liberal subject whose environmental concern is predicated upon notions of personal choice and agency that cannot necessarily cope with the radical aporias that climate change engenders. This is the arena Blühdorn has called a 'simulative politics'. Simulative politics deceives itself into thinking that it takes action against the unsustainable ecological situation while actually failing to address the complexity of the issues at hand, therefore becoming complicit in sustaining the unsustainable. In other words, an environmentalist way of thinking

> which had once been launched as a critical weapon against ideological deception has itself become ideological: it [simulative politics] tells a dubious story of eco-political oppression and alienation; it conceals the post-ecologist resolve to defend the ecologically exploitative and destructive system of democratic consumer capitalism.
>
> (Blühdorn, 2007: 264)

Mahon's pervasive irony encourages a way of reading which attempts to cognise and resist global ecological crises while acknowledging both the thresholds of ecopoetic thinking and the limits of individual agency

'Rage for order': ironies of time and place

In Mahon's collections before the 1990s, overt environmental concerns remain oblique, occasionally surfacing in poems such as 'The Antigone Riddle' ('a plover flops in his oil slick') or the 'Monet-monoxide sunset' of the poem 'Brighton Beach' (2011: 65, 138). There is however a pervasive fascination with the detritus of industrial modernity which, from vehicles to condoms, accumulates on the poetry's streets, fields and shorelines. In 'Apotheosis of Tins', the filthy modern tide sees 'imperishable' washed-up tins turn into Yorick-like memento mori, lying 'like skulls in the hands | Of soliloquists' (1999: 69). Technologies and commodities encroach on the countryside; the nymphs are gone – 'neraid' are transformed to 'coke bottle[s]' ('Ovid in Tomis', 2011: 140). In 'A Garage in Co. Cork', Ovid's hospitable rustics Baucis and Philemon change 'to petrol pumps' rather than trees – a metamorphosis of animal-bodies into oil that reoccurs in several late poems including the 2008 collection *Life on Earth*'s 'An Indian Garden' and 'Homage to Goa' (2011: 122).[1] These desacralising transformations and the constant focus on the junked, wasted and marginal are part of Mahon's fascination with those obsolete objects and abandoned spaces which highlight the transience of individuals and civilisations.

One of the key features of Mahon's poetry is the way that he uses other spaces and times to modify the here and now, hence the frame-breaking or shifts in perspective that typify many of his poems. These linkages across space and time are the counterbalancing force to a detachment that has been a source of ire for readers like Tom Paulin for whom Mahon is 'an intransigent aesthete who rejects life almost completely' and who writes poems yearning for 'a place of pure being which exists outside history' (1984: 55, 58). Though right, to an extent, about Mahon's gestures toward an ahistorical or even apocalyptic sphere, Paulin overstretches his argument. Poems from the 1960s and 1970s do indeed thrill in the contemplation of the apocalyptic, reaching out beyond the (corrupt and corrupting) human sphere into 'a world without cars, computers | Or nuclear skies' ('The Banished Gods', 2011: 77). In another poem from 1975's *The Snow Party*, Mahon's Frazerian 'Fire King', encumbered by the 'barbarous cycle' of violence, harbours 'cold dreams | Of a place out of time' because he is 'through with history' ('The Last of the Fire Kings', 2011: 63–64). However, what Paulin fails to properly acknowledge is that the irony and aestheticism that Mahon uses to hold history at a distance is marked by an awareness of this tactic's limitations.[2] The poet knows his ironic voice is encumbered by the same traditions he seeks to undermine. His engagement with history often generates an anxiety about complicity which also prevails in his later poems which disrupt any sense of Romantic ecology or localised dwelling with the contaminations of global ecological crisis.

While Mahon resists the pull of his roots he acknowledges that they exert a gravitational drag. He knows the charm of an aesthetic which foregrounds rootedness in the face of modern disaffection, echoing this sentiment through the mouthpiece of Knut Hamsun in the poem 'Hunger' (first published as 'Knut Hampson in Old Age' in 1981): 'Born of the earth, I made terms with the earth, | This being the only thing of lasting worth'. With his notion of the 'agriculture where all cultures start', Hamsun lies close to the nationalist eco-logical consciousness of Heidegger, and Mahon does not let us forget that he too was associated with Nazism – 'I shook hands with Hitler; knew disgrace'. However, as the nod to Yeats in the final stanza ('perfection of the life or of the work') indicates, it is not only Norwegian Nobel Prize winners who have sailed uncomfortably close to *Blut und Boden* (2011: 109–110). Such anxieties over the inter-pollination between rootedness and political violence means that Mahon can never fully make 'terms with the earth' as manifested in a single place. In this he contrasts himself to Heaney who has also used a mesh of his-tory and landscape to approach the violence of contemporary nationalisms. Mahon highlighted this schism in an interview – 'Seamus is very sure of his place; I've never been sure of mine' (Brown, 1985: 11).

The title poem of the 1981 collection *Courtyards in Delft*, blends two features we find in several Mahon poems – *ekphrasis* and an interest in gardens – and in doing so draws out the relation between a domestic exterior and a violence which the scene excludes but with which it is intimately bound up. The poem begins with an 'Oblique light on the trite', the thin slice of life depicted in a De Hooch painting (2011: 96). Mahon has proposed that the poem explores the interrelationship between 'the life-denying instincts and the rage for order' ('The Living Poet', n.d.). He challenges 'the chaste | perfection of the thing and the thing made' – Dutch Protestant society and the painting depicting it. The painting resits sexual and organic energy, no breeze ruffles the trees' 'trim composure',

> No spinet-playing emblematic of
> The harmonies and disharmonies of love,
> No lewd fish, no fruit, no wide-eyed bird
> (2011: 96)

Haughton argues that Mahon constructs his reading of the painting 'round its logic of violent exclusion (and the exclusion of violence)' (2007: 159–160). Here 'nothing is random, nothing goes to waste' – a problem for Mahon's sensibility which tends to reincorporate the wasted and marginalised. Moreover, the painting hides wider political and imperial violence which still resonates and operates in Mahon's present.

'Courtyards in Delft' ends with a typically Mahonian vision of inter-connected elsewheres that modify the sense of place. The speaker has 'lived there [the painting] as a boy',

> A strange child with a taste for verse,
> While my hard-nosed companions dream of war
> On parched veldt and fields of rainswept gorse.
> (2011: 97)

The regent of Delft in 1658 was William of Orange whose legacy in Ireland is still keenly felt. De Hooch's work was also painted just after the Dutch East India Company established a foothold in Cape Town. The painting's rage for order is extended to take in both the Dutch imperial project of the 'veldt' and the speaker (a portrait of a young Mahon) surrounded by the gorse of Ulster. Given that the poem was written when the Apartheid order was still raging in South Africa, we should 'remember not to forget' just how life-denying this rage for order was, something elucidated by a stanza Mahon inserted when the poem was published a year later in *The Hunt by Night*, but has left out of subsequent collections. In that version the 'pale light of that provincial town'

> Will spread itself, like ink or oil,
> Over the not yet accurate linen
> Map of the world [...]
> And punish Nature in the name of God.
> (1995: 10)

The apocalyptic vision is a nightmare of biblical colonialism described in terms of a pollutant, an ideological and literal wash that will sully rather than purify the world (or sully in the name of purification). But Mahon also includes an apocalyptic timescale which, Ozymandias-like, suggests not only the closure of the historical period, but the destruction of the artefact itself. The figures in the painting 'Will wait till the paint disintegrates | And dikes admit the esurient sea' as if it is only the apocalypse which will cleanse the nightmare of history (2011: 96).

Here, as so often in Mahon, two sorts of irony operate. The first is what we might commonly call 'communicative irony' or 'verbal irony' (or just plain 'irony') which relies on the tension between surface meaning and another layer of meaning. Authorial intention is the core distinguishing feature of 'ironic' writing for theorists of literary irony such as Douglas Mueke and Wayne Booth who treat irony as a type of speech act with a set rhetorical function. Such approaches privilege the moment when 'two minds meet in symbolic exchange' and argue that 'it is always good for an irony to be grasped when intended, always good for readers and authors to achieve understanding' (Booth, 1974: 204). Claire Colebrook has argued that such approaches position literary irony as primarily a question of stable and *decisive* communication where the reader picks up that there is more than meets the eye (and ear) and tries to uncover the author's deeper 'intended' meaning. She shows ways this approach to literary irony has been problematised both by theorists drawing on Derrida's challenge to communicative intentionality or those like Linda Hutcheon or Richard Rorty who argue for a 'postmodern' irony appropriate to an era which can no longer lay claim to commonly held values and assumptions. These more recent approaches raise a broader question of the relation between communication and politics that will become more important later in the chapter because:

stable or simple cases of verbal irony tend to prove how shared and clearly recognisable our social norms and assumptions are. If we think of irony as primarily stable, or as exemplified by clear and simple cases, then we will also think of social and political life as primarily reciprocal, common, and operating from a basis of agreement.

(Colebrook, 2004: 16)

Mahon's irony is often not simply resolvable or decisive, and this is crucial to the tone of his work. Indeed, while they are part of the same trait, it is this general ironic disposition or tone, the perception of a degree of aloofness or remove, rather than any specific instances of irony that generates his reputation as an 'ironic' poet. Ted Hughes remarked on Mahon's curious tone when judging a selection of early work for a Gregory Award in 1962:

I found these poems extremely likeable and, at the bottom, full of an interesting imagination of a rather visionary sort. If he has the temperament to do something with all that, I wouldn't be surprised what he'll do. The main thing against him seem [sic] to be a sort of facility, a youthful glibness about everything, though charmingly done. There's no real concern, so the language nowhere comes to grips with anything.

(Hughes, 1962)

What Hughes perhaps could not know at this point is that the strength of Mahon's poetry and the nature of his 'concern' would rest in the interplay of and the disjunction between his visionary imagination and his seeming-glibness.

The presence of multiple layers of meaning is often created through Mahon's supplementing his communicative irony with what, following Szerszynski, I call 'situational irony', where the 'understanding of a situation possessed by one or more actors acting within that situation is in dramatic tension with the reality of it as perceived by an outside observer' (2007: 341). This is a broad term and covers what we would normally call 'dramatic irony' as well as what Colebrook calls 'cosmic irony' (where 'we do not see the effects of what we do, the outcomes of our actions, or the forces that exceed our choices') (2004: 14). I use Szerszynski's term as he develops it specifically with the contradictions of contemporary environmentalism in mind. It also usefully captures how Mahon's poems often use a telescoping point of view or an instance of frame-rupturing to locate readers as privileged observers granted an alternative perspective to the figures within a poem, something which becomes particularly interesting when thinking through the ironies of the late poetry in relation to climate change.

In 'Courtyards in Delft' a kind of situational irony plays out at the level of the speaker who wants to distance himself from the horrors of imperial and religious violence. Mahon plays on the fact that readers familiar with the Belfast context are very likely aware of the irony surrounding the 'young Mahon' in the final stanza: that the 'bookishness' which grants him the ironist's aloofness to escape his coevals' nationalist fantasies is itself sponsored by the privileges afforded the Protestant middle classes with their grammar school educations. This is an economic and social privilege built on the imperial injustices from which the speaker seems to have successfully separated himself.

In his *Paris Review* interview, Mahon flags-up this question of complicity in relation to his generation of Ulster poets:

> Protestants like James Simmons, Michael Longley, myself could think that this was not our quarrel – our peculiar upbringing as middle-class, grammar-school educated, liberal, ironical Protestants allowed us to think of ourselves as somehow not implicated.
>
> (Grennan, 2000)

'[S]omething rotten in the state' of Northern Ireland has engendered an uneasy relation to the poet's home context (Mahon, 'The Sea in Winter', 2011: 107):

> Owing, perhaps, to the peculiar circumstances of life in Northern Ireland, where I was born, brought up, and now live, I have always felt something that might be described as 'dispossession' – a cultural dislocation, a nostal-gic (and slightly guilty) independence of community, and a resulting self-consciousness.
>
> (Mahon, 1968)

Poems like 'Courtyards in Delft' and 'The Snow Party' deal with this cultural dislocation through an aestheticising transmutation of social or political problems – a gesture which both holds these issues at a distance and admits their continual operation. Mahon links his preference for ironic aloofness over pernicious commitment to his formative interest in existentialism and his Protestant upbringing about which he claims it is not possible to be innocent:

> Irony is a feature attributed to liberal Ulster Protestants generally, the tone having been set by MacNeice, as if to absolve us of responsibility for our reprehensible heritage: one might write a love poem, or a plea for the wretched of the earth, and someone would say, 'Oh, he's a liberal Ulster Protestant, he's being ironical'.
>
> ('Yeats and the Lights of Dublin', Mahon, 2012: 67)

Though over time he has often excised ('Sisyphus') or heavily edited ('Camus in Ulster') poems which bear an overtly existentialist influence, Mahon has admitted to being 'what is now [and even more so since he wrote this in 1985] a very old fashioned term, I'm an existentialist with a small "e"' (Brown, 1985: 13). Brian Burton (2004) has shown that existentialism can be a fruitful philosophical context for reading the poetry's overarching tone of alienation and doubt. However, while Mahon may well have protested too much when he claimed that 'It's no good asking me for a program of ideas: I'm a poet, not a philosopher, a historian, or even an intellectual properly speaking', I do not think that he harbours a systematic approach to existentialism, or any philosophy for that matter (Mahon, 1984). What perseveres in his work is existentialism's disaffected tone as well as its insistence that existence precedes essence and that the individual is therefore condemned to choose or risk bad faith. Crucially, the emphasis on private choice does not, for Mahon at least, abnegate the political sphere: 'When you choose', he writes in an article on Sartre's appeal 'remember that your choice takes place in the human arena and is of necessity political'. Moreover, *l'existentialisme est un humanisme*, 'it is humanistic but it must also be humane' (Mahon, 1996: 147).

Brendan Kennelly has argued that Mahon, like MacNeice, evinces a 'humane', and fundamentally Protestant, irony. He sees their poetry as a 'source of alternatives, another way of seeing, another way of experiencing', one which 'perceives, tolerates, cherishes and celebrates difference'. Similarly, suggests Kennelly, Mahon uses 'the painful language of the Protestant humanist; words at war within themselves, or at least in argument with each other, ironical, loving, wild, reticent, fragile, solving' (Kennelly, 1989: 145, 150–151). The key word here is solving. Irony does not necessarily provide solutions, rather the poem's rage for order resolves the plural perspectives into the same poetic frame. These are held in ironic counterpoint to one another, destabilising ideological and political fixities, allowing for the play of interior differences and the inclusion of contexts that did not appear immediately apparent.

Kennelly's argument chimes with a statement Mahon made near the start of his career that

> The war I mean is not, of course, between Protestant and Catholic but between the fluidity of a possible life (poetry is a great lubricant) and the *rigor mortis* of archaic postures, political and cultural. The poets themselves have taken no part in political events, but they have contributed to that possible life, or to the possibility of that possible life; for the act of writing is itself political in the fullest sense. A good poem is a paradigm of good politics – of people talking to each other, with honest subtlety, at a profound level.
>
> (1970: 93)

The crucial question though is whether this irony that enables plural perspectives engenders or morphs into a kind of pernicious detachment or disaffection. Mahon himself lamented in an interview that

> I'm still a pretty cold fish in some ways – it becomes second nature, first nature, even, to get out of all community, and to turn into an antinomian, nasty character. The dangers are solipsism, inhumanity, intolerance. It's the first step towards, on the one hand, Rimbaud, and on the other hand, the serial killer.
>
> (Grennan, 2000)

Mahon's resistance to being grouped within a community or society becomes important later in this chapter when I examine whether Mahon's distancing himself from the causes of climate change risks turning him into an ecological beautiful soul, refusing to acknowledge his own complicity in perpetuating the corrupt world he rejects.

'Rage for Order', from the 1972 collection *Lives*, exemplifies the tension in Mahon's work which emerges from his aestheticisation of the political. On the one hand this aesthetic distance allows for a detached appreciation of multiple perspectives, but on the other, it risks alienation and self-deception. Amid the detritus of an industrial wasteland the speaker tells us of art emerging from chaos, 'An eddy of semantic scruple | In an unstructurable sea'. Mahon does not allow us any final knowledge of where we are – the 'scattered glass' and 'burnt-out | Buses' are reminiscent of Troubles-era Belfast but, as he says later in 'A Garage in Co. Cork', this scene of destruction 'might be anywhere' (2011: 47, 123). The tension between the aesthetic and the political emerges through Mahon's intertext, Wallace Stevens's 'The Idea of Order at Key West' where a 'blessed rage for order' alters Stevens's speaker's perception of the natural world, 'Arranging, deepening, enchanting night' (Stevens, 1997: 106).

Mahon's declared interest 'in a sort of secular numen' locates his poetry, partly, in the tradition of Stevens (Brown, 1985: 13). Here however, the adjectival switch from 'blessed' to Mahon's 'wretched rage for order' positions the poet not just as lowly but as 'one driven out of or away from his native country; a banished person; an exile' ('wretch, n. and adj.', *OED*). Mahon's poet is marginalised from the space of political violence but unlike Stevens's speaker at Key West – whose relations to the political, if existent, are at best oblique – is still forced to engage. As 'Rage for Order' closes, the poet struggles to make himself heard over the 'drums' – possibly those of the Orange Marchers.

> When the drums start –
> For his is a dying art.
> Now watch me
> As I make history,
>
> Watch as I tear down
> To build up
> With a desperate love,
> Knowing it cannot be
> Long now till I have need of his
> Terminal ironies.
>
> (2011: 48)

The artistic rage is contrasted with the rigid ordering of the political sphere – the dividing of community by class, religion and the 'desperately soul-constricting world view […] the punitive reactionaries and thick-witted demagogues who do so much harm' (Mahon, 1984). The artist responds to the political, transmuting the 'unstructurable sea' of historical material and allowing it to provide an aesthetic counterpoint to self-interest and violence. But, as 'Courtyards in

Delft' showed, the artistic ordering can become complicit in a similar logic of exclusion and control. With that in mind, Mahon ensures that his artistic resistance to historical nightmare occurs concomitantly with his gaze towards the margins, acknowledging what exceeds both the spatial and temporal frames of the poem so that when he 'make[s] history' he does not simply re-enforce a dominant narrative but knocks down to build up, enabling imaginative reconstructions which undercut essentialist positions.

After the double couplet that announces the drums and allows, for the first time, the poem's half-rhymes to begin to march together, Mahon instantly disrupts the movement toward stability of rhyme with the unrhymed 'down', 'up' and 'love'. The repetitive /ee/ sounds – me, history, be, need – peter-out in the slant-rhyme of iro*nies*, the final /s / hissing off as a ghostly demarcation of those remainders which cannot be contained by the rage for order but which must still be acknowledged.

The penultimate word of 'Rage for Order' has variously been 'germinal' in *Lives*, 'desperate' in *Poems 1962–1978*, before finally settling on 'terminal' as the modifier for 'ironies'. The irony is terminal, final, there can be no escape into a static position. But in Mahon the ironising, especially when 'desperate', is often 'germinal'. The undercutting of stable ground provides artistic spaces where a thought might grow, spaces of mutation and new 'possible life'. But while such humanistic thinking and liberal politics ('people talking to each other, with honest subtlety') might resist nationalist violence, they are not necessarily equipped to deal with crises which are unamenable to gradual progress and which operate at different spatial and temporal scales to conventional notions of human agency.

A 'chaos of complex systems': economy and ecology

Ways of thinking which prove useful in resisting atavism and sectarianism stall when confronted with the global scale of climate change. Notions of individual freedom and personal choice are not best placed to address the mass extinction of flora and fauna, overpopulation, pollution or ecological processes which exceed human control. In the face of climate change, 'cultural politics and criticism'

> need to incorporate a futural dimension as a space of both responsibility and contestation. For instance, work in environmental ethics has under-lined the alarming clash between the assumptions of mainstream liberalism and the demands of environmental – i.e. long term – issues.
>
> (Clark, 2008: 49)

Mahon is aware of this tension between short and long term issues. The question of how he tries to negotiate the conflicting demands of his ironic, liberal and humanist sensibility and his ecological awareness is at the heart of this chapter. Before turning to the specific engagement with climate change in the later work, I want to develop the broader foundations of Mahon's ecology, the way it revolves around a sense of, and an anxiety about, ecological and economic connectivity.

In Mahon's later work water constantly features as a medium of (and metaphor for) interconnection. It is a vehicle for expressing interrelationships and the transport of materials across space and time, as well as emerging as a concern in its own right when the economic impacts directly on the aquatic in terms of rising sea levels or polar melt. Mahon's use of water metaphors to destabilise inside/outside boundaries, binding the body to both its local and global environment, is not new. In 1979's 'Heraclitus on Rivers', 'Nobody steps into the same river twice | The same river is never the same | because that is the nature of water'. This insistence on transience is repeated on a micro level – 'your changing metabolism | Means that you are no longer you. | The cells die' – and in macro, 'the precise | Configuration of the heavenly bodies […] will not come again in this lifetime' (2011: 105). His 2005 version of Lucretius extends this liquidity, emphasising water as transport vector for human substances within their environment – 'a multitude of life-germs, water-sperm, unites | with cloud stuff'. The clouds contain the sea salt but also the corporeal 'serum, gism, | sweat, whatever fluid is in the organism' (2006: 19–20).

The continual binding of the human subject within global hydrological cycles is typified by 'A Swim in Co. Wicklow' (first published in the 1999 *Collected Poems*), with its epigraph from Montale: 'the only reality is the perpetual flow of vital energy'. The swimmer-speaker, and his syntax, 'swirl and spin'

> in sea water as if,
> creatures of salt and slime
> and naked under the sun
> life were a waking dream
> and this the only life.

In many ways these water poems can be read in the terms of Haughton's description of Mahon's Romantic materialism, re-enchanting the world with a fusion of mind, body and Nature. However, that final 'as if' bespeaks an undercurrent of anxiety within the water metaphors. The simile attenuates the fusion of 'vital energy'. The 'other life' of economic and historical conditions is always already bound up with the 'only life' of an organic 'waking dream' (2011: 242–243). Mahon's thinking in these poems is along similar lines to Alaimo's notion of trans-corporeality, discussed in Chapter One, and David Wood's early attempt to bring ecology and deconstruction together where he argues that the 'blind construction of inside/outside that needs to be re-evaluated parallels the sense that the environment may not be, as we suppose it to be, what surrounds us; it may equally be what pervades us' (2007: 267).

The 2005 collection *Harbour Lights* begins with a poem promising to 'study clouds and their formation ('Resistance Days', 2011: 252). The long seaside poem which closes the collection and gives it its name adds new environmentalist complexity to Mahon's watery images. Biting Swiftian couplets highlight the interconnected world the Cork-based speaker inhabits. Mahon shifts between the landscape and a range of concerns including foreign policy ('the Bush gang are doing it to Iraq'), tacky commercialism ('tourist coaches and our slot machines'), oil companies ('Exxon'), overdevelopment ('one more building site') and waste disposal ('dump our rubbish on the moon'). Water is an agent of and metaphor for connectivity, 'everything is water, the world a wave' and so the seaside skyline is 'transnational, the skies are Indian skies, | The harbour lights Chinese or Japanese' (2011: 281–286). In other poems, water and climate are linked even more directly with economics, particularly in the quasi-apocalyptic deluge of a 'cascading world economy' in 'The Thunder Shower', 'the global hurricane, the rule of money' in 'Dreams of a Summer Night' and in 'America Deserta' where

> our cherished rainfall is a thing of the past,
> our climate now that of the world at large
> in the post–Cold War, global warming age
> of corporate rule
> > (2011: 335, 372, 222)

In *Harbour Lights* these mutually affecting processes undercut any movement toward a Romantic ecology of dwelling – 'as for the re-enchantment of the sky | that option was never really going to fly'. Pastoral retreat away from ecological imperatives is not an option, for there is no non-implicated space: 'Magic survives only where blind profit | so quick on the uptake, takes no notice of it'. But 'everything [is] noticed, everything known in the knowledge era'. Mahon, like Prynne, implies that the drive toward systematic knowledge is concomitant with a logic of exchange – hence the importance of unpredictability. But here everything seems implicated:

> I toy with cloud thoughts as an alternative
> to the global shit storm we know and love,
> but unsustainable levels of aviation
> have complicated this vague resolution;
> for even clouds are gobbled up by the sun
> not even the ethereal clouds are quite immune
> these too will be marketed if it can be done.
> > (2011: 283–285)

An *Irish Times* article pasted into his notebooks indicates that the above lament is not just speculative and specious rhetoric; Mahon is genuinely interested in actual attempts to capitalise on clouds. He circles a passage about 'weather derivatives [...] the meteorological versions of financial instruments already used in financial circles to hedge-against interest rate fluctuations and currency variations' – such instruments would map and model clouds in order to monetise this information by selling it to investors and insurers (Mahon,

2002). This process of recasting ecological uncertainty as a new financial opportunity is central to Blühdorn's suggestion that industry adapts to a changing climate not by halting their damaging practices but by finding new arenas in which to exploit them:

> the unprecedented technological, environmental, economic and cultural uncertainties which Beck had conceptualised as the non-insurable and unmanageable threats that are characteristic of the risk society have successfully been re-conceptualised as unprecedented opportunities which are to be realised. The new opportunity society is no longer governed by Beck's imperatives of risk avoidance [...] but instead by technological optimism, aggressive innovation and the pursuit of first mover advantages.
>
> (Blühdorn, 2007: 261)

The long poems from this period, including 'Harbour Lights', tend to be direct and even polemical, incorporating the looser style of Mahon's mid-1990s New York and Dublin sequences and, before that, verse letters like 'Beyond Howth Head'. The strong rhymes and varied rhythms, packed full of what some felt to be excessive layers of quotation and allusion, do not have the tightly wrought economy of his most popular early poems.[3] Still, this light-verse approach sits well with the plastic chaos of the hyper-modern reality he sets out to describe, with its accumulation of jargon from advertising and popular media. Moreover, the long poems provide the framing concerns through which to read the shorter, more ambiguous and ambitious lyrics.

A notable feature of this period is for Mahon's poems to suggest a movement back to a kind of first Nature only to undermine that possibility, as shown in the Frankfurt School-influenced 'St. Patrick's Day'. Looking round Dublin on March 17th, 'St. Patricks Day' modifies the 'reality' of 'A Swim in Co. Wicklow' by replacing 'vital energy' so that now, 'the one reality is perpetual flow, | chaos of complex systems'.[4] Here 'corporate scheme' usurps 'ancestral dream', traditional calendar celebrations are co-opted by the tourist industry, the organic is commodified – mapped onto 'site-specific daffodils' and 'designer genes' (2011: 245–247). Mahon laments the lost city of his university years while realising that nostalgia is central to the touristification of Dublin – a process he describes in his essay 'The Poetry Nonsense' as the transformation of the city 'from the delightful old dump it had always been into an enormous ATM' (2012: 31).

It is not the 'complex systems' themselves that Mahon resists. The fact that these systems are rendered chaotic (and consequently unpredictable) through their mutual relation means that they are not finally knowable, ownable or controllable and therefore remain unamenable to the 'corporate scheme'. The poem links the excesses of 'consensual media, permanent celebration' to the control of information, referring to Swift to condemn 'yahoos triumphant in the market place' (2011: 245). Yahoos here indicate both crass consumerism and the control of information flow by the eponymous internet search engine.

(Of course, the rise of Google means that Yahoo is no longer as triumphant as it was in 1999 when the poem was written.)

With these Swiftian versions of rampant appetite triumphant, Mahon, in an earlier version of the poem, reacts against 'the entire universe known, owned and reified' with 'a tiny glitch that says to hide' (1999: 287). Glitch implies an internal error or mistake which resists things being known and owned – a remainder, a kind of germinal irony or non-identity that refuses quantification. Mahon associates this remainder or excess with both the artistic and the organic worlds. Poetry becomes a site of resistance

> to a world engineered for the maximum 'efficiency', competitive 'growth', 'global excellence' and 'world-class' foolishness of all kinds. The poetry nonsense sets itself up against regulation, system, utility. It's a last ditch of sanity in a naff world of exploitation and lies. It has no function and no exchange value [...] It is indeterminate, marginal, unimportant; and therein lies its importance. What we need is a dimmer, dreamier universe.
> ('The Poetry Nonsense', 2012: 33)

The urge to 'hide', the desire for a kind of non-commodified (internal or external) space, is a key feature of his 2007 David Cohen Prize acceptance speech where he praised a part of London (a bench near Soho) for being 'not *for* anything; it's a waste of space, and that's why it's important. Waste Space, the marginal and the overlooked: that's where the poetry starts'. Mahon draws together the ecological and the artistic under the same sign; when 'we talk about thinking globally and acting locally [...] the apparently "marginal", so vital to the arts, becomes visible, estimable and finally unignorable' ('Acceptance speech', 2007, emphasis in original). The late work is concerned with both the spatial aspects of waste (i.e. the margins, wastes of space or indeed waste land) and waste's materiality (including junk/rubbish, pollution and excess emissions).

For example, take 'The Bronx Seabirds', a poem stemming from a newspaper headline about rare birds escaping from a zoo. These birds become potent indicators of the ecological health of the city and for the concerns of the collection the poem appears in, 1995's *The Hudson Letter* (now retitled 'New York Time'). Like humans in the Anthropocene, the birds must exist outside the habitat they evolved in (or the controlled and presumably stifling zoo), coping with the 'mutant cloud-cover and air thick with snow-dust, | toxic aerosol dazzle and invasive car exhaust'. The speaker worries that these birds 'won't be fit to compete' for they '"won't touch garbage"; so where and what will they eat' (2011: 171). The poem begins with a rush of headlines and stock market quotations. Haughton sees both birds and poet as being forced to now survive amid the garbage 'that is intimately linked to the economic culture embodied in the headlined companies at the start' and suggests that this implies that 'for poetry to stay news, it has to compete with the newspapers and those electronic headlines' (2007: 239). However, a slightly different reading is available. The rare birds must compete with other avian scavengers not with the garbage they feed on. Hence the suggestion here is perhaps that for poetry to survive it must nourish itself on whatever sustenance is available, including the junk of corporate culture. Otherwise it will starve itself into irrelevancy.

The range and scale of Mahon's later poetry as it zooms between macro and micro, academic and demotic, lends itself to thinking about the sheer number of variables, inputs and unpredictable outcomes associated with climate change. Everything becomes potentially important, meaning nothing can be marginalised, whether it is purchasing habits, fuel efficiencies or melting rates. Mahon's poetry aims at making these complexities apprehensible if not conceptualisable, hence the importance of his emphasis on the chaos of a world where political, biological, geophysical and economic systems all interact.

In the Anthropocene there is no 'out there' definitively separable from human influence – a sentiment echoed by 'A Country Road', from Mahon's most overtly environmentalist collection, *Life on Earth*.

> We belong to this –
> not as discrete
> observing presences but as born
> participants in the action
> (2011: 309)

The physical and mental spaces of resistance that Mahon's work imagines are not finally outside the influence of technology and economics, but they elude control and systemisation. A poem like 'The Dream Play' (published in 1999) ranges after this sort of ecological consciousness. Riffing on *A Midsummer Night's Dream*, Mahon turns the fairy forest into a space where the sensory overcomes the rational, 'brain yields to nose and ear' making perceptible the 'dawn silence of the biosphere'. But local and macro scales are matched by a consciousness of the micro. The grove's inhabitants – 'Wild strains and viruses', 'shifting identities, mutant forms' – connote a kind of mutative potentiality. These are shaping fantasies which apprehend things beyond the comprehension of cool reason with its attempts to know, own and reify (2011: 244).

On the one hand this speaks to a sensory re-enchantment, on the other a kind of scientific awareness of the imperceptible ways humans are enmeshed within the biosphere; both are ramified by the Shakespearean frame. As Robert Watson has argued, *A Midsummer Night's Dream* can be read as an ecologically minded play. The interspecies couplings and metamorphoses assert a continuity of humans with other animals. Watson also compares the effects of the invisible fairy actors to the workings of microbes and genes, so that Shakespeare 'codes the world we do not know, but could not live without' (2011: 36). Like Theseus' Athens and the fairy forest, the domains of humans and micro-organisms become two interpenetrating worlds. The play asserts the continual operation of the forest's mutating, metamorphic forces within the rational, human space of Athens – Lysander returns permanently transformed, and it is Puck, not Theseus, who closes the play. These are spaces where a thought might grow.

But Mahon also acknowledges that resistance can itself become co-opted. As the poem which follows 'St. Patrick's Day' puts it, 'even dissent has long been marketable' (2011: 250). Now, he says in a related essay, 'critique itself is one more product [...] Adorno, the old curmudgeon, was wise to all this seventy years ago' ('Red Sails in the Sunset', 2014: 89). Moreover, Mahon writes to himself that 'my atavistic Ulster negative now re-surfaces as a resistance to US cultural imperialism, as eagerly embraced by the Dublin Crowd' ('Dublin Diary', 1997–1999). What is implied here is both that a renewed focus on the local provides a form of resistance to 'US cultural imperialism' and that Mahon knows that this resistance risks slipping into the regressive and reactionary thinking his early work had sought to subvert. The late poetry asserts the importance of resisting a drive to commodify and control the organic, while tacitly admitting that these sites of resistance – the hidden glitches, fairy forests and waste spaces – are themselves always potentially compromised and, as becomes important in regards to the simulative politics of climate change, sometimes compromising.

Beautiful souls and simulative politics

The first naming of Gaia in Mahon's work comes via Auden in *The Hudson Letter*'s 'St. Mark's Place'. The goddesses of Auden's 'Homage to Clio' and 'Ode to Gaea' both make an appearance: 'When will she – Gaia, Clio – send downpours | To silence the "gnostic chirrup" of her calumniators' (2011: 177). The apocalyptic undertone of these downpours is central to the distance the poem opens up between Mahon and Auden. Gaea and Clio, as described by Auden, are marked by withdrawal and silence, 'Earth, till the end, will be Herself. She has never been moved'; Clio, the muse, does not look as if she 'ever read' the poets (Auden, 1991: 556, 613). Edward Mendelson reads this aspect of the later Auden as evincing 'silence of historical choice, not an existential emptiness but the silent medium in which free acts are possible' (1999: 394). For Mahon, historical and ecological conditions mean that Gaea at least becomes a more dynamic entity – the earth has been 'moved', she is not herself and as such the nature of 'free acts' and socio-ecological responsibility changes. In 'St. Mark's Place' Mahon gently critiques Auden for his 'self-contempt', and, perhaps surprisingly, for being 'a victim, of nothing but irony, Gramsci's new | "disease of the interregnum"' (2011: 177). The question of why Mahon, as consistent an exponent of the ironic voice as Auden, should challenge his irony in this way highlights a tension in Mahon's climate change poetry.

Szerszynski argues that irony can function as a 'tactic' (in Michel De Certeau's sense of the term) for exposing the contradictions of contemporary ecology – the gaps between intention and outcome or between (corporate and think tank) truth claims and actual states of affairs. Irony though is also a 'symptom' of contemporary inertia on ecological matters and can function as a strategy of power to avoid responsibility: 'Strategies of dissimulation or denial rely on a deliberate or unconscious disconnecting of public language and conduct from private belief and intention' (2007: 347). Szerszynski accuses Rorty of this sort of evasion, and this is significant because, for all that Mahon is liberal and ironic, he does not fit the description of Rorty's key figure of the 'liberal ironist' – a figure who faces up to the insurmountable gap between the individual's self-creation and self-fulfilment on the one hand, and the demand for public solidarity on the other, and who is consequently marked by a 'spirit of playfulness and irony' (Rorty, 1989: 39). Indeed, differentiating Mahon from Rorty helps show what is most valuable about his poetry's ironic environmentalism.

For Szerszynski, Rorty's insistence on the disjunction between public solidarity and private irony reduces the power of the moral demand for solidarity. Part of the reason for this is that, as Colebrook has suggested, Rorty's belief in the power of irony is not alive to the ways the liberal ironist 'who speaks with an enlightened sense of his difference and distance from what he says, remains blind to the ways in which this discourse of detachment has its own attachments' – in Rorty's case an attachment to a capitalist liberal democracy which is proving ecologically disastrous (Colebrook, 2004: 173). As C.A. Bowers puts it, 'the form of liberalism Rorty proposes we adopt in the name of progress is reactionary in terms of bringing our cultural patterns into sustainable balance with the life sustaining eco-systems' (Bowers, 2003: 6). This is an instance of what Clark describes as a disjunction 'between specific environmental issues and the ideals and norms of inherited thought (e.g. in liberalism)' (2010: 145).

A debate with Robert Harrison held shortly before Rorty's death provides a telling example of the problems his thinking faces when it engages with global ecology. His liberal irony clashes quite violently with Harrison's (Heidegger-influenced) ecological concern. Resisting Rorty's claim that, despite what might be lost culturally, the rest of the world should 'try to be more like America', Harrison suggests that in an era of anthropogenic global warming (AGW) this would keep civilisation on this track for eco-disaster. Rorty's response – which, while pragmatic, is also alarming – is to resign himself to a fatalistic techno-managerialism: 'we've accommodated environmental change before. Maybe we can accommodate it again; maybe we can't. But surely this is a matter for the engineers rather than the philosophers' (Harrison, 2005).

What Rorty perhaps fails to do then is to think through the force of his own liberal irony and the ways it serves to justify and solidify what Simon Hailwood has described as Rorty's 'anthropocentric instrumentalism' (2009: 48). His liberal irony risks a kind of stasis that will not admit the sort of societal evolution that climate change might demand. A valuable aspect of Mahon's later poetry lies in the way it frames human behaviours and technologies within the context of AGW. It thereby offers a radical challenge to his own liberal, humanist perspective and a challenging interrogation of the role of irony both as a stimulus for critique and as a potentially destructive inertial drag.

Gramsci's 'disease of the interregnum', the phrase from 'St. Mark's Place' which appears several times in Mahon's notebooks, refers to the Italian Marxist's description of the stasis that ensues during an interregnum. For Gramsci the interregnum does not just mean the interlude in the routine transmission of power but, as Zygmunt Bauman explains, when the extant legal frame of social order loses its grip and can no longer keep burgeoning social life on track, and a new frame, made to the measure of the newly emerged conditions responsible for making the old frame useless, is still at the design stage, has not yet been fully assembled, or has not been made strong enough to be enforced and settled in place.

(2010: 120)

This engenders a crisis of stasis which for Gramsci 'consists precisely in the fact that the old is dying and the new cannot be born; in this interregnum a great variety of morbid symptoms appear' (1972: 276). As Bauman points out, Gramsci's interregnum also works well as a description of the new, globalised era. The

planet as a whole seems indeed to be in a state of interregnum these days. Extant political agencies bequeathed by the times before globalization are blatantly inadequate to cope with the new realities of planetary inter-dependency, while political tools potent enough to match the steadily rising capacities of powerful, though manifestly and self-admittedly non-political, forces are prominent mostly by their absence.

(2010: 121)

Likewise, Mahon's later poetry treats the contemporary moment as constituting a kind of morbid interregnum, caught between industrial (post)modernity and a new ecological era.

Mahon works with the knowledge that the ironic voice can, as well as opening up the space for change, contribute to stasis.

The question of wit, humour, irony etc. may seem unimportant but is actually quite central. Antonio Gramsci, in his prison writings, called irony 'the disease of the interregnum': while the world got on with the business of history, specifically the mutation of societies, irony remained and per-haps remains a resource for rueful aristocrats, Ivy League humanists and, no doubt, liberal Ulster Protestants like Louis MacNeice.

('Yeats and the Lights of Dublin', 2012: 67)

Though he refers here to a different period, the question remains as to how Mahon's poetry, with its close affinity to MacNeice's, deals with the inter-regnum of contemporary global ecology without snaring itself in irony and nostalgia for a lost space and time. As Hutcheon notes, the relationship between nostalgia and irony is a complex one. Even ironic modes which seek to expose the risks and lures of nostalgia inhabit the structures and positions they seek to disassemble:

Given irony's conjunction of the said and the unsaid – in other words, its inability to free itself from the discourse it contests – there is no way for these cultural modes to escape a certain complicity, to separate themselves artificially from the culture of which they are a part.

Ironic self-awareness both undermines nostalgia and allows its continual operation:

> the knowingness of this kind of irony may be not so much a defence against the power of nostalgia as the way in which nostalgia is made palatable today: invoked but, at the same time, undercut, put into perspective, seen for exactly what it is – a comment on the present as much as on the past.
>
> (Hutcheon, 1998: 206–207)

In another poem from *The Hudson Letter*, 'The Travel Section', Mahon, adapting Laforgue, looks West:

> I'm reading about life on the prairie and frontier
> when a voice cries: 'Hey, you could live here!'
> outcast from the old world, a desperado
> without God or government, where could I not go?
> out there I'll scalp my European brain,
> run like a wild colt on the open plain
> a sort of post-literate, Huck Finn child of nature
> or existential citizen of the future

This reads like a libertarian manifesto but Mahon's readers know that 'God or government' are not so easily divested, that the open spaces are not available in the same way as they were to Laforgue's imagination a century before and that the middle-aged and urbane Mahon makes an unlikely candidate for a new 'Huck Finn'. The 'mystique of campsites' that fire Mahon's imagination are *camp*sites, sites of affected, theatrical performance which send up macho, frontier mythologies while still keeping the idea of a more authentic lifestyle in sight. The dream of a less compromised 'outside' co-exists with our knowledge that it is inspired by the newspaper 'travel section', and therefore connotes the pervasiveness of commodified space rather than its limits. Moreover, the poem suggests the darker side of this 'post-pastoral' dream, with its allusions to the extrajudicial (in)justice of 'Lynch law'. The speaker claims he might start 'a new cult of the Golden Age' but Mahon's career has been spent resisting such prelapsarian metaphors (2011: 172). Given that the poem was published a year after the Waco massacre, it is impossible not to read the word 'cult' as challenging the sort of communities which head to a 'wild' West and seek to seal themselves off.

The pressures of climate change complicate Mahon's approach to the complex function of irony. The dangers of climate change lend themselves to a call for immediate action. The inertial drag of irony and nostalgia may engender a critical focus which uncovers the ways in which individuals are implicated within a complex whole and the adaptability of the political and corporate elites, who initiate self-evidently partial and inadequate change (Blühdorn describes this as 'symbolic politics') or seek to capitalise on the situation (as with the 'opportunity society').

Ecocriticism and environmentalism strive to move beyond the farce of symbolic politics. The danger is that, in an attempt to get on with the 'mutation of societies', the call for new thinking and practice actually allows for the same underlying problems to continue, because, despite 'their declaratory resolve to take effective action, late-modern societies have neither the will nor the ability to get serious'. This is the arena of simulative politics. The poetics and politics of authenticity (e.g. moving to the country for a sustainable 'good life', ecotourism, getting back to Nature) become complicit in the closure to the pervasiveness of ecological crisis:

> as a tool for the management of the late-modern problem that cannot be resolved, this performative regeneration of authentic politics is indispensable. It stabilises the narrative of ecological (and other) sustainability.
>
> (Blühdorn, 2007: 252, 267)

Irony, not least in its capacity to interrogate and undermine a misplaced authenticity, provides one tactic for challenging and uncovering the artificial solutions of supposedly authentic politics, solutions which do not actually address fundamental problems of unsustainability but sustain the unsustainable. However, the irony which distances the individual from corporate structures, hyper-information and carbon emissions risks abnegating individual responsibility. This is the realm of what Morton, after Hegel, calls the ecological 'beautiful soul'. One who 'washes his or her hands of the corrupt world, refusing to admit how in this very abstemiousness and distaste he or she participates in the creation of that world' (2007: 13). It seems to me that ecological beautiful souls, as described by Morton, are key players within the simulative politics described by Clark and Blühdorn.

Mahon's work often sees him working around and through these multiple levels of irony. Continually acknowledging his relationships within consumer society obverts some of the pitfalls of the beautiful soul, but this can also feed into a paralysing cynicism; the issue Mahon has with MacNeice's 'morbid irony'. For all that it might satirise contemporary society and open up space for new thinking, the poetry's gaze toward an untrammelled first Nature coexists with an awareness that, in Blühdorn's words,

> the belief in authentic politics, i.e. the once popular suggestion that the fulfilment of the authentic self and its reconciliation with a liberated nature can only lie beyond the confines of the established system of consumer democracy, is an idea which late-modern individuals can no longer relate to.
>
> (2007: 264)

In which case the irony is no longer germinal but terminal and debilitating – a tacit admission that radical change is not really possible.

Mahon's ecological irony often relies upon the reader actively detecting the internal contradictions with which he laces the text. The reading experience is often similar to that which Helene A. Shugart describes where the text 'invites multiple, contradictory meanings that complicate a subversive function and that may even function hegemonically' (1999: 437). The key question to me is how the subversive function of Mahon's irony is complicated by the dual risks of simulative politics and morbid irony. The dominant discourse might not be that of the political and corporate elite, but rather the self-deceiving and self-interested late-modern individual who purports to critique hegemony while actually perpetuating it. Irony challenges consensus, but an ironic viewpoint is 'necessarily hierarchical, claiming a point of view beyond the social whole and above ordinary speech' (Colebrook, 2004: 151). All this contributes to the tangled tone of the late work as it shuttles between caustic satire, glib playfulness, hopeful eco-rhapsody, visionary gloom, faux-naïve optimism and resigned apocalypticism.

Another key risk for irony in regarding climate change is that it becomes despairing and elitist, engendering the possibility of 'solipsism, inhumanity, intolerance' that Mahon fears in his *Paris Review* interview. Casting society or humanity as incapable of understanding its perilous situation and as therefore beyond saving itself leads to the sort of pessimism that, as the next section shows, typifies the later Lovelock. Even work ironising the position of the ecologically concerned liberal consumer who knows their own inadequacies does not free us from the lures and contradictions of that position. Mahon's travel poems negotiate these difficulties, probing the ironic ecologist's drive to find a space for self-renewal and ecological thinking while simultaneously negotiating the ironies and anxieties of that that drive.

Harbour Lights' 'High Water' initially seems to be a call for a kind of aesthete's retreat from the glare of modernity:

> Starved for pedestrian silence and in flight
> from the 'totality and simultaneity' of data,
> we stand on the Gesuati steps at high water.

In escaping into the aesthetic via Venice's galleries and architecture and attempting to resist the quantifying glare of data which attempts to 'know, own and reify', the speaker becomes a beautiful soul whose actions actively harm rather than help; it is not for nothing that Mahon writes 'global warming theme' by the side of his draft. The rhyme between data and water carries on Mahon's conceit that the two are obscurely linked; economic flows (where data is crucial to knowing and owning) impact on hydrological cycles. Hence when the speaker refers to 'Year-round tourism, now a perpetual high tide' the 'tide' denotes not only the tourists who swamp Venice underfoot but also the threat to the city from the 'high water' of rising sea levels that these visitors contribute to with their airline 'flight[s] from the totality' (2011: 233; 'High Water', n.d.). This is, after all, a poem from a collection which, in its opening poem, criticises 'unsustainable levels of aviation'.

Climate change and a new look at *Life on Earth*

Life on Earth (2008), the collection which followed *Harbour Lights*, takes its title from Lovelock's now cult 1979 book *Gaia: A New Look at Life on Earth*. Mahon also nods to Lovelock's autobiography *Homage to Gaia: The Life of an Independent Scientist* (2000), entitling the collection's central sequence 'Homage to Gaia'. Auden's 'Homage to Gaea' is another allusion at play, as is Mahon's own 'Homage to Goa' from the same collection. The central sequence contains nine lyrics dealing with planetary ecology, the relations between local and global, the threat of apocalypse and the new technologies that might enable a more sustainable society.

The aim of the final third of this chapter is certainly not to argue the scientific validity of Lovelock's controversial thesis that treats the Earth as a self-regulating system where 'organisms do not evolve independently of their environment' and 'organisms are part of the larger whole that includes the chemical and physical environment which they change' (2010: 114). Rather, I want to show how the use of Gaia foregrounds certain ironies and anxieties within Mahon's work and suggests certain ways of reading his later poetry and thinking about climate change literature in general.

There are multiple reasons why the figure of Gaia lends itself to Mahon's ecology. Gaia theory, certainly after the work of Lynne Margulis, emphasises the interpenetration of micro and macro, from geologic formations to micro-organisms to megafauna. It constructs a highly complex picture of planetary ecology, typified by unpredictable feedback loops which regulate climate, providing suitable conditions for the flourishing of life but, crucially, not necessarily for life on Earth as it currently manifests itself. Indeed, it is this dynamic regulation that means that, for Lovelock, the planet might kill us rather than the other way round: 'we can neither understand nor forecast the Earth's behaviour. Keep in mind that it is hubris to think that we know how to save the Earth: the planet looks after itself' (2010: 9). Gaia theory raises questions about the evolution of species and environment; it expects 'the evolution of physical and chemical environments and of the species to proceed always together' (Lovelock, 2000a: 54). Humans may not be Gaia's evolutionary future.

The figure of Gaia does not necessarily lend itself to a notion of liberal consensus or international cooperation. In 1979 Lovelock wrote against 'the fierce, destructive and greedy forces of tribalism and nationalism', suggesting that an awareness of Gaia might generate 'the compulsive urge to belong to the commonwealth of all creatures' where 'the rewards, in the form of an increased sense of well-being and fulfilment, in knowing ourselves to be a dynamic part of a far greater entity, would be worth the loss of tribal freedom' (see Lovelock, 2000a: 140). This sort of sentiment typifies parts of Mahon's later poetry with its meshing of local ecosystem with global environment. So it is hard to square his thinking with Lovelock's more recent claims that

> Effective action to sustain this island community will come from some form of internal tribal coherence and rare leadership, not from international or European good intentions [...] There will be time enough for internationalism during the stability of the long hot age. We have no option but to make the best of national cohesion and accept that war and warlords are part of it.

Lovelock now rejects the 'trendy populism that now attaches itself to everything green', preferring instead a 'radical pessimism' (2010: 61–62, 51). He has lambasted 'sustainable' energy as an expensive waste of time and advocates oil, gas and nuclear power. His notion of planetary ecology manifests itself as a reassertion of local and national politics, where Britain must defend its interests in the face of mass global deaths.

The way aspects of Mahon's superficially hopeful sequence is problematised by one of its own central figures is indicative of a broader problem for anyone trying to read his later work on climate change without paying attention to the different modes of irony. If it were not for the counterweight of its irony, the late poetry would offer a highly selective mode of ecological thinking and promote a politics of simulation which purports to tackle the amalgam of issues surrounding climate change while ducking the complexities of the issues at hand. There has been a tendency for reviewers to ignore the dominant patterns of Mahon's writing career and read the collection fairly straight, that is, without attentiveness to the irony. Some have found it laudable – Richard Rankin Russell sees the late collections as 'superabundant, ecstatic, poems of nature' which 'show us anew the delights that spring forth from the earth' (2012: 487, 489). Others find the late work frustrating – Bill Tinley laments the 'caustic poet' now 'mellowed to one transfixed by ripening fruit, cloud movements and solar power' (2009: 70). Tony Roberts reads the poetry of eco-concern as too often polemical, suggesting that Mahon does better when he approaches the subject 'obliquely' (2010: 69). However, when subjected to more careful analysis, the poetry's shifting layers of (self-)critique come to the surface, as evinced by Eóin Flannery's recent chapter which, while it ultimately sees the collection as more celebratory than I do here, also notes moments of 'typically Mahonian unease' and 'disarming facetiousness' which modify the late poetry's 'recalibrated ecological temperament' (2015: 33–35).

Employing a range of devices familiar throughout his work – the ironic voice, situational irony and disruptive allusions – Mahon undermines his own ecological project. Ultimately I hope to show that this irony is germinal because it moves toward an ecological engagement while working to free the poetry from the complicity and complacency of simulative politics. In doing so it explores the complex and often troubling relations between concerned individuals and their environment.

The first poem of the 'Homage to Gaia' sequence, 'Its Radiant Energies', begins

> A world of dikes and bikes
> where yoghurt weavers drive
> on gin and margarine [...]
> This is how to live
>
> in the post-petroleum age
> (2011: 311)

How do we read this poem? As a hymn to the sun and solar power or as an ironic take on the hopefulness of sustainable energy? On the surface its opening satirises the green movement, turning it into a fantasy realm of cooperation and sustainability dreamed up by 'Yoghurt Weavers' – generally understood to be a pejorative term for the affectations of bourgeois ecology.[5]

The trouble is that cars running on gin and margarine – or alcohol and vegetable oil – are not pie in the sky notions but sustainable technologies adopted in major cities. This *is* how to live in a post-petroleum age. But just when it seems that the poem embraces yoghurt-weaving trendy ecology Mahon tells us that

> Our micro-climate gives us
> gentle winters here.
> Spring starts in January
> and lasts throughout the year
> (2011: 311)

The yearlong spring of this 'world of dikes and bikes' makes the poem an (eco)utopia in the fullest sense, both 'good place' and 'no place'. In fact, given that this mild 'micro climate' smacks of a warmer world, this utopia might also speak to dystopia, the sort of temperate lifeboat-island that Lovelock suggests the UK will be – an atoll in a hot and flooded apocalyptic world.

The poem closes with a suggestion that 'we can never die' as long as the sun shines, providing energy for the poem's 'clean | photoelectric frames'. But of course the sun remains central to global warming (not to mention that, eventually, it will expand and engulf the earth). This lends the poem's final plea to the sun and nod to Lovelock – 'Remember life on Earth' – a darker hue (2011: 311–312). The poem's awareness of mortality raises the question of what the pronoun 'we' denotes. Gaia theory refers to a planetary totality of which humans are a constituent part – but they are not necessary to the continual operations of life on Earth.

The next poem, which lends the sequence its name, also addresses the role of humans within a geophysiological system, as well as their destructive tendencies.

Here humans 'babble about the world | while you [Gaia] sustain the earth'. The disjunction between human 'world' and the Earth as planetary totality serves as a reminder of anthropocentric arrogance; life on Earth does not need a species which has evolved so that its actions within its environment are no longer conducive to survival. Gaia 'will prevail of course | if in a different form' (2011: 313). If Gaia does exist then she will, as Lovelock has it, 'look after herself', reaching a state which provides the optimum conditions for life, but this need not imply human life. Indeed, this is one of the key mistakes made about Gaia theory – that the holistic vision necessitates a belief in an essential stability when in fact the opposite is true. J. Hillis Miller provides a particularly striking example both of this mistake and of what happens when the (critical) theory is put before the scientific claim. He argues that those who are interested in Gaia rely on an

> assumption that climate change cannot be real because nature is a benign maternal presence who has mankind under her protection. The whole earth is one living organism controlled by self-correcting homeostatic feedback processes. These will keep it a stable and happy environment for mankind worldwide. It is a wonderfully reassuring belief.
>
> (2012: 18)

Mahon, who unlike Hillis Miller, has grasped that Lovelock's argument essentially says the opposite may be true, gives us a poetry which shows how Gaian holism lends itself to an apocalypticism by positioning life as a pan-species phenomenon that confounds the anthropocentricism and humanism that Hillis Miller projects onto others. At the same time the global range of Mahon's view poses a challenge to individual agency and impact, especially for a consciousness which was honed on an (impossible) urge to withdraw from the political realm. In the Anthropocene all human and non-human life is caught up in political questions.

The sequence's apocalyptic strain surfaces most directly in the drowned world of 'Sand and Stars' where water levels have risen until we have

> High tide amongst the pines
> cod caves in the boughs,
> plaice flap in the ruins
> of sunken bungalows.
> (2011: 316)

The collection's green technologies co-exist with an uneasy awareness of the apocalyptic; there is always the danger that the discourse of sustainability becomes a form of technological optimism that negates an awareness of ecological limits. Take the eighth poem, 'Dirigibles', where airships are offered as an alternative, more leisurely, mode of aerial transport to 'unsustainable aviation'. As they float,

> […] slow idealists
> gaze at refrozen ice,
> reflourishing rain forests,
> the oceans back in place
>
> at sand and stars, blue skies
> clear water.
> (2011: 323–324)

The attitude here is ambiguous. Of course slower, more ecologically sound air transport remains a noble ideal. At the same time the benefits advocated seem drastically naïve. These 'idealists' are intellectually 'slow' if they think that this sort of emission reduction could do more than curtail the degree of climate change's impact. Readers should know that such activity certainly would not reverse its effects in the short–medium term – refreezing the ice-caps and lowering the oceans. The reader is lulled into an idealist dream but the reference back to the flooded world of 'sand and stars' seen two poems earlier, reintroduces the whisper of apocalypse behind the 'clear water'.

The notion, central to discussions about Anthropocene, that all places, however remote, are implicated in climate change appears as the guiding thought behind poems five ('At Ursula's') and seven ('Ode to Björk'). In his drafts Mahon calls these two pieces 'climate songs' although the former – a poem about a café and its menu – seems a long way from the ecological anxieties of the rest of the sequence. Only in the final lines does an intimation of outside space disrupt the cosy 'atmospherics, | the happy lunchtime crowd':

> Boats strain at sea, alas,
> gales rattle the slates
> while inside at Ursula's
> we bow to our warm plates.

Despite that division between privileged inside and an outside at the mercy of the elements, the poem's eatery-interior is so seemingly incongruous with the rest of the sequence that the reader is forced to pick back over the implications of this dinner poem, allowing its subtle relation with the rest of the Gaia poems to come to the fore. The waitress is namelessly international 'a nice girl from Cracow, | Penang or Baltimore' – migrants from three corners of the globe blend into one another.[6] The food is similarly non-local:

> Once a tomato sandwich
> and a pint of stout would do
> but them days are over
> I want to have a go
>
> at some amusing fusion
> Thai and Italian both
> (2011: 317–318).

As with his travel poems, the poet's own patterns of consumption in a global economy are drawn into his thinking about climate change, with a tacit admission that he revels in the new gustatory adventures and that there is no going back. If traditional lunch is firmly extinct then the refrozen ice caps of 'Dirigibles' are even more unlikely to be on the menu. In the draft version, the 'frosty but delightful' ice cream was 'arctic but delightful', suggesting that Mahon was thinking about the wider ramifications of even the most banal consumer choice ('Ursula's Place MS', n.d.). What we have here is one of Allenby and Sarewitz's third-level technology groupings discussed in Chapter One. Such groupings bring together factors from across a variety of spheres: the farming and transport technologies that facilitate global food production and import; the energy that it takes to freeze dessert or heat a café; the Ryanair flights and EU treaties that allow a (probably overqualified) Polish waitress to work in Ireland. In the poem all these factors now seemingly impinge on arctic temperatures in a manner that confounds expectation and control. With Mahon, as with Clark's ecological reading of Derrida's *On Hospitality*, domestic space's 'supposedly inviolable interiority [...] is already de-constituted, turned inside-out, by its multiple embeddings in public space'. Things have 'now become overwhelmingly more political than people', the ramifications of their material properties confounding assertions about individual consciousness and choice in an era of 'scale effects' (Clark, 2012: 154).

The tension between individual and global plays out in 'Ode to Björk' which positions the singer as a challenge to 'corporate brainwash rock'. Her music – such as the 'Anchor Song', which the poem namechecks – sometimes expresses Mahonesque sentiments of finding non-contaminated space:

> I live by the ocean
> And during the night
> I dive into it
> Down to the bottom
> Underneath all currents
> And drop my anchor
> This is where I'm staying
> This is my home.
> (Björk, 1993)

Mahon describes her retreat into arctic *terra nullis* as a need for

> mystery and mystique,

> the hidden places where
> the wild things are and no one
> can track you to your lair.
> (2011: 322)

But such an escape is impossible. As in Maurice Sendak's (1963) children's book, the realm of the wild things and 'home' bleed into each other. There are no hidden places and one cannot get 'underneath all currents', as the parenthetical insertion of the next stanza shows.

> (Sea levels rising annually,
> glaciers sliding fast,
> species extinct, the far north,
> negotiable at last ...)

This inserts an unignorable reminder into the aesthetic retreat. The pun on negotiable implies both the fabled northern passage potentially discoverable as the ice melts and the current political wrangling over Arctic sea-bed resources – as arctic space becomes knowable it becomes ownable; even Björk's hyperborean sea-bed is caught up in a global network of interrelation, no space exists unaffected by the currents of finance. The ellipsis moves out into an unknown but potentially terrifying future, cuing the final stanza which might be both arctic wilderness and apocalyptic waste:

> Up there where silence falls,
> and there is no more land
> your scared, scary voice calls
> to the great waste beyond.
> (2011: 322)

Throughout the sequence the apocalyptic clashes with a kind of hopeful reimagining of collective responsibility. 'London Rain' sees Mahon tracking the hitherto unseen impact of humans on climate by meshing biblical downpour with an economic storm to give

> [...] a new rain
> the rainmakers have sent,
> corporate and imported
> to swamp a continent.

Rain falls across London, the populace fly 'To shops in crowds' as if 'from an air raid' (2011: 319–320). This is a double allusion, firstly to Swift's 'Description of a City Shower' where rich and poor, Tory and Whig take shelter from the same storm and, secondly, to the hard rain which falls in MacNeice's own 'London Rain'. The MacNeice poem which flows underneath Mahon's sounds out an important base note to Mahon's ecology:

> Whether the living river
> Began in bog or lake,
> The world is what was given,

The world is what we make
And we can only discover
Life in the life we make.
          (MacNeice, 1966: 162)

Like MacNeice, Mahon asserts the need for individual responsibility amidst a collective threat. The fluid superconnectivity of individuals within global networks means that there is no longer any escaping into blinkered aestheticism or atavistic localism without succumbing to the abstemious distaste that typifies the beautiful soul. We are all rainmakers. MacNeice haunts Mahon's poem, reinventing an existential notion of being condemned to choose for the ecological era. Taken alone the poem remains open to the charge that, despite its purportedly Gaian viewpoint, it is perhaps a little too all-subsuming and potentially undermined by a lack of specificity: the effects of climate change are not likely to be uniform. However, the collection's multiple ironies and anxieties indicate that any ameliorative intervention might be inadequate, too little, too late, part of a self-deceiving simulative politics, providing superficial, ineffective and potentially destructive *pharmakons* that con-stitute just another arena for corporate exploitation. Still, even in the threat of the apocalypse, Mahon suggests that we must act as if we can choose a different future.

This multivalent awareness is central to the third poem in the sequence, 'Wind and Wave'. Its combination of allusion and rhyme-play complicates the tone and offers the sequence's most interesting approach to green technologies and the difficulties in conceptualising the realities of societal adaption alongside the imaginative force of dreams of untrammelled space. Superficially the poem reads as a stern critique of nimbyism and a defence of wind and wave turbines:

Quixote would pick a fight
with wind turbines, more
bad giants gesticulating
on shore and offshore
          (2011: 314)

The gap between Lovelock and the collection which borrows from him is significant here. Lovelock has raged against those that blindly support 'that great religious symbol of spin, the giant white wind turbine and sing hymns for the salvation of the planet' (2010: 151). Mahon's poem sings hymns for the planet and implicitly positions people like Lovelock as quixotic doom-mongers, yet 'Wind and Wave' is encumbered at several levels by irony and apocalypticism. The poem was initially called 'Aeolian Harp' and this figure for Romantic poetry comes out in the fourth stanza:

Coleridge kept an Aeolian
harp like a harmonica
lodged in an open window
to catch the slightest flicker.

Mahon extends the comparison to the turbines which transform (or, we might say, order) 'chaos and old night' into 'clean and infinite | source of power and light'. This enables us humans

> to light our homely lives
> with an unearthly glow.
> (2011: 314)

The adjective 'unearthly' provides an important cue for the reader to recognise the air of disquiet that blows through Mahon's turbines. The short lines stand in sharp contrast to the unrhymed, searching long lines of Coleridge's own 'Eolian Harp' but it is in the poem's use of rhyme where the tension between instrumentalised energy and 'chaos and old night' is most keenly felt.

'Chaos and old night' is a phrase which has an interesting heritage, calling up the writing of Milton, Emerson, Thoreau and indeed early Mahon. In *Paradise Lost* Satan discovers Chaos sitting on a throne with his consort 'Night, eldest of things' (2003, bk. II, lines 959–964). Walter Clyde Curry describes them as 'two deities, ruling over a wild abyss represented as being the womb of Nature and perhaps her grave' (1947: 38). We are given a kind of וָבֹהוּ תֹהוּ (tohu wa-bohu) that stands in contrast to the ordered creation – something akin to 'And the earth was without form, and void; and darkness was upon the face of the deep' (King James Bible, Genesis 1:2). Emerson, in a journal entry from 1839, draws on Milton in his description of rhyme as creative or generative, saying that he wants

> Rhyme that vindicates itself as an art, the stroke of the bell of a cathedral bell. Rhyme that knocks at prose & dullness with the stroke of a cannon ball. Rhyme which builds out into Chaos and Old night a splendid architecture to bridge the impassable & call aloud on all the children of the morning that the Creation is recommencing. I wish to write such rhymes as shall not suggest restraint, but contrariwise the wildest freedom.
>
> (1979: 98)

There is a certain irony in invoking the canonical non-rhyming poet in a defence of rhyme, but for Emerson, unlike Milton, rhyme is a 'necessary Adjunct or true Ornament of Poem or good Verse' (Milton, 'The Verse', 2003: 355). As Peter MacDonald notes, 'this species of rhyme is being promoted in Emerson's thoughts as something fundamentally purposive, and the sounds he invokes – that tolling bell, and the thundering cannon ball – are there to make their purposes felt, and not to jingle prettily in the background' (2012: 5). Emerson's famous lines from 'Merlin' are an example of such tolling-rhymes which similarly call up the harp as a metaphor for poetry through which Nature sings.

> Thy trivial harp will never please
> Or fill my craving ear;

Its chords should wring as blows the breeze,
Free, peremptory, clear.

(1883: 130)

In an illuminating essay Mutlu Konuk Blasing explains that rhyme has a complex function for Emerson. She sees his use of rhyme as generative in its 'freedom' to couple unlike senses, but in Emerson's work a 'second function of rhyme is to embody fate – as music and as Nemesis' (1985: 17).[7]

Whether or not he is consciously channelling Emerson, and I think he is, it seems to me that there is an interesting fatalistic progression in operation in Mahon's use of rhyme in 'Wind and Wave'. In every stanza there is a full rhyme on the second and fourth lines. However, as the poem progresses the level of rhyme between the first and third lines moves from virtual non-existence to resounding fullness: in the first stanza we have the very slight play on /g/ and /t/ in 'fight/gesticulating' and nothing in the second stanza pairing of 'these/long'. By the fourth stanza we have the off-kilter vowel-rhyme 'Aeolian /Window' and in the fifth the strong consonantal chime of 'breeze | dozing'. The sixth gives us a strong pararhyme of 'breath/froth' and the last two stanzas have (almost) full rhyme: drives/lives and seize/estuaries.

The question remains as to how this dextrous rhyme play fits with the poem's approach to green technology and 'chaos and old night'; Mahon's position seems neither 'peremptory' nor indeed 'clear'. Are the turbines forms of building which disclose the world in a certain way – if not quite an eco-version of Heidegger's temple in 'The Origin of the Work of Art', then something like Stevens's (ordering) 'Jar in Tennessee', with added rotor-blades? Or are they merely another instance of modern technology which commodifies the organic, albeit in a less deleterious way? The poem recognises the importance of decarbonised energy – not to do so would be tilting at windmills – and it is certainly possible to read the gradual strengthening of rhyme as an instance of human behaviour and technology falling into step with the 'song of the earth', expressing its rhythms and forces as the wind blows through rotor blades or harp strings.

At the same time there is a sense of disjunction. Given the previous poem in the sequence's assertion of the 'earth' over the human 'world', the fact that in 'Wind and Wave' humans, and their new technology, are seen in an 'unearthly light' thrusts them out of synch with the rest of the organic world. It is not just that the human relation to the world is always already technical, these technologies modify the totality of which they are a part. The final lines might be read less as a belief in sustainable technology than as a desperate plea or command:

Blow, wind, and seize
the slick rotors! Race
tide, to the estuaries
so we shine on in space!

(2011: 315)

The images paired by the rhymes further the sense of human uncanniness. For all their worth, green technologies will 'seize' estuaries and other parts of the landscape (the longstanding row over conservation and the proposed barrage over the Severn estuary is a case in point). As in Mahon's 'Rage for Order' the hissing /s/ obverts a totally full rhyme, the rhyme of 'seize' does not fully capture 'estuaries'. As so often in Mahon there is some sort of excess, a germinal remainder that resists the rage for order or the demand for human mastery encapsulated by the 'space race' that the final rhyme suggests. The sentiment in this poem is similar to that found in an untitled couplet next to some notebook jottings on Baudrillard and reality withdrawing from technology, where Mahon displays his anxiety over technological optimism which perpetuates 'the remake of reality, the enormous lie | which says we own the world and will never die' ('Notebook', 2000).

The untypical use of exclamation marks in the final stanza ushers a sense of the propaganda slogan into the final plea. The poem's uneasiness about harnessing new forms of energy is also deepened by the way 'Blow, wind, and seize | the slick rotors' contains more than a whisper of Lear's 'Blow, winds and crack your cheeks!' Mahon appeals to elemental forces that 'owe [him] no subscription' while raging against a potential dying of the light-bulb (*King Lear*: III. ii, 1, 17). Also at play is *Macbeth*'s 'Blow wind, come wrack | at least we'll die with harness on our back', lines which, in the context of this poem, intimate a doomed effort to face down fate (V.v. 49–50). Interestingly Mahon described the wind as 'a lost | Lear spirit' in 'North Wind', a 1981 poem which also used an allusion to 'Chaos and Old Night' to indicate the type of untrammelled and uncommodified space which we find in Thoreau's 'Ktaadn' (Mahon, 2011: 91).

> This was that Earth of which we have heard, made out of Chaos and Old Night. Here was no man's garden, but the unhandselled globe. It was not lawn, nor pasture, nor mead, nor woodland, nor lea, nor arable, nor waste-land. It was the fresh and natural surface of the planet Earth, as it was made for ever and ever, – to be the dwelling of man, we say, – so Nature made it, and man may use it if he can.
>
> (Thoreau, 1985: 645)

The ecological situation requires technological innovation and intervention; it does not afford the privilege of acting locally without thinking globally. But the assertion that 'chaos and old night' will be transformed into clean energy does not sit well within the apocalyptic frame of the collection's Gaia motif where the dynamics of the geophysiological whole remain indifferent to human need. Instead of embodying the necessity of environmentalist progress where society begins to march in step with its ecological constraints, the gradual strengthening of rhyme might indicate an altogether darker kind of fate. However, where Emerson dealt with the inevitable fate of human mortality, Mahon's frame of reference is apocalypse and extinction. If they 'shine on in space', and perhaps even if they don't, the glow from humans is 'unearthly';

they are part of the Gaian totality but have drastically altered it, and their attempts to survive this alteration may make them more, not less, technologically dependent. Throughout the sequence everything, from Ursula's café to Björk's seabed, is implicated within a global web. Despite the need for better modes of technological engagement in the form of wind farms, dirigibles or solar panels, there is no deep ecological dream to be had but only different forms of mitigation and adaptation that may or may not be enough to avert catastrophe. In contradistinction to Auden's 'Ode to Gaea' the Earth is not 'herself'; she has 'been moved'.

'Homage to Gaia' is a sequence about thinking futurity. Faced with eco-apocalypse it tracks the interregnum between an unsustainable society that can no longer remain unchanged and ecologically orientated behaviours which have not yet evolved and may yet not. This difficult dialogue between no longer and not yet generates the conflicting tones and positions within individuals and societies – from millenarian doom to ironic gloom to yoghurt-weaving loons. It is these shifting degrees of engagement and affect that Mahon attempts (and struggles) to invoke and negotiate in his later work.

Pious hopes

Mahon's later poetry can be read as a negotiation between two versions of futurity. The first sees the future as open, seeking to imagine societies and modes of being which, although potentially compromised by their implication within the workings of corporate modernity, might germinate into a more sustainable, more ecologically sound form of global habitation. Running contrariwise to this sense of *l'avenir*, or the possible to come, is an apocalyptic extension of the present, which is circumscribed by what seems presently possible. This future will admit no genuine change, even in the face of the ecological crises that will happen or, given the temporal derangements that climate change constitutes, has already happened.

Hence the important parallel between the notion of a morbid interregnum when 'the old is dying and the new cannot be born' and Clark's argument about the problems of era-closure. For Clark, broad awareness 'of even the probability of climate change marks a moment at which a historical epoch is discerned as such in its *closure*, rendering its intellectual structures both newly perceptible and philosophically exhausted'. The epoch whose closure is signalled is that which ignores the unpredictability of global ecosystems and their connectivity with global production. However, Clark also argues that 'one does not leave the epoch whose closure one can outline' (2010: 133).

In certain ways these paradoxes appear isomorphic with the contradictions Mahon has struggled with throughout his poetry. They lie behind his developing irony as a tactic for thinking inside and outside tradition when he attempts to think beyond both atavism and industrial modernity while still admitting their continual operation. Within his later poetry this becomes even more difficult because the kind of openness to multiple possibilities and perspectives he learns from MacNeice is compromised by the awareness that many of these constitute a failure to act appropriately to a desperate ecological situation, leading to a morbid irony.

By way of conclusion I want to turn to two poems from his 2010 collection *An Autumn Wind* which engages with the difficulty of moving forward in the face of this knowledge:

World Trade Talks

Downturn Means CO_2 Targets Now Achievable

A 'Hindu' growth rate,
hedges against the winds
of double-edged finance; organic crops
and comely maidens, is it too late
to push for these demands
and pious hopes?

The great Naomi Klein
condemns, in *The Shock Doctrine*,
the Chicago Boys, the World Bank and the IMF
the dirty tricks and genocidal mischief
inflicted upon the weak
who now fight back.

(2011: 339)

On the surface 'World Trade Talks' attacks the organs of neo-liberalism. Hence a Hindu Growth Rate (a term used to describe the slow rate of growth of India during its socialist economic period) might resist the worst excesses of global economics. But, like 'double-edged finance', the poem 'hedges' its bets both ways. The emissions targets not only re-assert the economic logic which seeks to control the unpredictability of ecological systems, but are also themselves constructed partially in accordance with the perceived needs of the economy (it is the talk of the world's trades and traders that gets listened to). These targets are types of opportunity for Chicago School economics to create markets and competition in the form of carbon credits and carbon management. Likewise, 'organic crops' offer a new opportunity for iniquitous consumption. In the Anthropocene it is not enough for these crops to be labelled organic, without asking a series of questions: which purportedly organic crops? Grown where? In what quantities? Distributed to who? Disposed of how? The global ramifications of production are always at play. In fact, this is part of the central thesis of *The Shock Doctrine*'s notion of 'disaster capitalism' where 'orchestrated raids on the public sphere in the wake of catastrophic events, combined with the treatment of disasters as exciting market opportunities' offer the 'opportunity society' new arenas of exploitation (Klein, 2007: 6). Hence the 'pious hopes' – echoing

Auden's 'clever hopes' in 'September 1 1939' – become avenues for superficially green consumption and the perpetuation of structural iniquities.

The 'Hindu' growth rate is itself an interesting choice. Economic liberalisation meant that India enjoyed massive growth in the 1990s and, despite a blip in the most recent recession, has continued to do so. Hence the 'Hindu' growth on display here is either anachronistic or belongs to other economies – one candidate sticks out more than others. 'Comely Maidens' is a quotation from Eamonn De Valera's 1943 St Patrick's day speech which reads

> [T]he Ireland that we dreamed of, would be the home of a people who valued material wealth only as a basis for right living, of a people who, satisfied with frugal comfort, devoted their leisure to the things of the spirit – a land whose countryside would be bright with cosy homesteads, whose fields and villages would be joyous with the sounds of industry, with the romping of sturdy children, the contest of athletic youths and the laughter of comely ['happy' in the broadcast version] maidens, whose firesides would be forums for the wisdom of serene old age. The home, in short, of a people living the life that God desires that men should live.
>
> (quoted in Lee, 1989: 334)

But while 'frugal comfort' and declining materiality might contain the seeds for a more sustainable future, de Valera's nationalist and religious vision with its dreams of a Golden age was a large part of the stagnant and regressive society Mahon critiques so vehemently in his 1970 verse letter, 'Beyond Howth Head':

> who would change self-knowledge for
> a prelapsarian metaphor,
> love play of the ironic conscience
> for a prescriptive innocence?
> (2011: 53)

Nostalgia for an imagined past forms a type of resistance, but it is also compromised by insularity in a situation that demands thinking globally. These anxieties regarding tradition resonate with those in the word 'Hindu'. Though Hinduism and 'Hindu Growth' are not specifically related, the poem's assertion of the 'weak fighting back' calls up the continued operation of the caste system and the ways in which tradition has worked alongside liberalisation within new, corporate India to produce just the kind of iniquities lambasted by Klein and, even more vociferously, Arundhati Roy, an author whose polemics Mahon quotes in his essay 'Indian Ink' (2012: 279).

For all his anxieties, the late poetry's dominant tone is choice and cautiously hopeful change in the face of paralysing irony. For Mahon this is a condition for the possibility of artistic expression in the face of crisis:

I think of it in dramatic terms: if you surround yourself with hesitation and constraint and so on, and yet manage to sing through, then you somehow earn the sound you make. Perhaps something like that is going on. But I suppose that you have to be able to speak without thinking all the time how it sounds – those peculiar moments when you are saying something and even as you are saying it, the objections, the laughter, all these things are going on simultaneously, and yet you are able to say it, without shame or horror or embarrassment. [...] Let's just say that you must, in order not to go mad, be able to speak.

(in Grennan, 2000)

The difficulties of speaking and writing under late capitalism in the Anthropocene emerge in 'A Quiet Spot'. As so often Mahon seeks a space outside the urban-corporate nightmare, a 'dozy seaside town' away from 'signage, carbon monoxide',

not really in the country, no
but within reach of the countryside,
somewhere alive to season, wind and tide,
far field and wind farm. 'Wrong life,' said Adorno,
'can't be lived rightly.' The right place
is a quiet spot like this

(2011: 333)

Michael Parker in the *TLS* reads the poem fairly straightforwardly, emphasising how 'a linked sequence of images ("expanding", "spills", "rich", "fertile") captures the fecundity and excess of his rural retreat', while suggesting that the play of rhymed consonants and vowels 'suggest the harmony it induces' (2011: 22). As should be clear by now I do not think this sort of approach to late Mahon is correct, especially given the cues he gives us in this poem.

The reaction of the ecocritic who does not pick up on Mahon's irony, but who also balks at the sense of dwelling, might be to apply the sort of 'futural' reading proposed by Clark, one which takes into account how '[t]echnology and infrastructures emerge not only as inherently political but as unpredictably doubly politicized in scale effects that deride the intentions of their users or builders', a criticism which is 'object-centred, aware of the capricious nature of nonhuman agency' (2012: 161). In such a reading the movement toward localised dwelling would be compromised by a knowledge that somewhere 'in reach' of the countryside probably requires a car, or is indicative of non-efficient land use for an elite minority, or that the spiritual good of this countryside retreat is negatively offset by the materials and energy needed to sustain this version of green consumerism. As Mahon's prose writing on Kinsale indicates, he is aware of such issues.[8]

What makes Mahon's poem interesting is the way it contains within it its own critique. The description of the town, particularly that conversational 'no | but', reads like an estate agent's brochure, a smug call to the good life. This might be the right place but it is still the wrong life; the following stanzas refuse the self-congratulation of 'the perfect work-life balancing act' because

> Gaia demands your love, the patient earth
> your airy sneakers tread expects
> humility and care.
>
> It's time now to go back at last
> beyond irony and slick depreciation
> past hedge and fencing to a clearer vision,
> time to create a future from the past,
> tune out the babbling radio waves
> and listen to the leaves.
>
> (2011: 333)

Parker notes the shift in tone but again shows how it is easy to miss the multiple levels of irony and turn the poem into a Romantic pastoral: 'At the lyric's pivotal point, however, the narrative voice changes tack and tone. Using language that leaves no room for compromise, he counsels us – like Wordsworth – to attune ourselves to nature's frequencies' (2011: 22). However, the 'patient' geophysical scales have, in the Anthropocene, become those of a sick 'patient'. Creating a 'future from the past' speaks to a kind of Blakean revolutionary nostalgia. But the poem's pleasant pastures are, unlike in ancient times, now trodden upon by specifically 'airy' footwear – manufactured abroad by Nike, probably to dubious labour standards. Going past 'irony and slick depreciation' asserts the importance of not falling into the morbid stagnation which strips the individual capacity to change things at any scale. At the same time, and this is what Parker misses, the poem's own ironising and slick depreciation of its smug, bourgeois country retreat (which has plenty of hedging and fencing) helps show that Mahon never can quite tune out the 'radio waves' of anxiety and ambiguity, those spatial, temporal and textual elsewheres that modify presence and present.

What makes Mahon's irony more pronounced is that the Adorno quotation is from a section of *Minima Moralia* (18 – 'Asylum for the homeless') which stresses, among other things: the impossibility of 'dwelling', the blind 'perpetuation of property relations', the plight of those who (unlike the speaker) cannot 'have no choice' where to live, the 'musty pact of family interests', the ideology of those 'wishing, with a bad conscience, to keep what they have', the knowledge that anyone 'seeking refuge in a genuine, but purchased, period style house, embalms himself alive' and, most of all, the moral responsibility 'not to be at home in one's home'. Knowing one's place becomes a fraught business indeed. Adorno suggests that the 'best mode of conduct, in the face of all this, seems an uncommitted, suspended one: to lead a private life, as far as the social order and one's own needs will tolerate nothing else'. However, not untypically for

Adorno, resistance to 'wrong life' has been etiolated into a potentially paralysing self-awareness. He warns us not to 'attach weight to [this mode of conduct] as to something still socially substantial and individually appropriate' (2006: 38–39).

We are returned to the double bind of the interregnum that Mahon's climate change poetry maps. It does not allow us to think the closure of the era or the poem; despite his rage for a new ecological order the irony here is 'terminal', it is also desperate – a desperation tied to the complex and perhaps not always successful tonal shifts of the later work. Mahon refuses to succumb to the closure of which Clark accuses ecocriticism – the irony is also germinal, allowing for both critique and the imagination of future possibilities. Mahon's germinal ironies search out modes and sites of resistance, qualities within the non-identical, the potentiality and operation of the wasted and the marginalised, consistently calling his readers to ask what – from microbes to multinationals – is implicated within the interpenetrating scales of his chaos of complex systems and how these might mutate in(to) an as-yet-unconceptualised future.[9]

Notes

1 'The Antigone Riddle' and 'Apotheosis of Tins' first appeared in *The Snow Party* (1975); 'Brighton Beach' in *Courtyards in Delft* (1981); 'Ovid in Tomis' and 'A Garage in Co. Cork' in *The Hunt by Night* (1982).
2 For a more thorough engagement with Paulin's critique of Mahon see Jarniewicz (2002).
3 Particularly critical was the normally supportive Peter McDonald, who, describing *The Yellow Book*, accuses Mahon of succumbing to 'lazy rhyming and rhythmic slackness', unnecessary 'reading lists' and 'academic jargon' (1998: 118).
4 In the pages surrounding a draft of the poem Mahon writes 'chaos theory: "unpredictability in complex systems"'. The drafts are also surrounded by notes on Adorno, his and Horkheimer's the Dialectic of Enlightenment and Benjamin's Angel of History ('Notebook', n.d.)
5 The online urban dictionary (www.urbandictionary.com), which is as good a resource as many for tracking the contemporary usage of slang, suggests that the term originated in a routine from comedian Alexi Sayle in the 1970s which expressed disgust at denizens of Stoke Newington 'all sitting around on the windswept concrete piazza, discussing Chekhov and weaving their own fucking yoghurt'. The definition which I suspect is closest to what Mahon is trying to convey is 'Pseudo middle class hippies who buy into aromatherapy etc. yet drive BMWs. Have no thought through politics. Buy Ecover, but have dishwashers' (2014). Mahon has used the term elsewhere to describe 'blow ins' from the city who move to West Cork ('The Bright Edge', 2014: 82).
6 The poem may of course mean either Baltimore in Maryland or Baltimore, Cork. Either reading speaks to a globalised world.
7 Compare Emerson 'Art': ''Tis the privilege of Art | Thus to play its cheerful part, | Man on earth to acclimate, | And bend the exile to his fate' (1883: 301).
8 Mahon, writing on his own 'quiet spot' in West Cork, remembers 'thinking of moving here [and remarking ...] how "handy" it was'. He also jokes that his article will 'encourage you lot to jump in your Porsches and come tearing down here in search for a little real estate' ('The Bright Edge', 2014: 85, 87).
9 This chapter is derived, in part, from an article published in *Green Letters* on 30 March 2014, available at: http://www.tandfonline.com/doi/full/10.1080/14688417. 2014.901897.

References

Adorno, Theodor W. 2006. *Minima Moralia: Reflections on a Damaged Life*. Translated by E.F.N. Jephcott. New York: Verso.

Auden, W. H. 1991. *Collected Poems*. Edited by Edward Mendelson. Revised and reset edition. London: Faber and Faber.

Bauman, Zygmunt. 2010. *44 Letters From the Liquid Modern World*. Cambridge: Polity.

Björk. 1993. 'Anchor Song'. *Debut*. One Little Indian Records.

Blasing, Mutlu Konuk. 1985. 'Essaying the Poet: Emerson's Poetic Theory and Practice'. *Modern Language Studies* 15(2): 9–23.

Blühdorn, Ingolfur. 2007. 'Sustaining the Unsustainable: Symbolic Politics and the Politics of Simulation'. *Environmental Politics* 16(2): 251–275.

Booth, Wayne C. 1974. *A Rhetoric of Irony*. Chicago: University of Chicago Press.

Bowers, C.A. 2003. 'Assessing Richard Rorty's Ironist Individual Within the Context of the Ecological Crisis'. *Trumpeter* 19(2): 6–22.

Brown, Terence. 1985. 'An Interview with Derek Mahon'. *The Poetry Ireland Review* 14 (October): 11–19.

Burton, Brian. 2004. *'A Forest of Intertextuality': The Poetry of Derek Mahon*. Unpublished PhD Thesis: Durham University. Available at: http://etheses.dur.ac.uk/1271/1/1271. pdf [accessed 21 January 2015].

Clark, Timothy. 2008. 'Towards A Deconstructive Environmental Criticism'. *Oxford Literary Review* 30(1): 45–68.

Clark, Timothy. 2010. 'Some Climate Change Ironies: Deconstruction, Environmental Politics and the Closure of Ecocriticism'. *Oxford Literary Review* 32(1): 131–149.

Clark, Timothy. 2012. 'Scale'. In *Impasses of the Post-Global*, edited by Henry Sussman. Ann Arbor, MI: Open Humanities Press. 146–167.

Colebrook, Claire. 2004. *Irony*. London: Routledge.

Corcoran, Neil. 1983. 'Flying the Private Kite'. *Times Literary Supplement*, 18 February: 160.

Curry, Walter Clyde. 1947. 'Milton's Chaos and Old Night'. *The Journal of English and Germanic Philology* 46(1): 38–52.

Elder, John. 2010. 'Introduction'. In *Out of the Earth: Ecocritical Readings of Irish Texts*, edited by Christine Cusick. Cork: Cork University Press. 1–4.

Emerson, Ralph Waldo. 1883. *Poems*. London: Macmillan and Co.

Emerson, Ralph. 1979. *Emerson's Literary Criticism*. Edited by Eric Carlson. Lincoln: University of Nebraska Press.

Flannery, Eóin. 2015. *Ireland and Ecocriticism: Literature, History and Environmental Justice*. New York: Routledge.

Gramsci, Antonio. 1972. *Selections from the Prison Notebooks of Antonio Gramsci*. Translated by Quintin Hoare and Geoffrey Nowell-Smith. New York: International Publishers.

Grennan, Eamonn. 2000. 'Derek Mahon, The Art of Poetry No. 82'. *Paris Review*. Available at: http://www.theparisreview.org/interviews/732/the-art-of-poetry-no-82-derek-mahon [accessed 20 November 2014].

Hailwood, Simon. 2009. 'Landscape, Nature and Neopragmatism'. In *Richard Rorty: Critical Assesments of Leading Philosophers*, edited by James Tartaglia, IV. London: Routledge. 48–66.

Harrison, Robert. 2005. 'American Philosopher Richard Rorty'. *Entitled Opinions*, 22 November. KZSU Stanford. Available at: http://french-italian.stanford.edu/opinions/ [accessed 15 January 2013].

Haughton, Hugh. 2007. *The Poetry of Derek Mahon*. New York: Oxford University Press.

Hillis Miller, J. 2012. 'How To (Un)Globe the Earth in Four Easy Lessons'. *SubStance* 41(1): 15–29.

Hughes, Ted. 1962. 'Notes on the Gregory Award Poets 1962, TS'. Box 114, Folder 4. Hughes papers, Stuart A. Rose Manuscript, Archives, and Rare Book Library, Emory University.

Hutcheon, L. 1998. 'Irony, Nostalgia, and the Postmodern'. *Methods for the Study of Literature as Cultural Memory* 6: 189–207.

Jarniewicz, Jerry. 2002. 'Derek Mahon: History, Mute Phenomena and Beyond'. In *The Poetry of Derek Mahon*, edited by Elmer Kennedy-Andrews. Gerrards Cross: Colin Smythe. 83–95.

Kennelly, Brendan. 1989. 'Derek Mahon's Humane Perspective'. In *Tradition and Influence in Anglo-Irish Poetry*, edited by Terence Brown and Nicholas Grene. Basingstoke: Macmillan. 143–152.

Klein, Naomi. 2007. *The Shock Doctrine: The Rise of Disaster Capitalism*. New York: Metropolitan Books/Henry Holt.

Lee, J.J. 1989. *Ireland, 1912–1985: Politics and Society*. Cambridge: Cambridge University Press.

Lidström, Susanna, and Greg Garrard. 2014. '"Images Adequate to Our Predicament": Ecology, Environment and Ecopoetics'. *Environmental Humanities* 5: 35–53.

Lovelock, James. 2000a. *Gaia: A New Look at Life on Earth*. Oxford: Oxford University Press.

Lovelock, James. 2000b. *The Ages of Gaia: A Biography of Our Living Earth*. Oxford: Oxford University Press.

Lovelock, James. 2010. *The Vanishing Face of Gaia: A Final Warning*. London: Penguin.

MacNeice, Louis. 1966. *The Collected Poems of Louis MacNeice*. Edited by Eric Robertson Dodds. London: Faber and Faber.

Mahon, Derek. 1962. 'Editorial'. *Icarus* 38: 1–4.

Mahon, Derek. 1968. 'Untitled [Reflection on Night Crossing]'. Box 25, Folder 21. Mahon papers, Stuart A. Rose Manuscript, Archives, and Rare Book Library, Emory University.

Mahon, Derek. 1970. 'Poetry in Northern Ireland'. *Twentieth Century Studies* 4: 89–93.

Mahon, Derek. 1984. 'Notes for BBC Northern Ireland Interview'. Box 34, Folder 1. Derek Mahon papers, Stuart A. Rose Manuscript, Archives, and Rare Book Library, Emory University.

Mahon, Derek. 1995. *The Hunt by Night*. Oxford: Oxford University Press.

Mahon, Derek. 1996. *Journalism: Selected Prose 1970–1995*. Edited by Terence Brown. Oldcastle, County Meath: Gallery Press.

Mahon, Derek. 1997–1999. 'Dublin Diary'. Box 226, Folder 1. Derek Mahon papers, Stuart A. Rose Manuscript, Archives, and Rare Book Library, Emory University.

Mahon, Derek. 1999. *Collected Poems*. Oldcastle, County Meath: Gallery Press.

Mahon, Derek. 2000. 'Notebook Circa. 2000'. Box 23, Folder 6. Derek Mahon papers, Stuart A. Rose Manuscript, Archives, and Rare Book Library, Emory University.

Mahon, Derek. 2002. 'Annotated Clipping of *The Irish Times*'. Box 48, Folder 7. Derek Mahon papers, Stuart A. Rose Manuscript, Archives, and Rare Book Library, Emory University.

Mahon, Derek. 2006. *Adaptations*. Oldcastle, County Meath: The Gallery Press.

Mahon, Derek. 2007. 'David Cohen Prize Acceptance Speech'. Box 48, Folder 7. Derek Mahon papers, Stuart A. Rose Manuscript, Archives, and Rare Book Library, Emory University.

Mahon, Derek. 2011. *New Collected Poems*. Oldcastle, County Meath: Gallery Press.

Mahon, Derek. 2012. *Selected Prose*. Oldcastle, County Meath: Gallery Press.

Mahon, Derek. 2014. *Red Sails*. Oldcastle, County Meath: Gallery Press.

Mahon, Derek. n.d. 'High Water TS'. Box 21, Folder 25. Derek Mahon papers, Stuart A. Rose Manuscript, Archives, and Rare Book Library, Emory University.

Mahon, Derek. n.d. 'St Patrick's Day MS'. Box 23, Folder 1. Derek Mahon papers, Stuart A. Rose Manuscript, Archives, and Rare Book Library, Emory University.

Mahon, Derek. n.d. '"The Living Poet", BBC Script Photocopy'. Box 28a, Folder 3. Derek Mahon Papers, Stuart A. Rose Manuscript, Archives, and Rare Book Library, Emory University.

Mahon, Derek. n.d. '"Ursula's Place", MS'. Box 22a, Folder 57. Derek Mahon papers, Stuart A. Rose Manuscript, Archives, and Rare Book Library, Emory University.

McDonald, Peter. 1998. 'Incurable Ache'. *The Poetry Ireland Review* 56: 117–119.

McDonald, Peter. 2012. *Sound Intentions: The Workings of Rhyme in Nineteenth-Century Poetry*. Oxford: Oxford University Press.

Mendelson, Edward. 1999. *Later Auden*. New York: Farrar, Strauss and Giroux.

Milton, John. 2003. *Paradise Lost*. Edited by John Leonard. London: Penguin.

Morton, Timothy. 2007. *Ecology without Nature*. Cambridge, MA: Harvard University Press.

Out of the Earth. 2010. Publicity material from Cork University Press. Available at: http://corkuniversitypress.com/Out_of_the_Earth:_Ecocritical_Readings_of_Irish_Texts/318/ [accessed 29 March 2015].

Parker, Michael. 2011. 'Homecomings'. *Times Literary Supplement*, 22 April: 22.

Paulin, Tom. 1984. *Ireland & the English Crisis*. Northumberland: Bloodaxe Books.

Roberts, Tony. 2010. 'The Pull of Home'. *PN Review* 37: 66–70.

Rorty, Richard. 1989. *Contingency, Irony, and Solidarity*. Cambridge: Cambridge University Press.

Russell, Richard Rankin. 2012. '"Can We Turn Now to the Important Things …?" Derek Mahon's Poetry and Prose'. *Irish Studies Review* 20(4): 487–492.

Sendak, Maurice. 1963. *Where The Wild Things Are*. New York: Harper Collins Publishers.

Shakespeare, William. 1997. *King Lear*. Edited by R.A. Foakes. London: Arden Shakespeare.

Shakespeare, William. 2014. *Macbeth*. Edited by Sandra Clark and Pamela Mason. 3rd edition. London: Arden Shakespeare.

Shugart, H.A. 1999. 'Postmodern Irony as Subversive Rhetorical Strategy'. *Western Journal of Communication (includes Communication Reports)* 63(4): 433–455.

Stevens, Wallace. 1997. *Collected Poetry and Prose*, edited by Frank Kermode and Joan Richardson. New York: Library of America.

Szerszynski, Bronislaw. 2007. 'The Post-Ecologist Condition: Irony as Symptom and Cure'. *Environmental Politics* 16(2): 337–355.

Thoreau, Henry David. 1985. *A Week on the Concord and Merrimack Rivers; Walden, Or, Life in the Woods; The Maine Woods; Cape Cod*. Edited by Robert Sayre. New York: Library of America.

Tinley, Bill. 2009. 'What Is Meant by Home'. *Poetry Ireland Review* 99: 70–74.

Watson, Robert. 2011. 'The Ecology of Self in *A Midsummer Night's Dream*'. In *Ecocritical Shakespeare*, edited by Lynne Bruckner and Daniel Brayton. Kent: Ashgate Publishing. 33–56.

Wood, David. 2007. 'Spectres of Derrida: On the Way to Econstruction'. In *Ecospirit: Religions and Philosophies for the Earth*, edited by Laurel Kearns and Catherine Keller. New York: Fordham University Press. 262–290.

4   The resistant materials of Jeremy Prynne

> *a single term like monogene reaches back into two entwined histories: the geochronology of*
> *land-formation and the cytochronology of biochemical evolution [...] the causal presumptions*
> *of over-humanised history can be displaced.*
>
> – Prynne (1969: 65)

Prynne's above words, from a review of Charles Olson's *Maximus*, consider the
mutations of biochemistry alongside shifting environmental conditions. Some of
the environmental shifts we find in Prynne's own work, such as the Pleistocene
thaws of *The White Stones*, are gradual. Others, like the post-Chernobyl irra-
diated landscapes that Simon Perril (2003) reads in *Bands about the Throat*, speak
to more sudden upheavals. Of course Chernobyl, like the agricultural chemicals
of *High Pink on Chrome* or the exploitation of the Tar Sands in *Sub Songs*, represents the capacity of human technology to radically transform an environment.
However, we should be wary of the presumptions of over-humanised history.
The materials which shape life in Prynne's poetry (including RNA, hydrocarbon
deposits, workable metals and genotoxic herbicides) are, Prynne reminds us,
resistant to human control; they exert a different kind of agency. This chapter
examines how Prynne treats different imbrications of technology, environment
and biology. As it does so it moves across different scales, moving in space from
the processes of gene-expression to pictures of the globe from lunar orbit, and
in time from the transhuman communities of prehistory to the marginalised
populations dealing with the repercussions of climate change.

   Prynne does not draw an analogy lightly. 'Analogy', he wrote to Olson, 'is
the means by which we finally do come to know; the cognate, parallel utterance'. But this is only the case if the 'whole pattern is allowed its substantive
integrity, and not merely employed as rhetorical ornament'. That is, the 'mind
must venture some real weight on the proposed image; commit a portion of
trust to its stability' (Prynne, 1964). Prynne's late-modernist poetics engage
with bodies of knowledge that extend beyond Marianne Moore's claims for
'business documents and schoolbooks' into stock market jargon and cutting-
edge biochemistry. This range of reference indicates an expansive purview for
poetry but also a profound interest in the ramifications of certain ideas across
different spheres. And so, Prynne tells Olson in another letter, 'there seems to

me a great need to take certain operating metaphors very literally indeed, to know as much as possible about them in some detail'. In this he distinguishes himself from 'that dolt E.P. [Ezra Pound] whose local ignorance is unsurpassed: wrong about Chinese syntax, and hopelessly stupid about the modern scientist's "shapeless 'mass' of force" [...] why in hell didn't he look for the facts?' (1963b).

Prynne has been rather more stably institutionally ensconced than Pound – and this afforded him the acquaintance of several scientists at Gonville and Caius. Over the years at Cambridge he interacted with Stephen Hawking, Rupert Sheldrake, Joseph Needham and, significantly for this chapter, Francis Crick, whom he met in early 1963 and stayed in contact with even after the Nobel Laureate transferred his operations to the USA.[1] In *Stars, Tigers and the Shape of Words*, Prynne's William Matthews lectures on linguistic arbitrariness and poetic language, he uses a term from biochemistry – 'reverse transcription' – to describe certain ways the linguistic sign might be partially motivated. This runs against the central dogma of Ferdinand de Saussure's thought which asserts the fundamental arbitrariness of the linguistic sign and that associations may not be attached to the 'system of sounds or graphs and coded back onto the level of sense or idea'. Prynne sees aspects of Saussure's argument as shadowing Crick's 'Central Dogma' of 'the biochemistry of genetic coding' which also

> excluded all reverse transcription. Francis Crick's hypothesis about the asymmetrical direction of intracellular data flow took the form (to put matters simply) that genetic information could and did pass from DNA to protein, but was barred from passing in the reverse direction: the mediating RNA characters would thus be, in Saussure's sense, 'arbitrary', as mere carrier templates of the coding. This feature was argued to be requisite in both systems, cells and language, and for the same reason, namely to preserve the integrity of the inner genetic material against the contamination of damaged forms.
>
> (1993: 6)

The 'data flow' Prynne refers to here is the way a cell's DNA is transcribed into RNA (ribonucleic acid) which is then translated into the amino acids used to build proteins. In fact, it would be found that retroviruses, including HIV, transcribe their genetic information back into DNA from RNA via reverse transcription, a possibility which Crick initially ignored or, in his own words, 'remain[ed] discretely silent' about (1970: 562). Neither Crick nor Saussure fully engaged with the way the materiality of the genetic or linguistic text challenged the neatness of their information flows.

Donna Haraway's work on cybernetics provides a hint as to why the rhetoric of information remains so important to Prynne's interest in biology. She reminds us that humans' imbrication in various communicative and bio-informational networks means 'information'

> is just that kind of quantifiable element (unit, basis of unity) which allows universal translation, and so unhindered instrumental power (called

effective communication). The biggest threat to such power is interruption of communication.

(1990: 163)

The products of science and technology are, as Lily Kay's history of genetic science argues, 'sociotechnical', embedded in material and cultural practices that 'stabilize and naturalize the technologies for producing knowledge and power'. For Kay, the informational-linguistic description of DNA provides a key instance of the dialectic between *technē* and *epistēmē*, where 'epistemic things become technical things' (2000: 18, 36). The history of genetics reveals a striking back and forth between conceptual and technological shifts, particularly in relation to cybernetics, telecommunications and the information theory that influenced Crick and other biologists. Prynne's looking 'for the facts' about biology led him to the figure of 'reverse transcription' – where the material properties of the text challenge the unidirectional 'flow' of information.

Prynne's interest in reverse transcription as both a biological and poetic process reveals much about his broader rejection of the calculative logics which infect conceptions of communication, biology, politics and environment. The supposed difficulty of Prynne's poetry is intimately linked to his sense that many materials are, in significant ways, resistant to human ways of knowing and doing.

Coal and metal: conditions of landscape and questions concerning technology

In 'First Notes on Daylight' from *The White Stones* (1969) Prynne writes of 'the history of person | as an entire condition of landscape'. This speaks to Prynne's enduring interest in the ways cytochronology (and humanity's survival across time) is related to geochronology – conditioned by landscape in terms of temperature, resources, flora and fauna. Landscape itself is conditioned as well as conditioning. In Prynne's early work shifts in agricultural and industrial technologies, emergent calculative techniques and mechanisms of exchange combine to change human relations with their environment. The Adornian reading of Prynne that we find in various guises in the work of Simon Jarvis, Keston Sutherland, Wit Pietrzak and others relates the difficulty of his philological strategy to a refusal to let the abstracting pull of the logics of exchange manifest themselves on a linguistic and conceptual level – an antipathy toward the question of transferable information vital to Prynne's approach to genetics.

While it is often hard to establish a Prynne poem's frames of reference, 'Die a Millionaire (pronounced "diamonds in the air")' – hereafter 'Die a Millionaire' – follows a more traceable pattern than most. The poem, the longest in *Kitchen Poems* (1968), begins and ends with questions of origin and these questions are related to philology's interest in the development of knowledge across time. The concern with origin bookends an interrogation of evolutionary, imperial and capitalist expansion which first appears translocal and transhistorical, and then focuses on the industrial maladies of Northern England. The poem is particularly interested in the political economy of carbon and in its different material properties.

The poem offers an implicit comparison between different 'self-optimising' systems suggesting the dangers of too-easy analogy between biological evolution, technological adaption and other forms of 'progress':

> the prime joy of
> control engineering is what they please
> to denote (through the quartzite window) 'self-
> optimising systems', which they like
> to consider as a plan for the basic
> living unit. And thus 'accelerating the con-
> vergence of function', we come to our
> maximal stance.
>
> Imperialism was just
> an old, very old name for that
> idea, that what you want, you by
> historic process or just readiness
> to travel, also 'need' – and
> need is of course the sacred daughter
> through which you improve by
> becoming more extensive. Competitive
> expansion: if you can designate a
> prime direction, as Drang nach Osten
> or the Western Frontier, that's to
> purify the idea by recourse to History
>
> *before* it happens. Envisaging the chapter-
> head in the historical outline as 'the
> spirit (need) of the age' – its primary
> greed, shielded from ignominy by the
> like practice of too many others.
> That
> of course is *not* expansion but acquisition
> (as to purchase the Suez Canal was merely
> a blatant example): the true expansion
> is probably drift, as the Scythians
> being nomadic anyway for the most part
> slipped sideways right across the Russian
> steppes, from China by molecular friction
> through to the Polish border.
>
> (2015: 13–14)

'Control engineering' is linked to the advances in cybernetics in the 1940s and 1950s associated with figures such as Norbert Weiner. It engages with the inputs, feedbacks and outputs of different systems; a self-optimising system would respond to environmental conditions to become more efficient or, to use the parlance of evolution, 'fitter'. It is unclear whether by 'basic living unit' Prynne means genes, organisms or communities (or indeed all three) but he appears uncomfortable with evolutionary tropes being simplistically applied in the human sphere. The poem resists the 'competitive expansion' of imperialist discourses which sail too close to a misplaced social Darwinism where only the fittest survive or flourish. The desire for acquisition, 'what you want', becomes the driving force of expansion. The poem's phrases include the imperial 'Drang nach Osten' (the German 'push to the east') and a nod toward the push of American manifest destiny at the 'Western Frontier'. Prynne refuses to let 'recourse to History' obscure the fact that this necessity is not evolutionary 'expansion' but rather 'acquisition'.

This figuration of expansion as pseudo-evolution stands in contrast to Scythians who, by virtue of their nomadic lifestyle, and integration with other communities, dispersed their genes throughout Eastern Europe. The key word here is 'drift' which has a specific meaning in genetics. Genetic drift is 'the statistical (stochastic) effect that results from the influence that chance has on the survival of variants of a gene'. Alongside 'natural selection, mutation, and migration, it is one of the basic mechanisms of evolution' (Bardini, 2011: 245). Genetic drift does not imply fitness but, in essence, sampling variation. There is no pressure of selection or an adaptive function arising from mutation that makes one group fitter.

The nomadic (drifting) Scythians might be read solely as an instance of migration, not of genetic drift. However, the word 'molecular' shifts the scale, harking back to the 'basic | living unit' and anticipates the later 'lives' put into 'strings of consequence into | molecular chains', phrases which foreground the gene as an important context within the poem and indeed throughout *Kitchen Poems* – for example, the 'genetic patrons' and 'genetic links' of 'A Gold Ring Called Reluctance' (2015: 21–23).

All this is indicative of Prynne's broader interest in the relations between humans, societies and their environments. As well as the movement of genes and populations the word 'drift' also implies the movement of the land. In their essay on 'The Glacial Question Unsolved' Matthew Sperling and Thomas Roebuck point out that Walter Brian Harland, an early theorist of Continental Drift, was at Prynne's college (2010: 55). Writing for *The English Intelligencer* a couple of years before the publication of *Kitchen Poems*, Prynne makes it clear that as 'with the migration of peoples, the earth too has her movements' ('A Communication', in Pattison et al., 2012: 5). 'First Notes on Daylight' asks readers to think about the 'history of person | as an entire condition of landscape', but here the landscape itself is on the move; its features, across a long enough timescale, are fluid. In a 1967 letter to Peter Riley, published in *The English Intelligencer*, Prynne notes that shifts in environmental conditions may favour certain species or may cause them to migrate:

For we can hope eventually to establish the sequence of environment-crises which helped to bring the refined hunting-societies into their long migrations, the movement of the reindeer herds itself consequent upon the climatic change and alterations in plant-cover.

These migrations meant that humans were not so much embedded in the landscape as moving across it

> in a semi-nomadic condition, as I take everything in Northwest Europe to have been until some point in the Mesolithic, the natural extension of man into landscape is not indicated at all, in a primary sense, by archaeological evidence. The natural extension is movement, literal passage across terrain, in response to some factors of which there are traces, and some of which there are not.

Prynne's laments about imperialism are related to 'developments in the Neolithic revolution which it is possible to resent: not that land is occupied, but that it's *owned*, possessed' ('Letter to Riley – 14 February 1967' in Pattison et al., 2012: 75–76, emphasis in original). Crucially, as 'A Note on Metal' shows, these developments are intimately related to the evolution of new technologies.

'A Note on Metal' (1968) tracks the historical and geographical ramifications of early civilisations' engagements with metals. Drawing together technological innovation, the development of conceptions of place and the evolution of systems of exchange and finance, Prynne begins by suggesting that the rise of metallurgy led to a different sense of quality in the history of substance. Developments in metallurgy meant efficient weapons which killed 'with new speed and power'. The new, cutting-edge technologies of the 'leading edge' (i.e. edges which cut better) engendered a technical and conceptual movement – the 'history of substance (stone) shifts with complex social implication into the theory of power (metal)' (2015: 128–129).

This shift from substance to power marks a parallel shift from nomadism to emplaced communities as peoples move from hunting into 'more settled expectation of reaping what you have already sown'; Prynne intends us to note the biblical whisper of investment and payoff. This itself 'produces the whole idea of *place* [...] which makes mining and the whole extractive industry possible from then on' (2015: 129, emphasis in original). Interestingly, Morton has also identified Neolithic settlement as containing the seeds of Anthropocene-era environmental destruction:

> this age is directly responsible for the Anthropocene, the moment at which human history intersects with geological time. This is because agriculture turns reality into domination-ready chunks of parceled out space waiting to be filled and ploughed by humans.

(2012: 16)

In 'A Note on Metal', settlement agriculture leads 'to value as a specialized function and hence dependent on the rate of exchange' and these abstractions from substance were 'in turn the basis for the politics of *wealth*: the concentration of theoretic power by iconic displacement of substance'. The specialisation of function allows for what Prynne calls, in 'Die a Millionaire', 'the weakness' of 'names' because it reduces to their exchange value; 'number replaces strength' (2015: 129, emphasis in original).

Hence, when Prynne speaks of an 'abstraction of *property*' it works in both senses. Property – as that which is owned – becomes conceptualizable in terms of number, whereas previously the condition of society had been one of 'power rather than of value'. Moreover, until this point weight had been 'the most specific carrier for the inherence of power'. With metallurgy 'weight coincides with other possible conditions which are less mixed and specific: brightness, hardness, ductility and general ease of working', hence, suggests Prynne, the notion of the properties belonging to a substance is abstracted, 'characterized as formal rather than substantive' (2015: 128, emphasis in original).

'Die a Millionaire' shows the dialogue between *epistēmē* and *technē* that characterised the relations between human and landscape in 'A Note on Metal', operating in a more contemporary context. The section following the spread of the Scythians begins:

> Otherwise it's
> purchase, of a natural course, the alteration
> or storage of current like dams in the
> river: what starts as irrigation ends up
> selling the megawattage across the grid.
> (2015: 14)

That which moved freely across the landscape – peoples, their genes, water – becomes technologically controlled. In order to transmit power across the grid we transform the water's current into electrical current and then increase our currency reserves by selling it as megawattage. The poem picks up the idea of the commodification of water current into currency via electric current ten lines later in 'divert the | currency' and a further seven lines later in 'the current chic of information theory'. The shared root of *currere* plays on both flows no longer *running* free, a shift from current to currency that defines society's relationship to 'natural' resources.

In the 1967 *English Intelligencer* letter to Riley, Prynne states that an 'overbalance of technology is clearly the genetic breakdown, the specialisation of function leading to the economies of exchange' (Pattison et al., 2012: 77).The shift from irrigation to power generation can be read as one such 'overbalance'. The instrumentalisation of the river begins with 'irrigation' – and irrigation itself denotes that shift from the nomadic to the agrarian that Prynne acknowledges in 'A Note on Metal'. He might well consider irrigation as one of those specialisations of function that produce an excess of resources, engendering the will and potential for trade.

One of the source-texts which flows through the river Prynne writes of in 'Die a Millionaire' is almost certainly Heidegger's *The Question Concerning Technology*. Prynne had been reading Heidegger since at least as early as 1961 as he appears in Prynne's first published essay 'Resistance and Difficulty'. For Heidegger, a river turned into a source of power has had its being violated; it has been enframed (*Gestell*).

> The hydroelectric plant is set into the current of the Rhine. It sets the Rhine to supplying its hydraulic pressure, which then sets the turbines turning. This turning sets those machines in motion whose thrust sets going the electric current for which the long-distance power station and its network of cables are set up to dispatch electricity.

The water's flow does not just create current, current is stored and, via a dam, so too is the water used to generate it ('storage of current like dams'). The river and its immanent power become a standing-reserve [*Bestand*]. In the same essay Heidegger explains that the same process of stockpiling also applies to coal, the 'coal that has been hauled out in some mining district has not been supplied in order that it may simply be present somewhere or other. It is stockpiled; that is, it is on call.' This process means that the landscape is also enframed: 'a tract of land is challenged into the putting out of coal and ore. The earth now reveals itself as a coal mining district, the soil as a mineral deposit' (Heidegger, 1977: 14–15).

'Die a Millionaire' also takes up the impact of carbon extraction on the landscape and its impact on the local populace. Although the poem challenges the approach of 'D.H. Lawrence' and other carolers of the 'industrial north and its misery', there is clearly a concern with the politics and economics of coal mining and other activities crucial to what Heidegger describes as 'the context of the interlocking processes pertaining to the orderly disposition of electrical energy', or, as this 'orderly disposition' is more commonly known, being plugged into the grid (Prynne, 2015: 13; Heidegger, 1977: 16). The poem continues:

> The grid is another sign, is knowledge
> in appliqué-work actually strangled & latticed
> across the land; like the intangible consumer
> networks.
>
> (2015: 14)

The 'latticed' structures strangling the land obviously suggest the pylons and wires of the National Grid (which had been upgraded in 1965) but also a conceptual latticing of the country, the division of space into knowable, and therefore ownable, sections. This second sense of the 'grid' appears on the cover of the American edition of *Kitchen Poems* which also displays sites for mining and oil processing along the East Coast of Britain. It is also worth remembering that

The UK Continental Shelf Act relating to 'natural resources' had come into force in May 1964. This sense of grid as the conceptual transformation of the landscape allowing its economic exploitation (including 'prospecting' for oil) returns again in the penultimate verse paragraph with the image of 'perversions' of knowledge which become a

> new feed into the
> same vicious grid of expanding prospects
> (profits) and are let through by the weakness, now
> of names
>
> (2015: 16)

This sense of the 'perversion' of knowledge and the 'weakness' of names is central to the poem's concerns with a rapacious economic expansion and, more broadly, can be taken as one of the key aspects of Prynne's early work. Teasing out what he might mean by 'perversions of knowledge' and 'weakness of names' is a difficult process but it illuminates how his concern with abstraction informs his poetic strategies. I take the 'perversion' of knowledge as referring to the sorts of enframing conceptual shift that allow the economic exploitation first seen in the second verse paragraph:

> what is known can be used to pick up
> or more usually to hold on and develop
> as what for the econometrist is
> 'profitable speculation'.
>
> (2015: 13)

Speculating, and indeed prospecting, implies looking forward and outward toward profits but also toward other lands and opportunities as in the expansions of 'Drang nach Osten | or the Western Frontier'. This speculation results in the technologically enabled exploitation of the landscape and its inhabitants which occurs when everything reveals itself as a resource. Here 'what is known' becomes part of 'profitable speculation' – *technē* (a way of revealing/knowing) and modern technology lead to the imprisoning and enframing 'grid' which is 'knowledge | in appliqué-work', knowledge co-opted for instrumentalising production. Because the poem associates looking-forward with exploitative prospecting and speculating-to-accumulate then one might expect resistance to take the form of a countervailing tendency to look backwards, which is exactly what Prynne suggests. The poem asserts the need to 'take knowledge | back to the springs' and for a 'back mutation' which is 'knowledge' in 'the richest tradition' (2015: 13–16). While this philological 'back mutation' does not constitute a reverse transcription, it is indicative of Prynne's interest in modes of resistance to enframing, quantification and instrumentalisation – resistance which, even in this early poem, is bound up with a suspicion of information theory.

The question as to why the 'weakness, now, of names' allows these tech-nological debasements and why a backwards looking knowledge might offer a form of resistance is an important one for Prynne's poetics. As Sutherland has argued, the 'names' in question refer to Prynne's philological project which involves 'the changing appearance of individual concepts throughout the history of language and considered under the aspect of their "names"' (2004: 23). Prynne's pre-*Brass* poetry tries to engender what Sutherland describes as a kind of immersion within language. 'Die a Millionaire' contains several cues to interrogate the history of concepts, to look backwards, helping reveal why the concept 'purchase' (and the associated word, 'grip') are so central to the poem's resistance against selling England by the pound.

The verbs in the phrase 'to *pick* up | or more usually to *hold* on to' might both be replaced with the word 'grip' which, in its older incarnations, means to 'seize firmly' with hand or mouth and 'to seize and encroach upon land' as well as the more recent use in 'gripping' our attention at the expense of other things. The *OED* also reminds us that to grip is also to find purchase on something. The poem relates gripping to purchasing; we are told that 'The grip is *purchase* again' and 'the twist-point is purchase – what the mind | bites on is yours'. When gears or mouths bite on something they grip. Drawing out the linkage between 'grip' and finding purchase is important because it forces the reader to think of purchase not just as exchange but as acquisition. In addition to its usual sense of acquiring in exchange for money, older senses of 'purchase' include: 'to appropriate or take possession' of territory or land; 'The action of attempting to bring about or cause something; endeavour; attempted instigation; contrivance'; the 'price at which something is or may be bought' and 'the action of seizing or taking something forcibly; pillage, plunder' or, as a noun, 'booty' ('Grip, n.'; 'purchase, n.', *OED*).

Prynne's prompting that the reader make enquiries into the history of purchase most obviously foregrounds a more rapacious and violent type of transfer behind the notion of monetary exchange, associating it with the corporeal acts of biting and gripping as well as drawing out the enforced 'purchases' of imperialist and capitalist expansion. But the resistance to purchase operates on a deeper level central to Prynne's poetics.

The notion of purchase as booty or plunder resonates strongly with Heidegger's description of 'knowing the world' in *Being and Time*. Heidegger resists knowl-edge being seen as a '"procedure" by which a subject provides itself with representations of something which remain stored up "inside" as having been thus appropriated' and so 'perceiving of what is known is not a process of returning with one's *booty* to the "cabinet" of consciousness after one has gone out and grasped it' (2009: 89, my emphasis). Just as Heidegger resists knowledge as booty-grasping, Prynne rejects knowledge as grip or purchase where 'what is known can be used to pick up | or [...] to hold on'. Both caution against seeing knowledge as (finding) 'purchase' – where 'what the mind | bites on is yours'.[2] This question of how we think is crucial to the technological exploi-tation of the landscape (its being purchased by industry) later in the poem.

Here, as throughout *Kitchen Poems*, Prynne's antipathy towards economic logic has an affinity with the Heideggerian notion that the drive to represent and the drive to control or master are profoundly implicated.

Clark reminds us that

> thinking, after Heidegger, cannot be the act of would-be sovereign consciousness seeking the security of an assured and totalizing system of watertight concepts [... it] is not a matter of 'grasping', 'securing', 'making certain', and 'mastering' but of 'following', 'hearkening', 'hinting', and 'being guided'. The reductionist process of analyzing something into a series of tightly secured separate items must give way to something far less familiar.
>
> (2002: 86)

Comparably, readers of Prynne's poetry find that he famously makes it difficult to secure purchase, to grasp, make certain or master meaning. In fact, as his writing has developed over the years, some readers have also lost the sense of hinting and being guided; a sign, for Pietrzak, of Prynne's moving away from Heidegger and towards something more readily describable in terms of Adorno's negative dialectics (2012: 93–100). What I want to emphasise here though is Prynne's poetry's constant refusal to offer easy resolution and its requiring the sort of reading process Ryan Dobran describes as

> the physiological intimacy with the texts, reading with recursive parafovea, attending to obscurity with curiosity and research; all of these approximate a rough ethics of thinking the text, rather than about the text as a completed or completable event.
>
> (2010: 1)

The flickering halo of connotation and secondary meanings require slow (re-)readings with an attentiveness to phonological suggestion and to the periphery of our conceptual vision, readings which move between the centre (or *fovea*) and the margins, spotlighting that which has been considered as waste, junk, noise or some other sort of invaluable but unvalued surplus. Hence 'Sketch for a Financial Theory of Self', another *Kitchen Poems* piece which warns against exchange debasing language, rejects the pricing of 'money' and our 'absurd trust in value' – 'where | the names are exactly equivalent to the | trust given to them'. Instead the poem suggests we might 'choose | to believe in the flotsam, the light glance | passing & innocent because unpriced' (2015: 19).

Such attentiveness to parafovea embodies the piece which closes *Kitchen Poems*, 'A Gold Ring Called Reluctance'. The reluctance stands against the efficiency of specialised function and abstraction – the 'splintered naming of wares creates targets for want'. Instead the poem looks toward 'Fluff, grit, various | discarded bits and pieces' as well as that which ducks the rate of exchange, including 'love' – 'a tangled issue, much shared; but at least we are neither of us *worth* it'. The hesitation and reluctance is a form of 'back mutation', an immersive engagement with the qualities of 'names' via the accretions of philology in order to counter the 'vicious grid' and the marketplace where 'the public assertion of "value"' risks 'seeping into our discretion'. Instead of efficiency Prynne is

> interested instead in
> discretion: what I love and also the spread
> of indifferent qualities. Dust, objects of use
> broken by wear.

In their inefficiency, dust and broken objects assert their substance rather than only what they can be used for or made into. The landscape is not merely an object for financial speculation and mineral abstraction,

> ground is suddenly interesting;
> not as metaphysic but the grave maybe,
> that area which claims its place like
> a shoe.
> (2015: 21–23)

Here, dust resonates with a sense of the materiality that we associate with Heidegger's notion of the 'silent call of the earth'. A call which, as it reveals itself in the peasant's shoes painted by Van Gough, remains resistant to conceptualisation ('The Origin of the Work of Art', Heidegger, 2002: 14).

Prynne's first published essay, 1961's 'Resistance and Difficulty', concerned itself with the ontological priority of the world to the observing mind and the need to do justice to 'substance', to 'make accessible the fact of its existence without impairing its status as a substantial, independent entity'. The essay rejects a

> position where the external world's main value to the subject lies in the graduated difficulties that it can provide him with, and by means of which the subject can render himself and his actions fully intelligible. I do not discover much about the nature of water, if I require it only to realize my ability to swim.
> (1961: 27, 29)

What the essay refers to as the world's, or the substance's, 'resistance' to appropriation by the subject is the way it refuses to offer any easy purchase point on which the mind might grip – hence the experience of 'difficulty'. Prynne's focus on 'substance' in 1961 clearly anticipates the concern with the quantitative supplanting the qualitative seven years later in *Kitchen Poems* and 'A Note on Metal', where he warns against seeing things only in terms of price or indeed purchasing power.

'Resistance and Difficulty' puts forward Gerard Manley Hopkins as a figure whose work enables readers to derive a sustaining sense of the 'complex variousness' of the world. Prynne's argument that Hopkins's use of the 'image of Christ's body as part of the natural order asserts the valid priority of substance' provides some valuable clues for thinking through the treatment of carbon in 'Die a Millionaire' (1961: 30). That the 'diamonds in the air' of the poem's subtitle appear nowhere within the body of the poem is striking, especially as the text deals with another, purportedly baser, form of organic carbon – coal.

'Die a Millionaire' plays on Hopkins's famous comparison of mundane coal and immortal diamond purity in 'That Nature is a Heraclitean Fire and of the comfort of the Resurrection' with its transition from worldly to heavenly carbon types:

> Fall to the residuary worm; | world's wildfire, leave but ash:
>   In a flash, at a trumpet crash,
> I am all at once what Christ is, | since he was what I am, and
> This Jack, joke, poor potsherd, | patch, matchwood, immortal diamond,
>   Is immortal diamond.
>
>   (Hopkins, 1994: 67)

The way Prynne asserts a different sort of 'priority of substance' secularises Hopkins's vision as part of his resistance to the idea that thinking means the capture of the 'watertight' concept and his preference for '[in]completable' communication; unlike Hopkins, Prynne refuses the crystalline finality of heavenly knowledge. Hopkins's 'trumpet crash' recalls the crashing trumpets of Revelation 1:10 which is also surely another source text for the springs and waters that flow through 'Die a Millionaire'. But where Revelation 22:1 has water as clear as crystalline diamond – 'And he shewed me a pure river of water of life, clear as crystal' – in Prynne's poem the 'water of life | is all in bottles & ready for invoice' (2015: 15). The poem refuses the comfort of the resurrection because this notion itself has been bottled and commodified. Prynne turns instead toward that which remains untapped, leading to his focus on substantiality, the 'fluff, grit' and other forms of interference and materiality.

As Prynne's thirty-two point list of 'Tips on Reading, for Students of English' circulated to matriculating undergraduates puts it, '[l]iterary reading is not a mere spectator sport' (2004: 4). Prynne has continually asserted that he believes reading must pay attention to the poem and not the poet, who is never the final arbiter of control.[3] Prynne's refusal to allow readers too much purchase on his poems also raises a question of the causality and temporality of the production of meaning when reading; it is worth thinking back to 'purchase' as 'to bring about or cause something'. When the mind's purchase on the 'watertight' concept is disrupted so too is its causal efficiency, the power of language to identify an exact referent. The sort of reading strategy proposed by Dobran and Jarvis means that the signal, to use the language of information theory (for reasons that will become apparent), is subject to different forms of interference. The poet is not in control of what his or her language does; *Stars, Tigers and the*

Shape of Words describes the way the reader's awareness of 'accumulated potential signification' stored in the past usage of words can

> weaken the lateral *grid* which connects the relation of a word with those on one side or the other within the system of differences, and is to promote instead the vertical connection *back* into the past and back up to the present, making words stand as the *name* for what the associations of sense and suggestion can bring into play.
>
> (1993: 16, my emphasis)

The notion that turning 'back' – in order to pay attention to the parafovea of sense and suggestion surrounding the 'name' – weakens the constricting grid which focuses only on relations is something that endures in Prynne's thinking.

Prynne's philological poetics in *Kitchen Poems* combines with the particularity of the individual reading experience to prevent the poem being the information 'transfer' of summarisable meaning. As 'A Note on Metal' asserted, to favour the quantitative over the qualitative is to make things exchangeable. Jarvis's Adornian reading of the early work illuminates how this operates on the level of language: 'Adorno argues that the belief that true thinking may simply be equated with correct predicative thinking both reflects and enables the imperative to a universal exchangeability of objects within organised economic life.' He reminds us of Adorno's claim that exchange is 'the social model of the principle of identification, and without the principle there would be no exchange; it is through exchange that non-identical individuals and performances become commensurable and identical.' This means that, Jarvis continues, the

> way in the which the qualities of concept and object are suppressed in a predicative proposition reflects and assists the way in which the different qualities of commodities (including commodified human labour) are regarded as irrelevant to their expression as exchange-value.
>
> (2002)

This Adornian reading of Prynne is a powerful one and addresses Prynne's philological interest and his political concerns by allowing form to be responsive to politics. It positions his disjunctive poetry with its lack of identifiable predicates as a mode of resistance to the quantitative logics that enable the exploitations of landscape and population we see in 'Die a Millionaire'.

While I would not deny the Adornian reading's potency or its general applicability as a common way of approaching Prynne, it seems to me that Adorno is not only *not* a key formative influence on Prynne but that Adorno's thinking lends itself to a human-focused critique rather than one attentive to those biological and geological forces that exceed and confound human intentionality. The ecumenical nature of Prynne's reading habits (as Jarvis points out in the same essay, the division of intellectual labour is itself a dangerous specialisation of function) means that other influences supplement, supplant and perhaps even prefigure the philosophical and critical positions associated with him. While it is hard to establish a clear trajectory or chronology of thought, science has always played a key role in his thinking. A letter to Ed Dorn indicates some of the models that interested and influenced him: 'It was pharmacology I invaded, together with plant hormone systemics: what price mere negative dialectics when necro-hormones can take you right through the reverse quotient' (1973). Elsewhere Prynne's correspondence, while admiring Adorno's approach to negation, cautions us against a too-easy rapprochement between himself and Adorno: 'much of the argument [in *Negative Dialectics*] is stupidly self-contradictory' (1978).

Adorno does assert the 'preponderance' of the object which destabilises the bourgeois subject's pretentions to autonomy (2004: 181). However, Jane Bennett, in her book on the function of objects and materials within ecological and political systems, argues that Adorno is 'quick, too-quick [...] to remind the reader that objects are always "entwined" with human subjectivity'. Accordingly, the emphasis in Adorno's writing falls on social conditions and not the material qualities of, say, workable metals, or carbon or ribonucleic acid. He is not as interested in what Bennett describes as the capacity of things 'not only to impede or block the will and designs of humans but also to act as quasi agents or forces with trajectories, propensities, or tendencies of their own' (2010: 16, vii). But the way such non-human agency operates alongside social, political and economic issues is vital to Prynne's writing about biology and ecology.

My tracking of ecological and biological contexts in Prynne's later work extends and complicates the key issues I have identified in my reading of his early work: concern with materiality, the focus on the qualitative over the quantitative and the way technological innovation and conceptual framing impact on the treatment of life, landscape and text. An attentiveness to the problems of abstraction means that Prynne questions approaches which, like information theory, enforce a calculative schema on communication.

Pertinent junk and the sound of information

Information theory has influenced conceptualisations of linguistics and genetics and, in some cases like the work Roman Jakobson, the relations between the two. Claude Shannon's 1948 paper 'A Mathematical Theory of Communication' forms the cornerstone of information theory. Developed at Bell Labs, where much of the research was still shaped by military imperatives (Shannon himself had been a cryptologist during the Second World War), this paper primarily focuses on ways of quantifying information rather than what the message means: 'semantic aspects of communication are irrelevant to the engineering problem. The significant aspect is that the actual message is one selected from a set of possible messages' (Shannon, 1964: 31). In this paradigm, information is encoded, transmitted and decoded – this section tracks some of the reasons Prynne is fascinated by the uses, abuses and unacknowledged legislation of ideas founded on quantifiable information.

Shannon's ideas were popularised in a 1949 book he co-authored with Warren Weaver. Mapping the communication system onto oral speech they suggested that 'the information source is the brain, the transmitter is the voice mechanism producing varied sound pressure (the signal) which is transmitted through the air (the channel)'; the receiver, which changes the transmitted signal back into the message is, in this case, the 'the ear and the associated eighth nerve' of the person being spoken to. In the communication channel there is the risk of noise when 'certain things are added to the signal which were not *intended* by the information source' (Weaver, 1964: 7). Questions of noise and interference are particularly pertinent to Prynne with his interest in philology – not least the way words accrue significance – but also because of his claim in *Stars, Tigers and the Shape of Words* that there might be a reverse transcription which violates the unidirectional data flow, where sound is coded back onto the level of sense.

Prynne's description of Saussure draws on the language of information theory. Prynne describes the 'sounds and shapes' as, for Saussure, part of the 'system of differences' onto which the 'quite unconnected' system of meaning – ideas in the mind of the language user – were mapped. Words become 'performable devices' which act as a carrier medium, and after transmission can be decoded in the mind of the recipient. The 'efficiency of the mapping or coding is determined by how clearly and adequately the differences within the idea system are displayed or performed by the sound (or graph) system'. Also significant for Prynne is the way that this perspective leads to Saussure taking the object of study as language at 'a given point in history, as a system of signs and signifying relations, rather than the sequence of its evolutionary history through time'. Moreover, Saussure is primarily interested in the 'abstract concept of human language' and not the moment of its articulation. Utterance becomes secondary, *langue* is emphasised at the expanse of *parole*; the 'drive towards a theoretic, non-historical scheme also leaves the performance aspects of language use at a more derivative and thus less decisive level than system' (Prynne, 1993: 5–6).

Prynne refers to Richard Hamming's explanation that information theory 'ignores the meaning' so as to better understand 'what equipment [like the telecommunications of Bell Labs] does to messages' (1993: 48). As Prynne argued in 'A Note on Metal', new technologies impact upon our conceptual apparatuses. Prynne, whose poetry's effect relies more than most on various interferences rather than direct communication, is interested in the question of what happens when the informational model shapes approaches in other fields. Shannon and Weaver, interested in efficient communication, ask how information theory can 'minimize the undesirable effects of noise' and also examine those aspects of the message which are 'unnecessary' or 'redundant'. These redundant aspects are unnecessary in the sense that if they were missing the message would still be 'essentially complete, or at least could be completed' (Weaver, 1964: 13). Prynne's work suggests that the sounds and shapes of words in poetic writing pose problems for Saussure's notions of arbitrariness. In a manner comparable to the way reverse transcriptions in the genome problematised

Crick's Central Dogma, there is a challenge to the model of unidirectional flow emphasised by information theory.

Prynne terms the sort of motivated sign that would violate Saussure's analysis a 'reverse transcription' because the transcription of RNA back into DNA is describable as noise in the communication channel becoming part of the message. Prynne's linguistic analogue sees the noise produced in the communication channel becoming part of a secondary motivation where the reader finds a connection at the level of sound that gets coded back on the level of idea.

Taking Saussure's own hunt for phonetic anagrams in classical literature as a cue, Prynne uses Blake's 'The Tyger' as an example of how the historical awareness and sonorous signification can combine in a localised part-motivation. He begins by examining the presence of certain letters:

> The <tig> of 'tiger' is within the letters of 'bright'; if the /r/ of 'bright' is permitted to stand in its transferred context as a vocalic /r/, then the whole of tiger in acoustic form can be recombined from the letters of bright.

What joins the two words is 'burning' so that 'the fearsome creature is at least half created by a back formation [...] from bright'. Prynne's notes nod to a kind of 'subject rhyme', the contrasting tiger stripes are brought out by the rhyme of bright and night: 'one value of the tiger's pelt rhymes by similar contrast with the other value: burning bright or carbon black' (1993: 25).[4]

Prynne galvanises his reading by moving from the play of sound and letters – the material of language – to the poem's own thematic concerns with materiality and technology at what is often taken to be the start of the Anthropocene. There needs to be a burning that makes the (black) night bright. Prynne turns toward the forests of Blake's second line and the industrial processes that use them: a 'furnace burns all through the night, enclosed within a surrounding darkness which looms like a forest'. The forest is also 'materially requisite' as to provide charcoal which would be used as a power source and a 'reactant in the metallurgical transformation' – 'blast furnace smelting' being the 'standard metal technology of the Industrial Revolution'. And the results of this smelting 'can subsequently be beaten into form'. Hence the tiger is

> the recombined and transformed product of its material combination, its colours and skin-pattern, its condensed power, and also the bright sounds and letters that make up its name are all formed into this new life by fusion and forge melting.
>
> (1993: 26)

The tiger burning bright is produced through the pounding trochees remoulding the letters and trees of the forest of the night, the 'words are both agencies of expression and also a material substrate for smelting into new forms'. The linguistic materials of poetry and the technologies and substances of the Industrial Revolution are forged together in the 'mind furnace'; it is, Prynne says, 'done with words and made of them' (1993: 30). Prynne's nod to J.L. Austin's *How To Do Things With Words* here is significant. As another critic of Saussure and Austin, who also sees a link between viruses and communication famously reminds us, iterability means we are not always in control of what we do with words (see Derrida, 1988: 1–25).

What Prynne's 'localized part motivations' allow for are

> secondary relations within the abstract schedule of language structure that ramify operative connections across the whole domain; which in turn become part of the social function of language because usage codes develop a history which can be written back into features of the system and then re-activated by recognized prompts and cues, either *from one side of the connection or the other*.

In other words, Prynne is not particularly hung-up on authorial intention, he explicitly states that 'authorial intention' cannot 'be the test' of whether sound is 'coded-back' onto the level of sense. Rather he sees literature as 'promoting expectancy of such classes of connection' between sound and sense where the noise that is a product of materiality becomes potentially significant – one of the functions of poetry is to create an arena where these sort of sense-generating engagements with sound happen (1993: 33–34, my emphasis).

We can apply Prynne's play of sound and sense to the first instance of information theory in his work, the concern we find in 'Die a Millionaire' with a quantitative approach which fails to adequately address the complexity of the living:

> The grip is *purchase* again, and the current
> chic of information theory will tell you how
> many bits of that commodity it takes to
> lift one foot/lb. of shit to a starving mouth
> or not starving actually, but just rather
> unthinkingly hungry.

In the poem information theory clashes with a poetic project concerning itself with problems of identification and exchange in linguistic or financial transactions and which posits non-identity and substantiality as a form of resistance. Coming nine lines after the 'currency' and 'current' of the 'grid', the 'current | chic of information theory' is shown as manifestly inappropriate for describing the marginalised 'real people' of the previous verse paragraph (2015: 14–15, emphasis in original).

The movement toward the quantifiable parallels the subsuming of surplus value, generated through labour, within the logic of exchange; the qualities of actual labour are displaced by units of work – (foot/lbs). The units denote the quantity of work done but not what form it takes. Information theory is not concerned with the meaning of the message, nor indeed with the implications of what 'redundancy' entails other than being surplus to requirements like those 'real people, slipping off | the face of that lovely ground'. Prynne uses the tribulations of the 'industrial North East' to show the parallel between the efficient information system and efficient economies in a human cost that is always too dear.

Again, in a type of reverse transcription, Prynne uses sound to disrupt the purely quantitative terms of information theory which focuses solely on 'surprise' information – those differences that make a difference. Reading the poem and enunciating the text 'foot/lb' as 'foot (per) pound' does not add any semantic content – in terms of information theory the 'per' is technically redundant. Only added by the human reader sounding the poem out loud (or with what Prynne would call their 'mental ears') the 'per' changes the sound but not the meaning. However, the combination of plosive /p/ and extended vowel sound stands out in sharp relief against two lines dominated by repeated dentals ('bits of that commodity it takes | to lift one foot [...] shit to a starving'). Prynne asserts that the bits – the units of information theory – have no worth in themselves, they are, as the internal rhyme enforces, shit. But the logic of exchange value means 'iconic displacement of substance [...] number replaces strength' despite, within the etymology of 'pound', the substance of weight (*lī bra pondō*) preceding the number of currency. The long vowel sound of (per) pound which stands in sharp relief against the dentals anticipates the corporeal 'mouth' at the end of the line. The vowel stresses and the reader's annunciation of 'per' bring the human back into the schedule of production and exchange, 'pound' foregrounding the fair flesh which is inimical to quantification whichever way you slice it. The abstract sign (/) is made flesh in the reader's articulation. The pounding of feet suggests a stamp of outrage at the economic situation and draws out the sound of human work (feet pounding) beneath the abstract informational foot/lb to remind us where the surplus value created by labour goes – into the 'vicious grid of expanding prospects | (profits)'. These are considerations that strain and stress poetry's metrical feet.

The grid's instrumentalisation of the environment which commodifies the river into current/currency parallels the gap between the informational 'bits' of labour and 'real people, slipping off | the face of that lovely ground'. Richard Dawkins has described Shannon's theory as a sort of 'economy of information' (2008: 297). One might suggest that Prynne's figure of a reverse transcription from sound to sense, where the phonic, contextual and historical operations contribute to the production of meaning through the materiality of the signifier, connotes an ecology – *logos* indicating a study of the *oikos* at a lower degree of abstraction.

Kay has detailed the fascinating range of political and technological factors that fed into the focus on information in the late 1940s and early 1950s, showing how theories of information spilled out of and across a variety of different areas. 'Information' was wedged at the intersection of military-sponsored research on both machines and living organisms: the mathematical theory of communication, modeling of the brain, artificial intelligence, command and control systems, cybernetics, automata theory, genetics and behaviorism.

(2000: 77)

Figures such as Norbert Weiner, Henry Quastler and George Gamow (founder of the 'RNA tie club' – a kind of genetically orientated gentleman's club of which Crick and Watson were members) were committed to the promise that information theory held for biology. Crick's writing on the informational flow of protein synthesis, which became the Central Dogma, was moulded by the transdisciplinary informational paradigm.

The key question for my reading of Prynne is not the overall scientific appropriateness of Crick's use of the discourses of information – it is hardly surprising that parts of Crick's work have been critiqued, challenged and modified over the last fifty years, particularly in relation to aspects of the roles of RNA and so-called 'junk' DNA, not mention his use of the word 'dogma'. Rather, I am interested in why Prynne suggests that the informational metaphor is sometimes problematic, and what this reveals about broader currents of thinking.

One central problem arising from information theory's use in genetics is identified by Emmeche and Hoffmeyer, two biologists who, in an article that Prynne cites in *Stars, Tigers and the Shape of Words*, challenge the

> tendency to see the 'information' (in genes or the written text) as the passive substance, being actively 'processed' or 'interpreted' by an organism or brain/computer which then restructures the message originally contained in the genetic 'memory' of the system.
>
> (1991: 37)

Drawing on his knowledge of the special information transfers that problematise parts of the Central Dogma, Prynne's figure of reverse transcription is formed round the idea that the materiality of the signifier can interfere with such restructuring – reading poetry is not a matter of reassembling the poet's thoughts which have been rendered into language, 'authorial intention' is not the prerequisite for a reverse transcription from sound to sense. This in turn is part of his broader interest in the evolution of phonology, language and concepts across time which are 'counterpart and compliment to essentialist analyses of structure' (Prynne, 1993: 34). Prynne's various public and private comments on Crick, not to mention his own poetry about genetics, show that he is aware of the warping influence of models primarily interested in the one-way information transfer.

In one telling letter he writes to Dorn to charge Crick with an obsession with specific function. Crick had co-authored an article on dreams which used the language of parasitism and information theory to suggest that dreaming worked at 'removing *parasitic* modes', a 'cleaning up mechanism' with which we might be exposed to certain ideas and feeling and without which our minds might produce 'unwanted responses to random *noise*', something which '*equalizes* the accessibility of stored memories and suppresses most of the spurious ones' (Crick and Mitchison, 1983: 112–113, my emphasis).

Prynne rejected Crick's 'biochemist's positivism' and suggested that his friend's

> notion that mammalian dreamwork may be a kind of purposeful overload scavenging, a feedback shunt to sump and dump, certainly raises (& maybe calls) the question of prosodic and political currencies at the lowest tariff barrier [...] holding hands with the Presbyterian abstraction of Freud (clinicians of the sacred), to set up dreams as mental weedkiller or (in the old-style idiom of hard-wiring) as voltage surges designed to blow all sub-threshold circuits ('parasitic or spurious modes') not earthed to positive connection in useful 'experience'.
>
> ('Letter to Dorn', 1983)

Crick's favoured genetic/informational models shape his speculative notions about cleaning up our mental landscape. It is worth noting that he also employed the language of parasitism to describe the operation of junk DNA.[5] Crick's overwhelming focus on the genes which code for protein synthesis amidst the sea of non-coding DNA that makes up over 98% of the genome, parallels his ideas about the clearing out of obsolete connections and obscure links in favour of efficient forms of neural communication with a 'useful' function. This positivism is anathema to Prynne with his cross-contextual focus on the junked and the marginal, on what might be redundant in informational terms but still significant; as one of his most quoted lines has it, 'Rubbish is | pertinent' ('L'Extase de M. Poher', 2015: 162). This rejection of (biochemist's) positivism, and the concomitant emphasis on the neglected junk, emerges in multiple ways throughout Prynne's thinking. Another letter to Dorn nicely indicates one of the reasons why this is so:

> Francis [Crick], airing his views about labs he's been visiting, says a sure test is whether there's junk in the corridors; if not the admin men have the place under control & no good will come of it. Ah yes thinks I, minds without junk ditto.
>
> (1978)

The secret lives of plants and viruses

While *Stars, Tigers and the Shape of Words* is the clearest re-deployment of the figure of reverse transcription from genetics to linguistics, Prynne had seized on reverse transcription as a significant model at least twenty years earlier in a series of prose pieces which blended questions of temporality, plant biology and academic politics. Some were printed in *Bean News*, Dorn's experimental newsprint project on which Prynne collaborated under the pseudonym 'Erasmus Darwin'. Others became 'The *Plant Time Manifold* Transcripts', a series of 'transcripts' from a fictional conference attended by academics such as 'Professor Lichen' and 'Dr Cypress'. This 1970s work, like his recent writing on Peter Larkin, uses plant biology as a means of challenging any too-simple, over-humanised insistence on causality, efficiency and intentionality.

In the fictional conference, 'Plant Time' describes an extension in both directions along the horizon of time's arrow. Unlike surface-dwelling mammals and their 'mammalian' time, plants extend themselves back into the past through 'root tip (r)' which grows down. These root activities impact on the transport of material within the plant and the activities at its 'stem tip (s)' (Prynne, 1972a). Here, Justin Katko explains,

> the surrounding earth is consumed into the backflow, as the root's 'appropriation' of subterranean mineral excavates the geological timeline of past organic life, now fossilised and compressed into plant food. Prehension defines the condition of the organism's relationship to past events.
>
> (2010: 269)

The past is reactivated in the present, and this provides a model that we find in Prynne's descriptions of poetics in *Stars, Tigers and the Shape of Words* and, more recently, in 'Mental Ears and Poetic Work' where he describes the capacity of poetry readers' 'mental ears' to tune into historical schedules of poetic composition 'so as to occupy a prior station already inflected by knowledge of successor historical conditions'. 'Mental ears'

> are also empowered by linkages of memory and retrospect, as reconstruction of what originally faced towards the undeclared future [...] 'Mental ears' will hear in older sounds the then new sounds of making and marking a track into forward space: a future in the past.
>
> (2010: 129, 133)

The correspondence surrounding *Bean News* shows Prynne occupied with temporal configurations of 'being' and thinking about his project in terms of both information theory ('*might be* minus relative entropy = *has been* minus noise') and genetic development ('hieratic centrocrats make the queen Been sit in the nucleus, with heredity, development and infection time bound from the throne in synchronic function substrates') (1971b, 1972b, emphasis in original). Given Prynne's ongoing concerns it appears that the issue at hand in terms of genetics is similar to that identified by Emmeche and Hoffmeyer – the problem of seeing the genome 'as a fixed blueprint or even a program with some "instruction" containing information telling the cell what to do' or 'as an inherent biological meaning processed by the cell and translated from the potential information to actual information' instead of 'a relational determined part of a whole developmental system' (Emmeche and Hoffmeyer, 1991: 37). The genes in the nucleus may be queen bee, but information does not only flow one way because factors such as reverse transcription may insert noise into the genetic message, impacting on ontogenesis.

Given its disruption of smooth linear progression in genetics, space-time and literary communication, it is significant that 'The *Plant Time Manifolds* Transcripts' is the first instance in Prynne's published writing of reverse transcription: 'RNA itself could have been transcribed backwards into DNA' (2015: 241). During the period of composition he wrote to Dorn excitedly that 'reverse transcriptase [...] is a functioning reality, you can read back out through the ticket into the box-office; the timewarp is deformable in so many vectoral combines that wit in this matrix needs more than front/back' (1972c). This spatial-temporal deformability is displayed in the roots and shoots of the notion of 'Plant Time', in the make-up of *Bean News* itself (parts of which read right to left), and in the strange film projector in Dorn's *Gunslinger* (a book partly dedicated to Prynne):

> Well, There's a Literate Projector,
> which, when a 35mm strip is put thru it
> turns it into a Script
> (Dorn, 1989: 76)

Dorn's image is telling for the thought processes surrounding the *Bean News* project. One could extrapolate the script from a film but if one were to reshoot the film with that script then one might expect a different movie dependent on other factors in the production. This insistence on not reducing everything to the text has implications for Prynne and Dorn's interest in biological development across time. As Emmeche and Hoffmeyer put it, the information of a

> developmental system is not 'inherent' in the DNA, but is being created in a continuous flow of events of interactions between the DNA and other parts of the cell. Therefore, the 'meaning' of the genetic 'message' is only discernible in the concrete process of development at the biochemical, the cellular, the organismic, and even higher levels.
>
> (1991: 37)

Despite what screenwriters and perhaps some information-orientated biologists like to think, the script does not tell the whole story. In *Bean News* and 'The *Plant Time Manifold* Transcripts', the unidirectional information flow is disrupted, or at least, as 'The *Plant Time Manifold* Transcripts' puts it, we have 'the operation of causality but not entailment' in relation to the genetic or linguistic text (2015: 234).

Recently Prynne has returned to the lives of plants to describe Peter Larkin's poetry in terms which are highly relevant to his own work. Prynne identifies a kind of 'mammal' or 'muscular' language, 'promoted by pronouns that are actions of agency with intentional structures, making and causing activities to occur through verb structures which are built into the habits of the human language community'. These are 'the kind of uses' to be expected from 'a TV commentator or a politician or any of those people who use language to exert muscular power over or within the development of human social practice'. What he finds in Larkin – who is himself a reader of Prynne and of ecocriticism – is something more botanical and associated with 'the organic world of plants and trees' with structures that are 'interrelational in a way that is not to do with muscular agency or with the deliberate causation of events' but instead 'not far different from the kind of rhizome structures which certain French theorists [presumably Deleuze and Guattari] have promoted as examples of alternatives to a world of muscular agency' (2013: 43–45).

Prynne draws a parallel between these organic networks and a sense of language different to that of mammalian agency, one aware 'of the deposits and relationships which comprise words before they are recruited into the action of human agency'. Instead their connected 'roots develop their own internal agency and activity' which is 'part of the world of the organic connection of the whole relation of language to world and to nature' (2013: 45). This challenge to human agency has a strong affinity to *Stars, Tigers and the Shape of Words'* resistance to the notion that 'authorial intention' is the final arbiter of significance.

It is also interesting that Prynne's comments on Larkin compare the strange workings of plant ecosystems and poetic language to the operation of 'some kind of microbes and some kinds of fungi' (2013: 44). While the question of whether a virus is a microbe is one of those vexed scientific issues well beyond the bounds of this book, it is clear that (reverse-transcribing) viruses are an embodiment of Prynne's interrogation of intentionality.

In *Stars, Tigers and the Shape of Words* it was the materiality of language that enabled reverse transcriptions; secondary motivations arise from poetry being 'done with words and made of them' rather than a conscious decision on the part of the poet when he 'encodes' ideas into text. Comparably, the interactions of ontogenesis exceed the sort of straightforward informational transfer that Crick envisaged. Derrida, whose own critique of Austin's belief in doing things with words has been so influential, makes a point about viruses and communication-interference that is illuminating of the role viruses play in *Bean News*. In an interview with Brunette and Wills he positions the virus as

> a parasite which disrupts destination from the communicative point of view – disrupting writing, inscription, and the coding and decoding of inscription – and which on the other hand is neither alive nor dead.
>
> (1994: 12)

The figure of the virus is an important one for the temporal distortions of *Bean News*. The self-help column 'Dear Flabbey' (penned by Dorn) makes clear why viruses are relevant to the project:

By itself, a virus is not really alive. When around the candy store dried up they form a crystal. They can wait like this for years! But when dissolved in liquid and allowed to penetrate a cell [...] Once inside the cell they fuck with its genetic machinery and use its rich stash of amino acids and nucleotides to make copies of *themselves*.

The motive here is to 'to reconsider an aesthetic which makes a distinction like Alive or Not Alive'; to assert non-human, and indeed non-living agency. Reverse transcriptions from sound to sense depend on tuning-in to the accumulated layers of signification accrued through a language's evolution. Hence it is not the 'deliberate and conscious' intention to include certain phonological effects that is important, but rather the way certain utterance-codes obtain or reactivate in shifting future environments. As Dorn's faux self-help column indicates, virology displaces intentionality, it 'takes care of all those decisions I've heard youre [*sic*] up against out there [on the scale of multicellular organisms]' ('Dear Flabbey', in Grossinger and Howe, 2015: 492–493, emphasis in original).

One of the virus' key properties is a period of latency known as the lysogenic cycle. The virus integrates with the host cell's genome, replicating along with it but remaining dormant until the right sort of conditions emerge for it to reactivate. The figure of that which is neither dead nor alive but which might re-emerge under certain environmental conditions (i.e. in the manner of viral lysogenesis) is resonant of the way past usage codes are 're-activated' in *Stars, Tigers and the Shape of Words* and 'Mental Ears and Poetic Work'. These reactivations are an instance of the 'contamination of damaged forms' that Crick and Saussure resisted.

Mutating code scripts

> *these chromosomes [...] contain in some kind of code-script the entire pattern of the individual's future development*
>
> – Erwin Schrödinger (1992: 20–21)

Schrödinger's 1944 musings on genetics proved inspirational to another young physicist-by-training, Crick (see Crick, 1990: 18). Schrödinger's book *What is Life?* focuses on a genetic pattern for 'not only the structure and functioning of the organism in the adult, or in any other particular stage, but the whole of its ontogenetic development' (1992: 20–21). For Judith Roof, Schrödinger reaches for 'the kind of performativity formulated by Austin in the speech act' where 'what the "code" is, is also the means by which what it says becomes an organic reality' (2007: 78–79).

Schrödinger's argument means that, even before the discovery of the role of DNA, the conceptualisation of morphogenesis has been haunted by a notion of performativity that feeds into the questions of informational transfer and the focus on DNA that this chapter has discussed. He argued that chromosomes contain 'code scripts' which are 'law code and executive power – or, to use another simile, they are architect's plan and builder's craft in one' (1992: 22). Schrödinger's foundational conceptualisation of the gene saw it as producing 'the effect it describes or enacts by its saying' (Roof, 2007: 54). The trouble is, as we have seen, that the closed-circuit of this model is contaminated by the interactions of code and the rest of the developmental system, including the interactions with rest of the cell and the environment. 'Plan' and 'craft' are well and good but, even having cast aside the previously thorny issue of who offers planning consent, there is still the question of available building materials, or the risk of subsidence in the local landscape. The replication of morphogenesis does not involve the repetition of the gene, but its being reiterated in a different context.

1999's *Triodes* queries the implications of the ways we conceptualise morphogenesis and his attempt to find a formal response to the (genetic or linguistic) textual element that is significant without being meaningful. Roof argues in her analysis of the rhetoric of genetics that 'the idea of a causal gene' allows it to become 'the mechanism that absorbs displaced causality from elsewhere, particularly from the realm of the social' (2007: 98). *Triodes* takes up questions of genetic causality, locating it alongside questions of the commodification of the living.

> Uh rusted mother says Irene she dispenses
> > patchy temper at the *pair rule*
> > slim kibbled and *engrailed* big-time under heaven.
> > > the pediment writes the balcony
> > with the *script of a gap gene code*
> > > not found back of the throat
> > gasping and retching.
> > > > > > (2015: 496, my emphasis)

The word 'gene' works to contextualise the usages around it. 'Gene code' initially seems shorthand for genetic code but in fact the important coupling is 'gap gene'. Gap genes are central to the development of segmentation in arthropod embryo development; they control the expression of other genes – the 'pair rule' genes two lines previously. Gap genes and pair rule genes both regulate Hox genes – the genes vital to organism structure. Hox genes work alongside a transcription factor that controls the informational flow from DNA to RNA. In the case of *drosophila* – the fruit fly so important to the history of genetics and to whose embryogenesis gap genes and pair rule genes are so central – the name for this transcription factor is 'engrailed'. Moreover, Hox genes contain the homeo*box* – a sequence which helps supervise structure. Given that figure of Pandora is referred to throughout the collection the 'box' appears to enclose some significance.

Some of the most important work on Hox genes was performed by Edward B. Lewis, for which he won the Nobel Prize in 1995. Prynne's letters show that he keeps a (not uncritical) eye on the awards of the 'Swedish royalty', especially its prizes for biology, and there is good reason that he would have found Lewis's work, and the discussion around it, particularly interesting.

Lewis researched the way that certain regulatory genes' proteins bind to regions which control the expression of other genes, thereby impacting on the way those genes are expressed. Engrailed is one such gene. Lewis's work plays an important role in an emergent field called 'evolutionary developmental biology' or 'evo-devo' which is pertinent to Prynne's work.

Evo-devo flags up epigenetic factors that impact on evolution – that is, changes in the expression of genes which do not necessarily include a change in the genetic information itself:

> Epigenetic factors, such as differential methylation patterns [chemical changes in the promoter region of a genome due to environmental factors], genomic imprinting, posttranscriptional control, and RNA editing, as well as biophysical properties of cells and tissues, geometrical patterns of self-organizing systems, and environmental factors such as temperature, all contribute to the regulatory machinery of developmental systems and their evolution.
>
> (Laubichler, 2008: 349)

It seems to me that even if *Triodes* is not thinking specifically about the advances in evo-devo discourse that were occurring in the 1990s, Prynne is very much interested in the way epigenetic factors impact on morphogenesis. Moreover, I want to suggest that Prynne does not just include certain advances in genetic research to direct his reader's attention to a set of scientific ideas that are important to thinking about biochemical processes, but that he also makes his poems perform them.

Gap genes control the transcription of the genetic code and here the 'gap gene' in a 'script of gap gene code' interrupts (and syntactically inverts) Schrödinger's code script. More important is the interjection 'Uh' with which the poem begins. 'Uh' appears thirteen times in *Triodes*' thirty poems including the first poems of each section – clearly a significant expression if not one that seems to code for a specific meaning. With its brevity and its role as a sub-articulate outcry 'Uh' shares certain similarities with the interjection 'O' that Prynne discusses at length in his essay 'English Poets and Emphatical Language'. 'O' is notable for its functioning as both an expression of an inner state and for being part of poetic convention; its 'exclamatory emphasis isolates the distinctive moment of its utterance, and yet its performance is kept within the margins of an intelligible context of expressive forms and rhythms' (1988: 155).

'Uh', unlike 'O', seldom marks the start of soliloquies and speeches. (Though 'Uh, what a rogue and peasant slave am I' works quite well, more so than 'Uh, Wild West Wind'.) Its reappearances throughout *Triodes* forces the reader to make decisions about how to either express it vocally or sound it with their 'mental ears' – as an expression of disgust (which might also be written 'urgh'), an indication of hesitation ('err'), a grunt of pain, or of pleasure. Perhaps it is the sound 'of the back of the throat gasping and retching'. In certain situations it might connote a blend of some, or indeed all, of these possibilities. *Triodes* does not give much by way of help in resolving the meaning of these utterances within the syntactical and lexical field of the line – they are pieces of homograph sound play. Maybe that is why the first poem announces a 'homonymous city' (2015: 481). Computing the informational worth of these repeated (and therefore, by some informational measures, redundant) pieces of poetic code is challenging. Yet they proliferate, a constant presence full of sound (and perhaps fury) signifying nothing in themselves and yet impacting on the expression of meaning from other parts of the text – the poetic code.[6]

Because it appears as a repeated piece of text-code that moves around within and between poems, one way to approach the 'Uh's in *Triodes* is to consider them analogous to 'Mobile Genetic Elements', that is sections of code that can move around the genome. Some of these, such as retrotransposons which arise through reverse transcriptions, can induce mutations in other parts of code. It is hard to imagine Prynne being unaware of these pieces of movable code given that McClintock had won the Nobel Prize in 1983 for their study and, more importantly, that some of their functions, including their role in gene expression, are discussed in the Temin article he recommends in *Stars, Tigers and the Shape of Words* (Temin, 1985: 460–461). It is also worth noting that it had become apparent that retroelements interacted in important ways with transcription factors (e.g. see Becker et al., 1993).

The comparison between transposable genes and phonemes is worth making because genetic retroelements parallel Prynne's phonic reverse transcriptions. These mobile elements infect and mutate the way we read. The first deployment of 'uh' in *Triodes* is

> Irene, plant group **moth**er you infix
> Shock limits, **uh** Pand**ora** your
> Leading kravatt will rise to the s**un**.
>   (2015: 481, emphasis added)

The bolded rhymes and half rhymes indicate that once the transposable element (uh) is introduced it begins to construct a field in which the syllables around it resonate. '**Uh** Pand**ora** read the **run**ning'; 'early **sun** | over tilting **uh**'; '**Uh** ru**sted moth**er'; 'dr**ug** hit on computed | **surg**e count, **uh** flesh b**ur**ns'; '**uh** Sharm | el-Sheikh will **run** and **run**' (2015: 488, 482, 496, 501, 502).

The interaction between the 'uh's and the surrounding words change the way the poem's phonemes might be emphasised or even pronounced (in the parlance of genetics, expressed) by a reader, showing that the text cannot fully prescribe its annunciation. As the search for /g/ and /t/ sounds in 'The Tyger' indicated, Prynne's reading strategies in the 1990s revolve around these localised motivations of sound play where the specific moment and site of utterance might exceed the intentions and code of the original. As *Triodes* puts it, 'The text | omits, the margin includes' (2015: 484).

Prynne's subsequent work indicates that there is nothing superficial in his engagement with this part of genetics. In *drosophila*'s embryogenesis, the transcription factor 'Engrailed', as well as interacting with pair rule genes and gap rule genes, expresses the protein Hedgehog. Hedgehog was isolated by Christiane Nüsslein-Volhard and Eric Wieschaus who shared the 1995 Nobel Prize with Lewis. Significantly, as Andrea Brady has detailed, the equivalent signalling protein in mammals, the memorably named Sonic Hedgehog (SHH), plays an important role in 2003's *Acrylic Tips*.

The titular tips are 'acrylic beads, used to insert genetic products into embryonic animals' (Brady, 2006: 82). The poem nods toward the issues of stem cell research ('unformed causal | stem') and genetic development ('gene expression resentment'), particularly the developments stemming from interferences with 'sonic [hedgehog] driven receptor sites'.[7] As Brady points out, mutations in the hedgehog protein cause a range of developmental mutations (2006: 81). These include cleft palates and lips ('lip trickle', 'cut your lip in mischief', 'punitive cleft', 'dental roof in spasm'); eye development ('eyes wide bridge mail', 'lens failure'); facial formation ('face value seared'); and the development of vertebrae, limbs and the forebrain development within the skull cavity ('Each neck attempted | forearm reversed nursing limpit prized, skull rims close to fusion') (2015: 533–546).

I agree with Brady that '*Acrylic Tips* is interested in linguistically mimicking the wounds and mishaps of the experimental body' and would suggest that a similar interest lies at the heart of *Triodes*. *Acrylic Tips*' linguistic deformations and derangements of sense make it worth 'considering what these experimental mutations in the linguistic field reveal about the directions our sensory and cognitive capacities can take' (Brady, 2006: 81). Similarly, *Triodes* forces readers to acknowledge the environmental field of factors, including mutative agents, that impact on the expression of genetic and linguistic codes. These formal mutations reflect a concern with pre-scribing genetic and linguistic 'meaning'.

Given Prynne's alarm over aspects of experimental mutation we might read Pandora, who opens and closes *Triodes*, as embodying the multiple evils visited upon humans when commercially motivated research prises open the Pandora's box of genetic engineering and commercial pharmacology. This is similar to what Heidegger feared: 'someday factories will be built for the artificial breeding of human material, based on present day chemical research' (2003: 106).[8] Indeed, Prynne has expressed his disgust at some of the driving motivations behind biochemical research both in the anti-Big-Pharma-concern of *Biting the Air* and in his letters to Dorn:

> The cleavage of active subsequences from precursor peptide chains is inferred [...] you can't fail to smell the rank stench of a vicious race for success. The prizes are not just the Swedish handout but immense spinoff from the drug empires: royalty and royalties. The biggest payout of all

must be reserved for a simple method of selectively focusing and binding specific pharmaceuticals on to the target sites of pathological activity.

(1975)

The fact that the letter also discusses serotonin and sleep as evolved mechanisms for 'pre-emptive wound response' indicates that Prynne is considering medication beyond the treatment of pathogens – that is, the medicating of what might, sometimes falsely, be described as pathological behaviour. *Triodes* also alludes to investment in chemical research which might target specific sites, be they neural or otherwise – 'designer drug options', 'a new drug | is the target' (2015: 512, 507).

On the individual level the ascribing of success simply to good luck or good genes is an ethical failure. Jarvis argues that Prynne's early work challenges a notion of election for removing agency to an external deity, but in *Triodes* 'gods [are] not in the sky' but 'plodding on [molecular?] strings' (Jarvis, 2002; Prynne, 2015: 494). The problem is similar: foregoing agency and responsibility for the genetic roll of the dice, forgetting about all the environmental factors that control gene expression or any other of the manifold determinates that impact on human development. Research in biochemistry may be able to alleviate certain problems but, as James Watson's justification for the Human Genome Project indicates, the language of these 'clinicians of the sacred' is dangerously over-zealous:

> The genetic dice will continue to inflict cruel fates on all too many individuals and their families who do not deserve this damnation. Decency demands that someone must rescue them for their genetic hells. If we don't play God, who will?
>
> (1995: 197)

This is the sort of reductive (and frequently one-way) thinking that Prynne has resisted throughout his writing life, something reflected in his gnomic 1967 statement published in *The English Intelligencer*:

> The ratchet is the mechanical equivalent of the non-return valve, and in either system what goes up can't then (or later) come down. And just because our economy is more or less arranged on this principle it does not follow that language is like that, nor either the kind of person a given life can induce.
>
> ('About Warning an Invited Audience', in
> Pattison et al., 2012: 168)

Wasted fields and digested hydrocarbons

One of the central thoughts of this chapter is that cytochronology and geo-chronology, the cell and the landscape/environment, feature in Prynne's work as parallel, and sometimes directly interrelated, matters of concern. 'Acquisition of Love', from *The White Stones*, sees a figure observing children as he or she tries to fix a broken mower. The poem combines the corporeal with the subtending level of the biochemical, 'I feel the | blood all rush in a separate spiral, each genetically confirmed', 'the gene pool itself defines these | lively feelings' (2015: 111). Peter Middleton describes the would-be mower as 'a product of a long evolutionary genetics, and also just suburban man doing his household chores' (1997: 350). But the mundane technology of this suburban vision impacts on the way the speaker regards the children, 'I guess their | capacity in pints'. The children are rendered in the language of the mechanical and the quantifiable, the

> poem suggests how close are different ways of thinking about the cause of human actions such as genetics and desire, and yet how difficult to connect when the result of optimistic conflation may be simply a grotesque image of the body as mere capacity.
>
> (Middleton, 1997: 350)

These children's bodies, and their future, are not only shaped by their genetics but by inherited concepts, 'they look outwards | to our idea of a planet. Their blood | is battered by this idea' (2015: 111).

Technology shapes conceptualisations of the organic as well as the organic itself. 'The Ideal Star Fighter' is *Brass*' (1971) engagement with the 'Earthrise' photo, the famous 1968 picture of the planet from space which provided an important image for environmentalism – 'we hear daily of the backward | glance at the planet, the reaction of | sentiment'. Joe Luna, who has assiduously detailed the poem's social, political and scientific contexts, points out that in his Vancouver lecture on Olson Prynne was clearly less than impressed by these various (sentimental) reactions to Earth taken from orbit: 'There was that unbelievably gross photograph of the Earth taken across the surface of the moon, which is now in all the soap ads' (Prynne, 1971a).

Like 'Acquisition of Love', the poem shifts between the technological and bio-logical to suggest that the ideas of the planet, affected and mediated by technologies (military, communicative, transport), will shape the future of the organisms on it: 'The permeated spectra of hatred dominate | all the wavebands, algal to hominid'. The poem's association of spectra and wavebands with both a range of lifeforms and broadcast media (via electromagnetic waves), speaks to the way that Prynne high-lights the physiological dimension of technologically mediated communication: the 'eye | converts the news image to fear enzyme' (2015: 165–166).

The poem's final section reverses the process. Instead of the physiological effects of media broadcast, the poem now speaks about the ethical and ideological in biochemical terms: 'we have already induced | moral mutation in the species'. The (moral) mutations wrought by technology and economics are thrown into relief by the poem's inclusion of the contemporaneous chemical attacks in the Vietnam War: 'Oriental human beings throw off | their leafy canopies, expire'. The herbicide Agent Orange not only defoliated the canopies of Vietnam's jungles (and destroyed its crops) but it is a mutational chemical which caused a variety of genetic diseases in the population and ongoing dioxin contamination of the landscape.

Luna has shown how the poem resists a 'maudlin, lopsided universalism' that accompanied the view of the Earth from orbit, highlighting the link between the development of cybernetics – themselves bound-up with studies of military efficiencies and related to the development of information theory – and some of the environmentalist discourses that emerged alongside the Earthrise photos. For Luna, the poem's 'hate system', where 'the whole object [i.e. the Earth from space] is loveable' serves as a critique of the 'whole systems' environmentalism of figures like Buckminster Fuller and Stuart Brand who 'encouraged the managerial cultivation of the global technocratic *oikos* called "Spaceship Earth"' (Luna, 2016). One of the most obvious ways this technocratic managerialism evinces itself is Brand's opening editorial to his *Whole Earth Catalogue*, 'We are as gods and we might as well get good at it' (quoted in Turner, 2006: 82).

The resonance of Brand's phrase with Watson's 'If we don't play God, who will?' is striking. Both are examples of how the ideas of cybernetics have an afterlife in conceptions of technoscientific control of the organic at micro or macro scales. Indeed, Brand is still very much a proponent of both geoengineering and genetic engineering as a mechanism of environmental adaptation.[9] Moreover, Prynne's poem positions the 'whole system' vision that sponsors notions of technological control alongside an older kind of anthropocentric holism. The split quotation in the poem's first section ('if fear is an evil why should there be danger') is from Samuel Johnson's critique of Soame Jenyns's writing on the 'great chain of being'. The 'great chain' is a kind of hierarchical depiction of creation which situates humans at the top of the non-divine categories, and finds perhaps its most famous rendering in Pope's 'An Essay on Man'. Pope's poem is also a target for Johnson; it contains its own 'mawkish regard' and concomitant hierarchical politics: 'Look round our world; behold the chain of love | Combining all below and all above' (Pope, 1978, Epistle III: lines 7–8).[10]

The kind of whole-Earth gaze which masks systemic injustices and neo-imperial violence finds a partial correlate in the contemporary anxieties of Nixon and others who feel that the Anthropocene itself might be a totalising concept that risks forgetting that some populations and communities are far more at risk of adverse effects than others. In 'The Ideal Star-Fighter', the despoliation of the poem's final section reminds us that even if we are 'as gods' (and one suspects this is a notion that Prynne, with his rejection of 'over-humanized history', would strongly resist), then humans are a long way from being and 'good at it':

> What more can be done. We walk
>   in beauty down the street, we tread
> the dust of our wasted fields. The
>   photochemical dispatch is im-
> minent, order-paper prepared.
>   (2015: 166)

The clichéd (and maudlin) simile of 'like the night' from Byron's 'She walks in Beauty' is transferred to the suburban literalness of 'down the street', an appropriate shift for a poem which shows what happens when the Earth is seen in a new light. The 'photochemical dispatch' speaks to the circulation of the newly developed photographic negatives of the view from the heavens, a world picture that perhaps obverts 'that tender light | Which heaven to gaudy day denies' (Byron, 1970: 77). For Lee Spinks, the poem mutates Byron's vision into a nuclear landscape, so that Prynne resists the

> privilege Romantic aesthetics accords to epiphany or moments of trans-cendence where the ideological and social divisions of experience can be temporarily overcome. Prynne's reinvention of Byron refuses to endorse the Romantic conception of nature as a restorative space for historical and cultural schism; the only moment of transcendence the poem offers us is the 'photochemical dispatch' of the nuclear instant.
>
> (2000: 163)

'Photochemical' processes involve the chemical impact of light, which in this instance imply both the instant of a nuclear blast but also what is known as 'photochemical smog'. This smog is a type of pollution which is a possible after-effect of a nuclear explosion and, more generally, a product of the reaction between sunlight and atmospheric particulates, particularly those stemming from industry and transport, providing a link back to the 'Exhaust washes' of the poem's previous section (2015: 166).

Four years later in *High Pink on Chrome* (1975) Prynne delves deeper into the technological (mis)management of the biological. The poem taps into the consciousness of toxic landscapes that followed Carson's work in the previous decade – and it is worth remembering that the link between military technology and pesticides is important to *Silent Spring*. This is probably Prynne's most overtly ecologically engaged collection, with its references to the toxicity of agro-industrial practices:

> The chisel plough meets tough going,
> we spray off with paraquat 2½ pints
> per acre. And the [51]CR label shews
> them and us in your same little boat
> (2015: 257)

Hugh Foley points out that paraquat is a (now banned) herbicide. Several compounds of Chromium (CR) are also toxic despite their uses in metallurgy, pigments and tanning. Foley argues that the '"same boat" we are in is the skin of the slaughtered animals from earlier in the collection whose pelts were tanned "with aniline"' (2012: 84). More significant is the way that the repeated /cr/ in acre inlays the contamination of heavy metals within the landscape.

Some of these metals used in agricultural and industrial processes have mutative power:

> There is no doubt that some of the toxic effects of
> these metals is the result of a cell-mediated immune-
> logical reaction against the body's own proteins
> modified antigenically by the metals and that this is in
> some way genetically controlled.
>
> (2015: 251)

Chromium (along with aniline) is not only a carcinogen (as famously documented in *Erin Brockovich*) but also genotoxic, that is it causes damage to the genome, changing the ways genes code for proteins. These new proteins, created by the body's own genes, prompt a damaging response from the immune response system. Another 'heavy metal' with genotoxic compounds, mercury, often used as a herbicide, can cause Acrodynia – also known as *pink* disease. It name is due to the fact that symptoms include pink discoloration of the skin, as well as itching ('lost into the burned skin'). Mercury poisoning also causes chest pain ('intense burning | pain in the chest') and shortness of breath ('shallow breathing') (2015: 257, 251). Kevin Nolan (2003) and, in more detail, Dan Eltringham (2015) have pointed out that an important context for *High Pink on Chrome* were the tragic deaths of up to 10,000 members of rural Iraqi communities in 1971, inadvertently poisoned by grain treated with mercury-based fungicides. The toxic foodstuffs had been turned pink.

The attempt to manage the organic leads to unforeseen and unpredictable consequences due to the diverse properties of the materials. Ian Patterson reads the collection as showing that metal

> is now not only a metonymic token of value, it is a circumambient and
> toxic presence in the foodchain, with consequent requirements to redefine
> the pastoral. What the eye doesn't see, the liver dies of.
>
> (1992: 242)

An interest in substance confounds a focus on quantification and the 'abstraction of property' tracked in *A Note on Metal*. In *High Pink on Chrome* Prynne continues to demand that we make connections:

> And this little biscuit is as much as anyone could ask
> for and more than many could take. Aliphatic
> hydrocarbons are its tacit basis, the explosive device
> was placed on a window ledge and the area sealed off.
>
> (2015: 256)

Putting aside the context of the (fertiliser) bomb, the poem reminds us that even little biscuits are part of much greater networks, something highlighted in the Vancouver 1971 reading when Prynne discusses the name of his collection *Kitchen Poems*: 'kitchens are a very good place to start getting clear about certain kinds of commodity link-up in the world around, which basically work down to what you eat' (Prynne, 1971c). Here, as so often, aliphatic hydrocarbons (which include methane and several compounds found in petrol) are the 'tacit basis', underscoring global production.

Carbon may be in coal or diamond, CO_2 or methane but in his collections since *Triodes* (1999), the concern for 'real people slipping off' the face of Northumberland, has shifted onto those impacted by oil wars and the agricultural and industrial policies of climate change. Prynne's late style is his most resistant, but paying attention to the constellations of phrases and imagery within and across the late collections reveals hydrocarbons and climate change to be crucial aspects of his late work.

Despite his antipathy towards any totalising world picture in *Brass*, the more localised concerns with chemicals and coal in the earlier work have gone global in the last decade, as indicated by *Unanswering Rational Shore's* (2001) 'planet auction', the 'planet ember' of *Acrylic Tips* (2002), *Biting the Air's* (2003) 'trading to a planet' and 'globe toll' and, in the uncollected 'Frag (2)' (c. 2010), a poem which appears to be referencing the polluting particulates of the Deepwater Horizon incident, the atmospheric 'planet pelt' (2015: 524, 544, 567, 629). The collections are peppered with words and phrases which carry a certain baggage due to their reference to contexts that are increasingly part of our discourse of global warming: aviation, carbon capture, resource wars and emissions limits.

In *Sub Songs'* 'Riding Fine Off' the reader finds that the phrase 'water slides up and up' gives a darker tinge to the words 'fear no more' a few lines later; we cannot help but hear *Cymbeline's* 'the heat of the sun', and the predicted consequences of the heat, such as the concomitant 'up and up' of sea levels (2015: 616). A similar phrase also pops up in the uncollected 'Never the Same' – 'no more the heat, fear the sun'. This is a poem marked by threateningly watery phrases (including 'waters followed | in laps to spoony fate', 'obdurate melt', and the Canute-like futility of 'fluid slay waves') alongside phrases suggesting atmospheric conditions ('average furnace overcast', 'Sky clip ozone', 'submit atmospheric'). The poem is also interspersed with the language of quantification and sufficiency ('pitch target', 'tag enough', 'several uncounted', 'ever offset') which makes a carbon footprint a more-than-useful fit for the second sentence's 'accurate | cast slipper animate', a phrase which reads as an accusation directed at the reader: if the glass slipper fits, wear it. Also interesting are the poem's varied images of combustion, especially those which, to me at least, suggest fracking: 'spark | fissures convinced to catch hot wick at cost margin', 'hot fume | notional gather' and in particular 'fumarole faucet' (2015: 630–631). A fumarole is a vapour vent in a volcano. Having it in conjunction with the American usage of 'faucet' calls up the flaming household taps linked to fracking in the United States, most famously in the documentary *Gasland* (2011).

The interpenetration of the economic and geophysical in phrases like 'planet auction' is important, not just because consumption fuels shifts in global temperatures but because this is 'carbon season' where carbon becomes both commodity and threat (2015: 546). The poetry touches on different kinds of carbon as 'scant fuel thins to vapour in vacant air' in *Unanswering Rational Shore* and the competition for untapped resources (*Acrylic Tips*' 'unslaked level fields') fires the Middle Eastern conflicts that also permeate the late work, most directly in the 'war for oil, oil for food' of 'Refuse Collection' – a poem which engages with the horror and disgrace of Abu Ghraib (2015: 531, 546, 578).

The later poetry also plays with the emergent technical and economic mechanisms that have been devised to reduce emissions such as carbon capture – 'emission drainer staple' (*Acrylic Tips*), 'Modest capture […] vapour banks' (*Biting the Air*), and *Kazoo Dreamboats*' 'particulate vapor to | consign into bedrock' (2015: 545, 554, 661). *Sub Songs*, published shortly after the failure of the 2009 Copenhagen climate talks, seems particularly interested in the constructing and missing of targets. 'Along the Wall', the poem most overtly engaged with issues surrounding climate change, nods toward the Copenhagen talks' key headline figure of a two-degree temperature rise – 'sufficient total not two'. Two degrees was seen as the tipping point after which a series of positive feedbacks would kick in, triggering runaway climate change. If there is any chance of reaching this figure, and there may not be, then some action has to be taken as 'drastic indecision makes for burnt living' (2015: 625, 613).

However, the solely calculative approach to the key figures of climate change does not sit well with the interpretation of Prynne that I have detailed within this chapter. The arguments over maximum possible temperature rises or concentrations of carbon particles in the atmosphere apply the calculative technics of the grid on a planetary scale – the complex systems of which are amenable neither to accurate modelling nor to human control. As Karen Pinkus has argued, market-driven carbon management propagates a fantasy of technological control manifestly inappropriate to the 'chaotic and unfathomable temporality of climate change' (2010: 51).

Locating carbon within a mechanism of exchange risks forgetting about both the complex feedback mechanisms which climate modellers and carbon traders must struggle to take account of – such as the 'clathrate denial' in *To Pollen* (2006) and *Kazoo Dreamboats; or, On What There Is* (2011 – hereafter *Kazoo Dreamboats*). Clathrate structures lock in elements like a 'lattice'; methane clathrate is a form of ice ('Braided up like | floss to a seizure named like water') that keeps methane trapped in arctic permafrost and under the seabed (*To Pollen*, 2015: 589). Or, in *Kazoo Dreamboats*

> A small fortune however, or not,
> more or less mostly sides contradiction lies further back in
> the bedrock of stich and mend and spin, threadwork clathrate
> to oddments if or not, digested monastic lunch-party while we
> also err, chew it over like sheep dyed in green.
>
> (2015: 658)

A change in temperatures, perhaps already in the offing, could destabilise these clathrates, triggering a massive release of methane, a far more potent greenhouse gas than carbon dioxide, which might constitute a tipping point in runaway climate change. In fact, certain companies are thinking of trying to exploit these reserves, something that seems to be happening in *Kazoo Dreamboats* with its reference to unconventional ways of sourcing hydrocarbons.

Something that lies dormant in a crystal structure and which emerges in the right sort of environmental conditions to negative effect obviously resonates with Prynne's interest in the reverse transcriptions of virology. We might refer to the properties of such phenomena as known unknowns which confound the (geo)political decision making process. Carbon structures that had been, literally, 'on-ice' become more politically significant than any set of Toyota Priuses or wind farms which, by comparison, come across as another instance of greenwash that we 'sheep dyed in green' buy into as we procrastinate ('chew it over') – a critique of readerly passivity which chimes with *Not You*'s (1993) 'causing the forest | to fail softly by watching leaves turn' (2015: 407). The potential impact of these carbon deposits ruptures the illusion of human sovereignty which thinks its emission reductions will necessarily enact the change they intend. The confounding nature of these materials and their resistance to being finally calculable or controllable means that the desperate attempts to bring the global economy up (or down) to speed with the demands of the global climate has to contend with the fact that, to misuse Schrödinger's words, the 'architect's plan' might be miscalculated and the 'builder's craft' reliant on techniques that are still in the process of development. Focusing on human emissions risks downplaying an awareness that the carbon in the biosphere and atmosphere is not just that quantified and exchanged on the trading floors of carbon exchanges but an unpredictable factor in the planetary feedbacks central to climate change.

The sort of concepts which pervade climate change discourses suffer from similar problems as those concepts Prynne examines in relation to genetics, economics and communication. Shannon's model of information transfer focuses on the efficient transfer from sender to receiver. As I have shown, this concern with intentional transmission forms a constellation with a more general exploration in Prynne's work of quality and the non-identical. These concerns are replicated in Prynne's exploration of that which is 'significant' but cannot be reduced to meaning, those reverse transcriptions from sound to sense – a type of connection readers' 'mental ears' tune-in to expect but which cannot be reduced to authorial intention. In genetics this evinces itself in the too-strict concentration on the movement from genetic code to phenotypic characteristic which ignores other factors and contexts in ontogenesis and morphogenesis, not to mention the environmental and social determinates. The 'given life' of genes does not fully pre-ordain the 'kind of person' it helps induce.

By the same token, to see too direct a correlation between carbon emissions (now measured in parts-per-million, exchanged on the market floor as credits) and temperature, risks forgetting the role phenomena exterior to human control play while also failing to address issues of over-consumption.

Situating carbon as exchangeable and controllable fails to address its qualitative properties and the way its materiality interacts with a developmental network of technologies, societies and ecosystems. As in *High Pink on Chrome*, the attempt to control the biological system has unexpected or unwelcome consequences.

In 'Along the Wall' the ramifications of a failure to attend to various materialities of carbon and its compounds plays out. After the (in)'sufficient total' of less than two degrees warming, the reader sees 'ice near dry now', connoting both melting ice and frozen CO_2 (dry-ice being frozen carbon dioxide) (2015: 625). Prynne's 'lark | rustles in ripe grain' is a clear allusion to the 'lark does rustle in the ripe corn' in Blake's 'Visions of the Daughters of Albion', a line from a passage which, significantly, calls up the image of a 'red, round globe, hot burning' (Prynne, 2015: 625; Blake, 2006: 61). The poem's disorientating play of images of cutting and reducing – 'file, sever, fall, nip, just cut it, cut ig' – shifts, at the poem's close, into the clearest contextualisation in the whole of *Sub Songs*.

> Oh love be so
> Blind to send to not roam
> Alien in cornfields, again
> [...]
>
> butt scorch,
> corn full of fire as men in oil dress swept from, hydrocarbon in
> digest evermore in chat fume, to regain from what then to not
> is done to be, known ejected all to spend ash ready support mesh
> the more given the more to spare
> there willing, hold to spring
> off block down desire zone each in peak interdict power line from
> sand rending, as or shale later chat through swamp mimic heartland.
>
> (2015: 626)

The desire to reduce emissions and ensure energy security (perhaps from the 'men in oil dress') has led to the growth of corn to be rendered into (bio)fuels through enzyme digestion (hence 'hydrocarbon in | digest'). By also having the poem ask to 'not roam | alien in cornfields, again', Prynne draws out the figure of Keats's Ruth and the cornfields she stands alien amidst. When new technologies and market conditions mean corn yields more as fuel than as food we are alienated from our cornfields' literary and emotional heritage, butterscotch fields become butt-scorching fuel destined for the automobile's tail-pipe.

Scorched corn also suggests the 'parched corn' which gives sustenance to Ruth in the *King James Bible* – a refugee-figure exiled from her own land (Ruth, 2:14). A pertinent reminder that the drive for biofuels led to drastic increases in food prices, the co-opting of land for biofuel farming and the concomitant driving of local farmers off their land. Those alienated from their cornfields, like those Canadian communities displaced or sickened by 'power line from | sand rending' (the Alberta Tar Sands) or the US citizens endangered by the fracking of shale gas ('or as shale later') are, as in 'Die a Millionaire', indicative of the human cost of the disjunction between the economy and the ecology of carbon.

In the Anthropocene, economic logics combine with new techno-scientific attempts to regulate local and global ecosystems. The ecological challenge of this contemporary 'carbon season' is not simply one more area of political concern for Prynne, but an extension of his attentiveness to the qualitative and the quantitative in the realm of the organic, something which, as I have suggested throughout, lies at the heart of his poetics.

This difficult matter

> *In studying a problem, we must shun subjectivity, one-sidedness and superficiality [...] To be one-sided means not to look at problems all-sidedly*
>
> – Mao Zedong (1965: 323)

Shunning subjectivity and looking at problems (and poems) 'all-sidedly' would serve, as well as many others, as a brief description of Prynne's later practice. Even if Prynne had not included large chunks of it in *Kazoo Dreamboats*, there is a good case to be made that Mao's 'On Contradiction', quoted above, is a much more important essay for thinking through Prynne's work than, say, Adorno's 'On Lyric Poetry and Society' because it brings dialectical thinking to bear at every scale, including the level of matter. Mao was not the first to do this but his emphasis on 'internal contradiction in every single thing' as being the primary cause for change differentiates him from Marx in that his focus does not only orientate around the human (cited in Prynne, 2015: 642). This sense of contrariness, or perhaps the resistance and indeed the liveliness of matter, is at the heart of Prynne's interrelated approaches to biology, environment, technology and language and part of what makes Prynne such an interesting poet to think the Anthropocene through.

The 1982 *Collected Poems* contains the following introductory note, which might be attributable to Prynne himself:

> Much early critical response to J.H. Prynne's work mistakenly took its cue from the first line in this book: 'The whole thing it is, the difficult', failing to establish that difficulty as being the ardent 'matter' and the accompanying breadth of imaginative and political reference.
>
> (quoted in Jarvis, 2002)

Jarvis's comment on the note is typical of many defences of Prynne's poetry from charges of obscurity: 'difficulty is claimed not to be a manner of presentation supposedly separable from subject matter, but to be inherent in the matter addressed itself' (Jarvis, 2002). Jon Clay, in his more recent Deleuzean reading, makes an astute point that Jarvis, despite his concern with quality in the face of quantity, does not emphasise; namely that 'difficulty is not denied but matter is insisted upon'. Moreover, that matter might not only refer to the 'situation under consideration' but that Prynne's note, in which

> he characterizes the matter as 'ardent', might suggest another reading that pays less attention to syntactic inconsistencies. 'Ardent' suggests that matter has its own force, its own enthusiasms and passions upon which it might want to insist. If 'matter' is read in the sense of 'material' then we are presented with the sense of a recalcitrant thing that exists in its own right, something in the world that offers resistance to expectations of easy co-optation by the reader.
>
> (Clay, 2010: 22)

Clay sees this secondary possibility as a factor which contributes to Prynne's anti-representational aesthetic.

> The poem might be taken as a material difficulty that readers do not simply assimilate intellectually but encounter as a transformative reality of the world, an intensity that produces an actual transformation of readers themselves in the process of reading.
>
> (2010: 35)

This intriguing aesthetic argument about what a Prynne poem does would be even more convincing if it dwelled more on Prynne's thematic interest in materiality. In 1961 a young Prynne described 'resistance' as 'an inescapable sense of the *given*, found to exist, and may not be fabricated or willed into being – like difficulty – to meet the continuing demand for palpable texture of human affairs'; hence the 'valid priority of substance' (1961: 30, emphasis in original). Should we not then consider the 'valid priority of substance' in Prynne's own work before hastily jumping to the difficulty of the 'texture of human affairs'?

Prynne's explorations in phonology see him focusing on how language's materiality can exceed intentionality, even to the extent that it can be productive of reverse transcriptions from sound to sense. As I have shown, this concern with the materiality of the signifier is related to Prynne's interest in biology, not least in the ways the material properties of the genetic code script have implications for ontogenesis and gene 'expression' that cannot be properly accounted for by the information transfers of Crick's Central Dogma. At another scale it is the way different technologies and techniques for calculating, commodifying and extracting carbon have profound ramifications for lives and environments at local and global scales.

Now of course these concerns have profound social, political, economic and ethical implications and dimensions; this chapter has shown how the 'accompanying breadth of the imaginative and political reference' is at times breathtaking in its ranging from microbiological mutations to maimed landscapes. But it is still 'difficulty' (of interpretation, of living ethically under late capitalism) that often dominates discussion of Prynne rather than questions of resistance and of materiality.

In a powerful recent essay which confesses to frustration with what he sees as the Adornian justification for Prynne's difficulty, Christopher Nealon (2013) suggests that:

> For all the praise given Prynne because he reads widely in the sciences, his poems feel less experimental than ascriptive, so that each new bit of scientific (or financial, or engineering, or programming) language comes about to seem merely as the latest support for Prynne's claim about the un-linear instabilities inside of seemingly linear time, and its capacity to model (if not actually enact) the undoing of the damage caused by linearity, grids, forward-thrustingness, and instrumentalization. More consistent even than the absence of any lightness in the poems is the absence of the scientific emotions of perplexity and wonder.

Remembering how he claimed that 'geochronology' and 'cytochronology' displace the causal presumptions of over-humanised history we should be wary of seeing Prynne's biology and ecology as simply something tacked onto, or even emerging out of, radical politics. Nealon describes Prynne's work as an Adornian poetics in which

> the reversibility (or at least non-linearity) of patterns of everything from migratory drift, membrane salinity, and word-shapes can be pitted against the relentless instrumentalization of time and persons by capital, without actually being 'pitted against it' per se.
>
> (2013)

This seems to apply more to the arguments of some of Prynne's advocates than his own work. While one should not hold Prynne fast to his early pronouncements in 'Resistance and Difficulty' it is important not to forget how, during his formative years, he positioned difficulty as the 'subjective counterpart to resistance' (1961: 28). His corresponding literary difficulty is not, or rather not only, response to the 'damage' of late capitalism but also evidence of an awareness of the material world's immanent 'resistance', and the contradiction or potentiality that is perhaps not adequately encapsulated by the Adornian 'non-identical'. Prynne himself suggests that his deep (and not just 'wide') engagement with the natural sciences is in some ways generative of his concern with quality and the non-identical – not only the other way round: at 'what price mere negative dialectics' when you can have 'necrohormones'?

An Adornian reading helps illuminate large parts of the concerns of this chapter, not least the technological domination of natural history. However, it strikes me that Prynne's recent comments that Mao's essay had interested him for decades and that Adorno's work was not revolutionary perhaps stem in part from the fact that Adorno's approach to Nature does not contain a sense of the inner dynamism of matter as in 'On Contradiction', nor indeed does it address the mutative potential Prynne draws on in his engagement with living systems.[11]

Written in an almost visionary mode quite unlike anything else in the latter part of his career, *Kazoo Dreamboats* reveals more than most collections about Prynne's processes, concerns and contexts – not least due to the extended list of 'Reference Cues' on the back page. Even so, the poem's exuberance – which, *pace* Nealon, might well be described as conveying the 'perplexity and wonder' of scientific discovery – provides many challenges for the reader. Prynne nods towards the ways his poetry might be (mis)read; those who see him as only purveying a 'Cranky-danky fear | of abstractions' or mistakenly think the poetry a kind of resolvable cryptic game where 'you get triple | points if you guess the connection' (2015: 660, 642). This is more than 'lightness' from a poet aware that he is approaching the latter stages of his writing life. Giving his poetics a turn in the spotlight forces the reader to consider the collection's constant references to forces and matter in relation to the work his poetry does.

As if prompted by one of the long embedded Mao quotations that argue that the 'internal contradiction in every single thing' is the 'fundamental cause of its development, while its interrelations and interactions with other things are secondary causes', *Kazoo Dreamboats* is awash with dynamic objects where matter itself appears ridden with contradiction (2015: 642). From the worlds formed by the 'cosmic whirl' of 'atoms' to the body 'From itself autoimmune' nothing stays still or exists in a harmonised state, everything appears 'by nature self-mutable': there is no peace past understanding, to seek the 'Still point of a turning world [is] self-deluded' (2015: 644, 650). Moreover, Prynne denies the possibility of empty space or noiseless communication channel

> "We now recognize that 'empty space'
> is a turmoil of electromagnetic waves of all frequencies and wave
> length. They wash through and past us" or say "we are all bathed
> in this 'Vacuum infinity' of all virtual electromagnetic waves" pro-
> voked and then quelled in reciprocal perturbation.
>
>   (2015: 640)

At another point we read that 'even the zero-field is in- | flected, by charge and currency'. There is no physical or conceptual (pastoral) space outside the fluctuations of different determining forces and tensions ('What's that humming sound? The so-called outside'). As with the focus on current before it was commodified into currency in 'Die a Millionaire', 'charge and currency' here nod back to the non-pecuniary meanings of 'load/substance' and 'flow' as well as to electromagnetism where positive and negative charge is a form of pre-organic contradiction (2015: 653–654). Prynne's emphasis on counter-tensional forces echo Mao's proposing of contradiction as an ontological principle that subtends politics:

Thus the contradiction peculiar to a certain field of phenomena constitutes the object of study for a specific branch of science. For example, positive and negative numbers in mathematics; action and reaction in mechanics; positive and negative electricity in physics; dissociation and combination in chemistry; forces of production and relations of production, classes and class struggle.

(Mao, 1965: 320)

I am hesitant about extrapolating what exactly this Maoist trans-scalar emphasis on contradiction says about Prynne's politics. However, in terms of his approach to ecology, technology and biology there is surely a telling implication in the fact that the word that comes up over and over again in *Kazoo Dreamboats* is 'dialectric' and not dialectic. Rather like the way Prynne's poetry approaches the transmission (or indeed conduction) of semantic meaning, a dialectric is a kind of material across which electric current acts but the dialectric does not itself conduct electricity, it is an insulator and therefore resistant to current's flow. As Gerald Bruns puts it, the dialectric's disruption of electrical charges results in

something like a trackless storm and so Prynne's 'dialectric' stands in marked contrast, for example, to the dialectic of Hegel (and Marx), which defines a history of reason that drives events forward (however explosively) toward some coherent end or purpose.

(2013: 60)

Prynne, as ever, asks readers to think beyond anthropocentric terms, including the ways the resistance of the world – its conflicting and dynamic materiality – exceeds both conceptual thought and technological control.

The stakes for resistance and contradiction are highlighted by the article on tomography in petrocarbon production from *Oilfield Review* that Prynne lists in *Kazoo Dreamboats'* reference cues. This article, Christopher Earley explains in his detailed analysis, explores the use of CAT scanning technology to map geological structures with potential hydrocarbon prospects. This technology

reads the density and opacity contrasts of the interior of the sample from multiple angles and, through the work of various tomographic-reconstruction algorithms, creates a 3D computer representation of its interior [...] From this model the potential for a yield of hydrocarbons from the specified oilfield from which the core sample in question was taken can be predicted.

(Earley, 2015: 92–93)

The 'vicious grid of expanding prospects | (profits)' is thus updated for the twenty-first century.

The *Oilfield Review* article begins with a claim that '[i]nformation gained through core analysis is invaluable in predicting the producibility of a reservoir pay zone'. It closes with an allusion to Blake's 'Augeries of Innocence', claiming that this new technology helps today's (often corporately employed) geoscientists 'to better see their world in a grain of sand' (Kayser et al., 2006: 4, 13).[12] Ironically, Blake's poem also says that 'The Whore and Gambler by the State | Licencd build that Nations Fate' (2005: 295). Increased 'information gained' through CAT-scanned core analysis means better odds for the (nationally licensed) petrochemical industry in the short term, but this information is inextricably linked to other gambles and uncertainties, not least with the markets and the climate. Prynne is not one for isolating different systems, materials or discourses; oil seeps across the globe's economies and ecosystems like no other substance. Ignoring the resistance of substance for the simplifying quantification of information facilitates this process. Whether they involve tomographic data-imaging or Brent Crude pricing mechanisms, these technologies shape the conceptualisation and usage of the hydrocarbons that are so central to the Anthropocene's uncertainties and injustices.

Prynne resists thinking that performs a simplifying conceptual violence on the complex interactions between living systems and their (technologically affected) environments. Castigating both the Wordsworthian Romantic subject and the myth of scientific omniscience, *Kazoo Dreamboats* tells us 'you do not see into the life of things, dimension- | less or not, except by harvest of data plotted against uncertainty' (2015: 655). This certainly speaks to the way Prynne shows how, on a practical and theoretical level, uncertainties, mysteries and doubts sometimes exist in the predictions and models of the scientists, economists and politicians. This is true in both biology and climate science, where the demand for accurate predictions for pharmacology or the modelling of emissions' correlation with potential temperature rises must be offset against an inherent uncertainty that challenges the depredations of techno-scientific capitalism. More frequently, his work reminds us of the danger of compartmentalisation and of the unpredictable (future) effects of different technologies, concepts or materials. Hence Prynne's poetry provides a fascinating way to think the Anthropocene because, while registering the impacts of human technologies from a genetic to a planetary scale, his poetry renders a world resistant to anthropocentric ('over-humanized') conceptualisation, commodification and, ultimately, control.

Surely then his warning that we do not really 'see into the life of things' also speaks to our reading of a Prynne poem with its 'gaps of explanation rolling like wheels contrary within themselves' (2015: 651). An attentiveness to the data – philological, phonological, historical, contextual, scientific – must be plotted against the uncertainty over what this resistant material will do to the mind that encounters and works with it.[13]

Notes

1 The meeting is described in Prynne's letter to Dorn (1963a). Interestingly enough his conversation with Crick revealed that the scientist 'knew about Black Mountain', the experimental liberal arts college where Dorn had studied.

2 Interestingly booty, or rather the German cognate from which it is probably adapted, *beute*, is influenced by the 'Old Norse *býti* meaning 'exchange, barter', and connected with *být* 'to exchange'. See 'booty, n.1', *OED*.

3 This also applies to the assumed authority by a poet reading his or her own work, an attitude Prynne satirises as 'Look, the poet is wearing red socks! Now at last we understand everything!' (2010: 130).

4 Derek Attridge makes the astute point that '[b]afflingly, given his historical scrupulousness, Prynne uses the modern spelling of *tiger* with an *i* rather than Blake's spelling with a *y*, which would have undermined the argument' (2013: 90).

5 See Orgel and Crick (1980). Much of this non-coding DNA, the not uncontroversial work of the ENCODE project suggests, is far from simply parasitic – it potentially has significant biochemical functions.

6 See the fifth poem which includes phrase 'Tomorrow and tomorrow in the micro'. Here Prynne alludes to Macbeth's words on that which struts around signifying nothing (2015: 500).

7 As well as referring to 'beads' the poem also states 'heparin | Regulation demeans' (2015: 538).

8 Given Prynne's interest in Heidegger and his use of non-commercial book-production it is worth noting that Heidegger continues: 'The need for human material underlies the same regulation of preparing for ordered mobilization as the need for entertaining books and poems, for whose production the poet is no more important than the bookbinder's apprentice.'

9 Take his comments in a 2009 interview: 'environmentalists don't like engineering. It's going to take a lot more science that environmentalists have to learn to be non-selective about. They like climate science but they are not interested in nuclear science. They like climate science but they are not interested in genetic engineering science. That's what needs to change' (Brockman, 2009).

10 For an extended discussion of Johnson on Pope and Jenyns see Spector (1997: 106–110).

11 Prynne's comments were made to a seminar on his work at the University of Sussex on 13 February 2013 which I attended.

12 Prynne's 'Reference Cues' list an article with the same title, journal and authors but he gives a different issue (16) and date (2004). There are no articles in that journal on pore geometry for 2004. It is unclear whether Prynne is playing a game with his readers or whether this is a transcription error.

13 An early approach to some of the ideas discussed in this chapter was published in the *Oxford Literary Review* 34(2) in 2012. Available at: http://www.euppublishing.com/doi/abs/10.3366/olr.2012.0046.

References

Adorno, Theodor W. 2004. *Negative Dialectics*. Translated by E.B. Ashton. London; New York: Routledge.

Attridge, Derek. 2013. *Moving Words: Forms of English Poetry*. Oxford: Oxford University Press.

Bardini, Thierry. 2011. *Junkware*. Minneapolis: University of Minnesota Press.

Becker, K.G., G. Swergold, K. Ozato and R.E. Thayer. 1993. 'Binding of the Ubiquitous Nuclear Transcription Factor YY1 to a Cis Regulatory Sequence in the Human LINE-1 Transposable Element'. *Human Molecular Genetics* 2(10): 1697–1702.

Bennett, Jane. 2010. *Vibrant Matter: A Political Ecology of Things*. Durham, NC: Duke University Press.

Blake, William. 2006. *Selected Poems*. Edited by G.E. Bentley. London: Penguin Classics.

Brady, Andrea. 2006. 'No Turning Back: Acrylic Tips'. *Quid* 17: 80–83.

Brockman, John. 2009. We are as Gods and Have to Get Good at it, Stewart Brand Talks About His Ecopragmatist Manifesto'. *Edge*. Available at: https://edge.org/con versation/stewart_brand-we-are-as-gods-and-have-to-get-good-at-it [accessed 20 July 2015].

Brunette, Peter, and David Wills. 1994. *Deconstruction and the Visual Arts: Art, Media, Architecture*. Cambridge: Cambridge University Press.

Bruns, Gerald. 2013. 'Dialectrics: Or, Turmoil & Contradiction: A Reading of J.H. Prynne's *Kazoo Dreamboats*'. *Chicago Review* 57(3/4): 57–74.

Byron, George Gordon. 1970. *Poetical Works*. Edited by Frederick Page. Oxford: Oxford University Press.

Clark, Timothy. 2002. *Martin Heidegger*. London; New York: Routledge.

Clay, Jon. 2010. *Sensation, Contemporary Poetry and Deleuze: Transformative Intensities*. London; New York: Continuum.

Crick, Francis. 1970. 'Central Dogma of Molecular Biology'. *Nature* 227(5258): 561–563.

Crick, Francis. 1990. *What Mad Pursuit: A Personal View of Scientific Discovery*. New York: Basic Books.

Crick, Francis, and G. Mitchison. 1983. 'The Function of Dream Sleep'. *Nature* 304 (5922): 111–114.

Dawkins, Richard. 2008. *The Oxford Book of Modern Science Writing*. Oxford: Oxford University Press.

Derrida, Jacques. 1988. *Limited Inc*. Translated by Samuel Weber and Jeffrey Mehlman. Evanston, IL: Northwestern University Press.

Dobran, Ryan. 2010. 'Introduction'. *Glossator* 2: 1–11.

Dorn, Edward. 1989. *Gunslinger*. Durham, NC: Duke University Press.

Earley, Christopher. 2015. '"What Is Not Rock Is Voidally Known": On J.H. Prynne'. *Hix Eros* 6: 87–98.

Eltringham, Dan. 2015. '"Pass the Mint Sauce": J.H. Prynne & Other Post-Pastoral Poetics'. Talk given at Senate House, 4 March [currently being written up as an article].

Emmeche, Claus, and Jesper Hoffmeyer. 1991. 'From Language to Nature: The Semiotic Metaphor in Biology'. *Semiotica* 84 (January): 1–42.

Foley, Hugh. 2012. 'The Age of Brass'. *The White Review* 6: 79–88.

Fox, Josh (Dir.). 2011. *Gasland*.

Grossinger, Richard, and Linda Hough. 2015. *Io Anthology: Literature, Interviews, and Art from the Seminal Interdisciplinary Journal, 1965–1993*. Berkeley, CA: North Atlantic Books.

Haraway, Donna J. 1990. *Simians, Cyborgs, and Women: The Reinvention of Nature*. New York: Routledge.

Heidegger, Martin. 1977. *The Question Concerning Technology, and Other Essays*. Translated by William Lovitt. New York; London: Harper and Row.

Heidegger, Martin. 2002. *Heidegger: Off the Beaten Track*. Translated by Julian Young and Kenneth Haynes. Cambridge: Cambridge University Press.

Heidegger, Martin. 2003. *The End of Philosophy*. 2nd edition. Chicago: University of Chicago Press.

Heidegger, Martin. 2009. *Being and Time*. Translated by John Macquarrie and Edward Robinson. Oxford: Blackwell.

Hopkins, Gerard Manley. 1994. *The Works of Gerard Manley Hopkins*. Edited by Emma Hartnoll. Ware: Wordsworth Editions.

Jarvis, Simon. 2002. 'Quality and the Non-Identical in J.H.Prynne's "Aristeas, in Seven Years"'. *Jacket* 20 (December). Available at: http://jacketmagazine.com/20/pt-jarvis. html [accessed 22 September 2013].

Katko, Justin. 2010. 'Relativistic Phytosophy: Towards a Commentary on "The Plant Time Manifold Transcripts"'. *Glossator* 2: 245–294.

Kay, Lily E. 2000. *Who Wrote the Book of Life?: A History of the Genetic Code*. Stanford, CA: Stanford University Press.

Kayser, Andreas, Mark Knackstedt and Murtaza Ziauddin. 2006. 'A Closer Look at Pore Geometry'. *Schlumberger Oilfield Review* 18(1): 4–13.

Laubichler, Manfred D. 2008. 'Evolutionary Developmental Biology'. In *The Cambridge Companion to the Philosophy of Biology*. Edited by David Lee Hull and Michael Ruse. Cambridge: Cambridge University Press. 342–360.

Luna, Joe. 2016. 'Space | Poetry'. *Critical Inquiry* [unpublished draft – manuscript accepted].

MaoZedong. 1965. *Selected Works*. Vol. 1. Peking: Foreign Language Press.

Middleton, P. 1997. 'Not Nearly Too Much Prynne'. *The Cambridge Quarterly* 26(4): 344–353.

Morton, Timothy. 2012. 'The Oedipal Logic of Ecological Awareness'. *Environmental Humanities* 1: 7–21.

Nealon, Chris. 2013. 'The Prynne Reflex'. *The Claudius App*. Available at: http://thecla udiusapp.com/4-nealon.html [accessed 7 June 2014].

Nolan, Kevin. 2003. 'Capital Calves: Undertaking an Overview'. *Jacket* 24 (November). Available at: http://jacketmagazine.com/24/nolan.html [accessed 18 March 2016].

Orgel, L.E., and F.H. Crick. 1980. 'Selfish DNA: The Ultimate Parasite'. *Nature* 284 (5757): 604–607.

Patterson, Ian. 1992. '"The Medium Itself, Rabbit by Proxy": Some Thoughts about Reading J.H. Prynne'. In *Poets on Writing: Britain, 1970–1991*, edited by Denise Riley. Basingstoke: Palgrave. 234–246.

Pattison, Neil, Reitha Pattison and Luke Roberts, eds. 2012. *Certain Prose of the 'English Intelligencer'*. Cambridge: Mountain Press.

Perril, Simon. 2003. 'Hanging on Your Every Word: J.H. Prynne's Bands Around The Throat and a Dialetics of Planned Impurity'. *Jacket* 24 (November). Available at: http://jacketmagazine.com/24/perril.html [accessed 30 December 2014].

Pietrzak, Witold Konstanty. 2012. *Levity of Design: Man and Modernity in the Poetry of J.H. Prynne*. Newcastle upon Tyne, UK: Cambridge Scholars.

Pinkus, Karen. 2010. 'Carbon Management: A Gift of Time?' *Oxford Literary Review* 32(1): 51–70.

Pope, Alexander. 1978. *Pope, Poetical Works*. Edited by Herbert Davis. Oxford: Oxford University Press.

Prynne, J.H. 1961. 'Resistance and Difficulty'. *Prospect* 5: 26–30.

Prynne, J.H. 1963a. '*Letter to Dorn*'. 22 January. Box 19, Folder 329. Ed Dorn Papers, Archives and Special Collections at the Thomas J. Dodd Research Center, University of Connecticut Libraries.

Prynne, J.H. 1963b. '*Letter to Charles Olson*'. 28 December. Series 2 Box 206. Charles Olson Research Collection, Archives and Special Collections at the Thomas J. Dodd Research Center, University of Connecticut Libraries.

Prynne, J.H. 1964. '*Letter to Charles Olson*'. 21 January 1964. Series 2 Box 206. Charles Olson Research Collection, Archives and Special Collections at the Thomas J. Dodd Research Center, University of Connecticut Libraries.

Prynne, J.H. 1969. 'Review of Charles Olson, The Maximus Poems IV, V, VI (London: Cape Goliard Press, 1968)'. *The Park* 4/5: 64–66.

Prynne, J.H. 1971a. 'Jeremy Prynne Lectures on Maximus IV, V, VI Simon Fraser University, July 27, 1971'. Available at: http://charlesolson.org/Files/Prynnelecture1. htm [accessed 22 June 2015].

Prynne, J.H. 1971b. '*Letter to Dorn*'. 24 November. Box 20, Folder 334. Ed Dorn Papers, Archives and Special Collections at the Thomas J. Dodd Research Center, University of Connecticut Libraries.

Prynne, J.H. 1971c. 'Reading in Vancouver'. 1 August. Archive of the Now, Queen Mary, University of London. Available at: http://www.archiveofthenow.org/a uthors/?i=77 [accessed 23 September 2015].

Prynne, J.H. 1972a. '*Letter to Dorn*'. 14 March. Box 20, Folder 334. Ed Dorn Papers, Archives and Special Collections at the Thomas J. Dodd Research Center, University of Connecticut Libraries.

Prynne, J.H. 1972b. '*Letter to Dorn*'. 30 May. Box 20, Folder 334. Ed Dorn Papers, Archives and Special Collections at the Thomas J. Dodd Research Center, University of Connecticut Libraries.

Prynne, J.H. 1972c. '*Letter to Dorn*'. 25 October. Box 20, Folder 334. Ed Dorn Papers, Archives and Special Collections at the Thomas J. Dodd Research Center, University of Connecticut Libraries.

Prynne, J.H. 1973. '*Letter to Dorn*'. 12 September. Box 19, Folder 334. Ed Dorn Papers, Archives and Special Collections at the Thomas J. Dodd Research Center, University of Connecticut Libraries.

Prynne, J.H. 1975. '*Letter to Dorn*'. 23 September. Box 20, Folder 335. Ed Dorn Papers, Archives and Special Collections at the Thomas J. Dodd Research Center, University of Connecticut Libraries.

Prynne, J.H. 1978. '*Letter to Dorn*'. 10 September. Box 19, Folder 337. Ed Dorn Papers, Archives and Special Collections at the Thomas J. Dodd Research Center, University of Connecticut Libraries.

Prynne, J.H. 1983. '*Letter to Dorn*'. 17 July. Box 20, Folder 338. Ed Dorn Papers, Archives and Special Collections at the Thomas J. Dodd Research Center, University of Connecticut Libraries.

Prynne, J.H. 1988. 'English Poetry and Emphatical Language'. In *Proceedings of the British Academy*, 74: 69.

Prynne, J.H. 1993. *Stars, Tigers and the Shape of Words: The William Matthews Lectures 1992 Delivered at Birkbeck College, London*. London: Birkbeck College.

Prynne, J.H. 2004. '*Tips on Reading for Students of English*'. Cambridge: Cambridge University.

Prynne, J.H. 2010. 'Mental Ears and Poetic Work'. *Chicago Review* 55(1): 126–157.

Prynne, J.H. 2013. 'On Peter Larkin'. *No Prizes* 2: 43–45.

Prynne, J.H. 2015. *Poems*. 3rd Revised edition. Hexham, Northumberland: Bloodaxe.

Roof, Judith. 2007. *The Poetics of DNA*. Minneapolis: University of Minnesota Press.

Schrödinger, Erwin. 1992. *What Is Life?: The Physical Aspect of the Living Cell; With, Mind and Matter; & Autobiographical Sketches*. Cambridge: Cambridge University Press.

Shannon, Claude Elwood. 1964. 'A Mathematical Theory of Communication'. In *The Mathematical Theory of Communication*, edited by Claude Elwood Shannon and Warren Weaver. Urbana: University of Illinois Press. 31–124.

Spector, Robert Donald. 1997. *Samuel Johnson and the Essay*. Westport, CT: Greenwood Publishing Group.

Sperling, Matthew, and Thomas Roebuck. 2010. '"The Glacial Question, Unsolved": A Specimen Commentary on Lines 1–31'. *Glossator* 2: 39–78.

Spinks, Lee. 2000. 'Writing, Politics, and the Limit: Reading J.H. Prynne's "The Ideal Star-Fighter"'. *Intertexts* 4(2): 144–166.

Sutherland, Keston. 2004. *J.H. Prynne and Philology*. Unpublished PhD Dissertation, Cambridge: University of Cambridge.

Temin, H.M. 1985. 'Reverse Transcription in the Eukaryotic Genome: Retroviruses, Pararetroviruses, Retrotransposons, and Retrotranscripts'. *Molecular Biology and Evolution* 2(6): 455–468.

Turner, Fred. 2006. *From Counterculture to Cyberculture: Stewart Brand, the Whole Earth Network, and the Rise of Digital Utopianism.* Chicago: University of Chicago Press.

Watson, James D. 1995. 'Values from a Chicago Upbringing' *Annals of the New York Academy of Sciences* 758(1): 194–197.

Weaver, Warren. 1964. 'Recent Contributions to the Mathematical Theory of Communication'. In *The Mathematical Theory of Communication*, edited by Claude Elwood Shannon and Warren Weaver. Urbana: University of Illinois Press. 1–29.

Conclusion

Evolution, agency and feedback at the end of a world

> *The primary goal of autopoetic systems is the continuation of autopoiesis without any concern for the environment, typically the next step in the process is more important for them than the concern for the future, which is indeed unattainable if autopoiesis is not continued. Viewed from a long-term perspective, evolution is concerned about reaching 'ecological balances'. But this merely means that systems pursuing a trend toward exposure to ecological self-endangerment are eliminated.*
>
> – Niklas Luhmann (1989: 14)

Luhmann's stark pronouncement was published (in German) five years before Bate argued that critics should bring 'Romanticism to bear' on the developing set of ecological crises (1991: 9). Luhmann's claim is built round his description of society as formed of multiple coevolving systems which impact upon each other, but not in any coordinated way. As Moeller explains, Luhmann's systems theory suggests that humans 'are no longer capable of their own development, but are simply an element within highly complex system-environment entanglements', a situation which undermines 'the concepts of intentionality, planning, and free will' (2012: 70). Underscoring the ecological concerns of this book has been an awareness that the future states of societies, species, ecosystems or the biosphere are determined not only by the relations between organisms and their immediate environment but, in the Anthropocene, by vehicle emissions, mutagenic industrial chemicals, farming practices, energy generation and other variables. What a social systems theory reminds us is that these ecologically significant processes are themselves not easily controlled by individual resolve, a centralised government or intergovernmental legislation. Rather, they depend on the way the elements of a society's different mutually affecting subsystems (Luhmann's 'function systems') orientate themselves towards ecology: what the economic system chooses to cost, how the media system codes environmental issues as news, what the legal system addresses as part of its jurisdiction, whether the participants in the political system see a 'green' agenda as important to electability and so on.

Not only does the operation of these communicative systems within Earth's geophysical systems make it hard to model the future state of either a society or its environment (particularly the local impacts of global phenomena such as average temperature rises) but the process of modelling itself resonates in different ways within these function systems causing different sorts of activity. In what follows I suggest that one of the things that makes poetry so interesting for ecocritical study is the way that it engenders reading strategies which help the reader observe the different ways subjects and social systems address their environments. I also show that questions of how we register unpredictability and uncontrollability in the development of living systems and societies are an important aspect of how I have read the poetry in this book and of any eco-critical formulation. As art and criticism evolve, we have to think about what these questions mean at a time when it is problematic to think about a non-technological human and a globe that has not been modified by humanity's technologies.

The life of the poets

In the second chapter I partially reclaimed Hughes from the treatment of his earlier (eco)critics, showing that his vaunted (and maligned) violence is not a poetics of unmediated reconnection but a subtler figuration of humans' various technologically mediated engagements with the environment and their own, and other animals', embodiment. Hughes's most interesting contribution to thinking about ecology lies in his evolutionary perspective that looks not just back toward an animal inheritance but forward to a posthuman future where the state of life on Earth will continue to be shaped through the relations between the organic and the technological. Hughes's emphasis on evolutionary processes means that he thinks about life-in-general rather than at an individual species level. This helps him to create a future-orientated ecology with an emphasis on error and adaptation. Everything is part of a 'strange engine' where Hughes plays down individual human agency; instead 'Life works at life using men and women' ('A Crow Hymn', 2003: 201).

In Hughes's work, humans are not in control of the biological processes of mutation and their evolutionary animal-inheritance – the 'secret governing mafia' which 'makes us catspaws of its archaic operations' (1994a). Nor can they control what he describes as the 'nearly autonomous technosphere' (1994b: 128). It is worth noting that, as with the word 'mafia', there is often a touch of anthropomorphism in Hughes's use of biological and technological factors to destabilise human agency: the apocalyptic 'word' of the *Crow* poem 'A Disaster', the ever-battling life-energy of the trickster, the iron giants as living symbols of technology.[1] Anthropomorphism can cause problems but, as Jane Bennett argues, it can sometimes be a useful means of disassembling the human fantasy of control that stymies ecological thinking:

> If a green materialism requires of us a more refined sensitivity to the out-side-that-is-inside-too, then maybe a bit of anthropomorphizing will prove valuable. Maybe it is worth running the risks associated with anthro-pomorphizing (superstition, the divinization of nature, romanticism) [all

accusations that could be levelled at Hughes] because it, oddly enough, works against anthropocentrism: a chord is struck between person and thing, and I am no longer above or outside a nonhuman 'environment'. Too often the philosophical rejection of anthropomorphism is bound up with a hubristic demand that only humans and God can bear any traces of creative agency.

(2010: 120)

For Bennett, agency does not presuppose intention. Her work on materiality assesses how, within the assemblages we find in the contemporary world, objects and substances have a kind of agency and so erupt into the political sphere. Her work is also useful for addressing something interesting about Hughes. Hughes's writing concerns itself with the way technologies and techniques (such as rods, poems, factories, calculus) change the physical conditions of the environment and the mental conditions of the individual. This poses an evolutionary question about the ways species and societies adapt, not necessarily positively, to these new conditions. In Hughes's evolutionary paradigm, a kind of agency is granted not only to technological objects and organic materials (including DNA, changes in which enable species adaptations) but also to myths which both evolve and are a form of evolutionary adaptation. Hughes figures myths as technologies, 'factories' for expression and understanding, circulating in communication media and partially shaping human behaviour. However, he also renders them in organic terms, as infectious, tricksterish, dynamic entities with unpredictable effects depending on their environment. They are an emergent property of life-in-general which shapes its future course. In works like *Crow* and *The Iron Woman*, Hughes models the way art, myth and other forms of communication play a role in societies' evolution by shaping our ways of thinking, doing, relating and making. His myths of transformation are intended to have a mutative effect and at the same time to mythologise the role of art as a force in modifying perception – Hughes depicts a kind of second-order observation of the ways we observe and communicate.

It is worth emphasising though that Hughes does not display a blind optimism about the power of humans to adapt – the apocalyptic maladaptation that loomed large in 'The Environmental Revolution' was still extant towards the end of his life. At the closing of the 'Creation; Four Ages; Flood; Lycaon' poem from *Tales from Ovid*, the progressive technologisation of the humans ends with them being obliterated by Zeus. Hughes adapts Ovid's own myth-adaptations for the current climate; the flood is rendered startlingly contemporary and full of ecological portent. Ovid's *Aeoliis Aquilonem* (the North Wind) is replaced by 'the blast | That fixes the Northern ice', couching Ovid's flood drama in the language of melting ice caps (Ovid, 2004, bk 1, l. 262; Hughes, 2003: 878). The error and adaption of Hughes's evolving world does not privilege the human but is underscored by the possibility of maladaptation and apocalypse which, by the mid-1990s, has been given a local habitation (the arctic) and a name (global warming).[2]

Of course, with a few exceptions, Prynne generally eschews the mythic and deals much more directly with the languages, injustices and contradictions of late capitalism. When Prynne writes about ecological issues he does it with a keen awareness of the specific ways that matter in various forms (carbon compounds, ice flows, DNA, mutagenic chemicals, workable metals) interact with and shape different landscapes and societies across history, indicating that 'culture', as Bennett puts it, is 'not of our own making, infused as it is by biological, geological, and climatic forces' (2010: 115). But again what is striking about his approach to the relationship between organic life and the ways it can be conceptualised, commodified, controlled and coerced is that his engagement with the sciences contributes towards his approach to this issue at the level of form, on the work the poem does to the reader when she works with it.

Resistance to the logics of exchange and freely transferrable information operates at a linguistic level. Prynne emphasises the materiality of genetic or linguistic codes and the agency of materials to encourage the reader to pursue etymological, anthropological-historical and scientific enquiries which complicate the reader's approach to the specialised function of individual units of meaning. When matched with the poetry's syntactical and semantic derangements and distortions, this makes the reading process radically unpredictable, the materials resistant to the poet's final control. Phrases, words, even phonemes, shift in significance depending on how the reader positions or sounds them at the level of line, sentence, verse-paragraph or poem. While this could be said of lots of poets, reading Prynne, perhaps more than any other writer, requires a constant process of re-reading, working with the poem to work at and work through 'the world and its layers of shifted but recognisable usage' (Prynne, epigraph to Riley, 1992). His poems enact a process of critique, interrogating language and society while engendering surprising connections and sensations. This process is intimately related to his engagement with biochemistry – words and genes are not discrete units of information that code for a specific meaning but are part of a 'continuous flow of events of interactions' (Emmeche and Hoffmeyer, 1991: 37). Likewise the objects and materials in the poetry's organisms and environments are not passive or easily controllable but do things (like melt or mutate) with unpredictable consequences. This bespeaks a kind of broader awareness of a materiality which, to use Bennett's terms, is 'vibrant' or 'lively', with crucial implications for thinking about ecology:

> In a world of lively matter, we see that biochemical and biochemical-social systems can sometimes unexpectedly bifurcate or choose developmental paths that could not have been foreseen, for they are governed by an emergent rather than a linear or deterministic causality. And once we see this, we will need an alternative both to the idea of nature as a purposive, harmonious process and to the idea of nature as a blind mechanism.
>
> (2010: 112)

Prynne, at least since *Brass*, barely lets in even the vestiges of the Romantic lyric or the identifiable lyric subject. It is not enough to do as Mahon does (and Prynne did in a different way in *The White Stones* and *Kitchen Poems*) and problematise the pastoral impulse by enforcing an awareness of the industrialisation and commodification of life and landscape and the poet's own potential complicity in that process. Where Mahon relies on an ironic awareness that identifies the lure of nostalgia, Prynne, in a manner that reflects the argument that there is always a degree of complicity even in an ironised nostalgia, develops an increasingly resistant language and in doing so risks the opposite to nostalgic recapitulation – suspicious disaffection. Prynne's and Mahon's divergent approaches point toward two broader tendencies within ecocriticism and ecologically orientated literature. The first attempts to find a way of expressing or modelling the forces and networks – biological, ecological, technological, economic, linguistic – which make worlds and shape the Earth. The second addresses what it feels like to live in a world thus shaped. This is certainly not to say that these are mutually exclusive or even strictly delineated inclinations. Many texts will contain both in different ratios and the best writing reflects on the relations and feedbacks between the two.

Of the three poets, Mahon deals most directly with the key issue of contemporary ecological thought, climate change. His poetry identifies climate change's global scale and its local effects; he articulates many of the ironies and contradictions inherent in being an ecologically concerned individual and positions the neglected and the marginalised (which he associates with the aesthetic) as a site of resistance and a space of mutative possibility. Moreover, often building on the figure of Gaia, he offers a 'chaos of complex systems' where technological and industrial forces operate on the biosphere with potentially apocalyptic consequences. The imagined apocalypses that swept away the malign forces that peppered his early poetry have become more pronounced; Mahon's sense of an ending has shifted from immanent fantasy toward imminent possibility.

Mahon's late ecological work is perhaps not his most accomplished but is amongst his most interesting in that it embodies a general problem of trying to describe an ecological conscientiousness which can engage with the politics and economics of climate change from within the borders of a liberalism that, as Blühdorn and Clark suggest, might be part of the environmental crisis. Mahon's focus on the ironical subject sometimes produces a jarring tone so that even when the poem calls us to 'listen to the leaves' in a 'quiet spot', readers are forced back into a process of self-critique. Such work skilfully embodies the clashing perspectives and emotions generated by contemporary ecology but it also indicates a poet running up against the limits of his own style. The quasi-Heideggerian sense of 'inhabitation' is counterweighted by an ironic and self-critical perspective reminiscent of Auden and MacNeice. Mahon increasingly acknowledges a world of shifting ecological forces and draws out the cognitive dissonance inherent in benefitting from industrial modernity while still professing environmental concern. Faced with the possibility of catastrophic climate change his poems oscillate uneasily between treading the path of enlightened adaptation and slouching toward the apocalypse along a road littered with toy windmills.

Therein lies the rub. The indeterminacy generated by Mahon's poetry – as opposed to the chaotic systems the poetry tells the reader about – normally belongs to the ambivalent subject rather than her physical environment. His late form and style are still well described by his early statement that a 'good poem is a paradigm of good politics – of people talking to each other, with honest subtlety, at a profound level' (1970: 93). Mahon's rendering of the activity of communication almost resembles a kind of Habermasian communicative action in that the irony enables an implicit dialogue between different subject positions, thereby modelling a process of consensus building in society or presenting the individual as working toward overcoming the conflicts within his or her own thinking and perception. This tension between rational communication and chaotic systems is a notable feature of Mahon's late poetry: while he identifies the complex ecological and social forces important to the Anthropocene, the sorts of (internal or external) dialogue the poems set up focus on the concerned consumer struggling to acknowledge problems with their own life(style) in a changing climate. This is partly because the ecological poetry emerges out of a sense of 'good politics' and individual resistance where the subject identifies and negotiates the difficult relationships between self and society. He faces the challenge that Luhmann constructs for ecological consciousness – namely that 'social communication' when facing ecological crises is not typified by consensus building or communicative rationality but by the mutually affecting yet uncoordinated function systems.

Luhmann emphasises that there 'is no superordinate authority that would provide for measure and proportionality here. Through resonance small changes in one system can trigger changes in another' (1989: 117–118). Prynne's 'Along the Wall' works with a telling instance of this lack of 'proportionality'. The poem speaks to a world where the carbon emission predictions of the science system lead to modest political incentivising of new carbon markets by the political system. This means that the economic system, aware of developments in energy-generation technologies, sees cornfields as being potentially 'full of fire', thereby driving a biofuels boom which sees developing countries' political and legal systems struggling to cope with their populations being deprived of their sustaining corn, their landscapes slashed and burned to make way for a new cash crop. This is the realm of the level III technology constellations described by Allenby and Sarewitz (2013) that I discussed in chapter one, where emergent effects defy attempts at control or prediction. In Prynne's poem the density of the language and the ways it slips between multiple referents and contexts reflects the fact that there is no 'superordinate authority' here; no individual or social system has final control over how the ecological issues are communicated and the consequences of that communication.

I am not wholly endorsing Luhmann's approach to ecological communication. Indeed I think the challenge to Luhmann from Habermas is an important one within an ecological context. Habermas makes the point that Luhmann, in his increasing focus on the a-centric function systems leaves very little room or 'point of reference for a critique of modernity' (1990: 374). In this way Luhmann's criticism of communicative rationality might actually facilitate a kind of pessimistic inactivity not dissimilar to the ironist's paralysis that Mahon fears. Nevertheless, contemporary ecological thinking must be prepared to adapt to the challenges of thinking about communication at both individual and societal-systemic levels. The relationship between different forces in society is something with which Mahon is clearly concerned but the fundamental model of his poetry is 'people talking to each other' (or themselves). The poems generate a play between perspectives which, while often contradictory, are nearly always identifiable and understandable. This implicitly enforces a sense, to use Luhmann's words, of 'measure and proportionality' rather than any 'chaos of complex systems' Mahon identifies.

It is worth asking whether Mahon's focus on the self-questioning individual is related to the fact that he is less interested than Hughes and Prynne are in the forces which subtend the human. Mahon presents a world of circulating materials and discourses. However, he seldom examines evolution, embodiment or animal drives in the way that Hughes does, nor does he, like Prynne, explore genetic mutation – though he does have a keen sense of technological adaptation to changing climates (and the lack of it). While biological mutation is not a key thematic concern for Mahon, 'A Dream Play' and other poems like 'Aphrodite's Pool' figure the aesthetic as a space of mutation outside the glare of modernity, a space where new possibilities emerge from the marginalised detritus of culture. But mutation is not central to the poetry's form like it is for Hughes with his 'radioactive' myths and symbols that inform and deform each other in different contexts. Nor, despite its occasional cacophonies of allusion, does Mahon's work engender the sort of strange connections and constellations readers encounter in Prynne's dense, distorting and resistant language with its mutation of linguistic and semantic codes.

Mahon's erudite and witty engagements with ecology, with their skilful formalism, emphasise the tensions within the individual's perspective but do not go as far as Prynne's or Hughes's poems do in attempting to challenge (or, indeed, mutate) the mythic, linguistic or conceptual structures that undergird communication and cognition. His ecological poetry is marked by a sense of indeterminacy that is still more stable than Hughes's visions of biological, technological and cultural evolution or Prynne's awareness of emergent unpredictability and radical uncertainty due to resistance and contradiction even at the level of matter. The value of Mahon's late work lies in its exploration of the modern liberal subject in the face of ecological crisis, but its strength is also its limit, and the limit recognisable for many writers addressing climate change. Despite problematising individual agency by locating the human in a network of economic, ecological, geophysical and political systems, it is ultimately a humanist poetry trying to negotiate a posthumanist world. Though of course negotiating a posthumanist world is what liberal, humanist individuals increasingly have to do.

Feedback loops

Claire Colebrook has suggested that critical theory's disruption of the human subject holds a lesson for contemporary ecology. She argues that psycho-analytic and poststructuralist theory have shown that the 'visual figural unity of the human body – the bounded organism we see in the mirror' is never the 'self-comprehending and self-affecting whole' it appears to be. Ecocriticism, she suggests, should similarly resist 'the figure of the globe – the ideally bounded sphere in which each point is in accord with the whole, and in which the whole is a dynamic and self-maintaining unity' (2012: 32, 34). This book has also sought to challenge notions of bounded harmony on at least two different scales. At one scale via what my first chapter described as the *Anthropos kainos*, the posthuman subject whose animal body and genetic structure can be modified by mutagens, microorganisms, viruses and biotechnologies and whose subjectivity is terminally bound up with different tools, inherited concepts and communicative systems. On another scale, via the Anthropocene's changing environments in which this subject, and other forms of life, exist. All this happens on a planet which is shaped by autopoetic systems and vibrant materials and which is now changing, thanks to human technologies, at an alarming rate. In this brave new world, different groups, individuals, species and social systems must adapt or, as the Luhmann epigraph to this chapter bluntly puts it, be 'eliminated'.

Although finding a text with a self-conscious ecological concern is not a prerequisite for a successful ecocritical reading, I have argued for the importance of reading writers who both engage directly with questions of how life might flourish (or not) in the late Anthropocene and whose work addresses these challenges as part of their poetics rather than simply as subject matter. A poem, as Morton's OOO defence of poetry puts it, 'is not simply a representation, but rather a nonhuman agent' (2012: 215). Prynne's analysis of the way poetry can enable reverse transcriptions from sound to sense reminds us that poems contain their own vibrant materialities, something central to their capacity to operate in unpredictable ways on their readers. Moreover, reading poetry involves a process describable in terms of feedback. The reader consciously enters the discoveries of a first reading – whether a submerged allusion, a striking symbol, a word's secondary definition, a rhythmic shift, a sonic resonance or structural irony – back into the poem in a process of circular re-reading, shifting the work's meanings as she does so.

This book has sought out poetry which not only addresses ecology but treats the poem's way of happening as an intervention into readers' ways of thinking and doing which may find broader resonances. Hughes's imagery crossbreeds old and new myths in an attempt to tune the reader into the operation of their society's constitutive mythologies. Mahon manipulates tone and irony to draw out the negotiation between different subject positions and ideologies which will emerge into different possible futures, implicating the reader as he does so. Prynne encourages research alongside critique: philological and phonological investigations engendering an unpredictable and unresolvable play of connotation and meaning which pulls the poem's possibilities one way then another. In other words, these poets draw attention to the way the readers feed their own observations and biases back into the processes of the reading-event. In each of their *oeuvres* we find examples of the way poems can model the process whereby a system's (an individual psychic system and in some cases a social system) observation of its own, or other systems', ways of observing, may impact on the future behaviour of that system. Lyric poetry's play of thought and affect provides a space in which society's concepts are tested and where, occasionally, new concepts can emerge.

When the poem in question is specifically about environmental issues, the power of the text to facilitate ways of thinking through ecology can be galvanised. Any process which can foreground the ways that humans perceive the world – and perceive themselves perceiving it – potentially has, in the Anthropocene, ecological consequences. To present the reader as a part of, and an actor in, the damaged world they are reading about, brings interesting types of affect and temporality into play. We can see this in the work of Jorie Graham, whose poetry I turn to here as an example of how the concerns and approaches in this book can be useful to reading other poetries which address the models, metaphors, ironies and emotions of the Anthropocene.

Graham's 'Positive Feedback Loop'[3] comes from a collection, *Sea Change* (2008), written 'after a very deep apprenticeship to the facts and issues involved in climate science' (interview with Blackie, 2012: 40). The poem begins:

> I am listening in this silence that precedes. Forget
> everything, start listening. Tipping point, flash
> point
> convective chimneys in the seas bounded by Greenland.
>
> (2008: 42)

There is no still point in this churning world. An individual's attempt to focus on Nature or to find a degree zero for contemplation is interrupted by the changing biosphere which they helped shape. A flash point is the temperature at which a substance ignites, a kind of tipping point between states. In Graham's poem there is a strong suggestion that the biosphere may already have met a key tipping point where positive feedback loops (exponential ice melt, destabilised currents, clathrate release etc.) kick in causing runaway climate change. The convective Arctic currents act like chimneys, playing a crucial role in regulating global temperatures. In the Anthropocene the effects of the chimneys of industry are terminally inlaid in arctic currents. Just as Mahon's Björk discovers, there is no pastoral escape to an uncorrupted outside. Graham has suggested that 'the whole machine is at work, and is us. We can no more step out of the machine we made that is ecocide, than we can step out of our own bodies' (Blackie, 2012: 37).

The opening phrases set a pattern for the poem as it lurches between the individual and the global across a grid of long, medium and short lines, deploying a scientific vocabulary that, if not as demanding as Prynne's, still requires a level of knowledge or research that exceeds the common reader's 'general competence'.

> In Hell they empty your hands of sand, they tell you to refill them with dust and try
>   to hold in mind the North Atlantic Deep Water
>   which also contains
>   contributions from the Labrador Sea and entrainment of other water masses, try to
>   hold a
>   complete collapse, in the North Atlantic Drift in the
>   thermohaline circulation, this
>   will happen,
>   fish are starving to death in the Great Barrier Reef, the new Age of Extinctions is
>   now
>   says the silence-that-precedes – you know not what
>   you
>   are entering, a time
>   beyond belief.
>
>   (2008: 42)

Water, not for the first time in this book, becomes a medium and metaphor for global connectivity. The infernally difficult attempt to contain its entrainment in the human mind results in damnation for multiple species in this new age of extinction (where melt-water changes the temperature and salinity of the thermohaline circulation, potentially leading to a collapse in plankton, which in turn leads to fish and other marine life 'starving to death'). As well as the movement of fluids the word 'entrainment' can refer to brain activity and other forms of synchronisation with an external pattern, such as circadian rhythms. Humans, here, cannot entrain themselves to (as the internal rhyme suggests, conceptually contain) the movements of the biosphere. The song of the earth is subject to technological interference and the grand spatial scale of these movements shows that human agency is not the only player in the world of positive feedback loops. Crucially, the current state of climate science means that our species is no longer able to claim that they know not what they do. The question now is not fully knowing what we have done, humans 'know not what' they 'are entering'. It is a time 'beyond belief' and beyond final control, a not-quite-not-yet-apocalypse where whether deniers 'believe' in AGW or not is secondary – 'this | will happen' whether they like it or not.

The accusatory 'you' anchored by the other monosyllable 'now' challenges the concerned artists and academics amongst whom Graham numbers herself:

>   [...] An orchestra dies down. We have other plans
>   for your summer is the tune. Also your

winter. Maybe the locks at Isigny
> will hold, I will go look at
> them

tomorrow
> [...]
> > count the cities you
> have

visited

> (2008: 43)

Graham, who often dwells in Normandy though she teaches at Harvard, does something similar to Mahon in his travel poems and 'A Quiet Spot'. She draws on the flippant bourgeois tourist's language of 'summer plans' (near Isigny) to acknowledge her own complicity and the impact of her own lifestyle choices on a changing climate. Temperature rises will change our summers (and necessitate different plans for them) and there is no escaping the fact that previous summer plans, the cities we 'have visited', have contributed to this process.

What makes the poem, and the collection, so compelling is the attempt to register this feeling of catastrophic futurity on a formal level via the play between line and sentence. In an interview, Graham described her shift to the 'alternation of the very long and very short lines, spread over cascading sentences' as a new stylistic choice:

> letting the sentences move along this grid of very long and very short lines – feeling both of those prior 'socially aware' poets [Whitman and Williams] in my ear – I also was able to enact a sense of a 'tipping point' – the feeling of falling forward, or 'down' in the hyper-short lines at the same time as one feels suspended, as long as possible, in the 'here and now' of the long line – so that the pull of the 'future' is constrained by the desire to stay in the 'now,' which is itself broken again, as a spell is, by the presence of the oncoming future. This also involves a tipping back and forth between hope and the brink of its opposite.
>
> (Wengen, 2008)

A tension forms between a line long enough to contain multitudes (currents, land masses, species) and the short sharp slap of a climate-future which is increasingly here and now although its most extreme effects have yet to manifest. Graham has also described how she tries to make the reader aware of different sorts of time:

> to enact the time in which it takes to see the thing, the time in which that seen thing is living and constantly changing, the time it takes to 'take' those actions down, the time in which my language is occurring, your

reading is occurring – to make of all that a piece. The mutability of the external meeting the mutability of the internal.

(interview with Gardner, 2003).

It seems to me that this poem in particular works to construct a kind of vertiginous concatenation of different sorts of time. This unsettles the reader by suggesting that parts of the world which had remained seemingly static for so long are changing even as she reads and even as the poem calls for a sustained mode of attention which might draw in the different constituent parts of the biosphere, moving across different spatio-temporal scales that take in place and planet.

Graham has spoken of a desire to draw out not just ideas about climate change but climate change itself – AGW 'experienced (as in watching the bees vanish, or the blossoming trees lose their natural cycle, or the birds species disappear) and researched' (Wengen, 2008). The poem closes with a Whitmanesque poking up of grass that also resonates with the uncertain awakenings of Williams's 'Spring and All':

> [...] we
>   shall walk
> out onto the porch and the evening shall come on around us, unconcealed
>   blinking, abundant, as if catching sight of us,
> everything in and out under the eaves, even the grass seeming to push up
>   into this our
>   world as if out of
> homesickness for it,
>   gleaming.

(Graham, 2008: 44)

But despite the Heideggerian 'unconcealing', an air of disquiet surrounds the image of the grass emerging into new life while materials, thoughts and perceptions flow 'in and out' across the threshold of 'the eaves'. Even if we read this as a moment of dwelling and care, where the home and earth are bound together as an *oikos* (i.e. as house or dwelling-place), there have been too many moments which tip the poem forward into the future to read this without an awareness of the non-human forces in operation. It is worth noting that the collection itself ends on an apocalyptic tone – 'there are sounds the planet will always make, even | if there is one to hear them' ('No Long Way Round', 2008: 56). And what, after all does the grass gleam in anyway? It glistens with the water and sunlight that the poem has presented as part of the interlocking processes of climate crisis. The cumulative effect of the poem's nods to climate change science and the strange connections created by the poem's long disrupted sentences cause the reader to feed the images of home and sunlight back into the poem's inextricable feedback loops. The lines which best show what is at stake are to be found toward the poem's middle:[4]

[...] invisible bog,
positive feedback loops – & the chimneys again, & how it is the ray of sun
is taken in
in freedom, & was there another way for
this host
our guest,
we who began as hands, magic of fingers, laying our thresholds stone upon
stone

(2008: 43)

As the (until now invisible) clathrates in the Siberian bogs melt and release greenhouse gasses which will trap those rays of sun, Graham turns back to the birth of the species. We who, as Stiegler and Hughes imply, 'began as hands' with the ability to shape tools: the originary technicity of the human-animal will end up engendering the 'machine which is ecocide', a machine we have as much chance of stepping out of as our own bodies. To build thresholds and build a dwelling is to use technology to set up boundaries between inside and outside. Graham appears to be acknowledging the late work of Derrida in whose writing on hospitality these boundaries are challenged by the relations between host and guest. For Derrida the host's hospitality depends on the guest who would be welcomed and not just the at-home host who polices the threshold; hence the host is held hostage by the one she hosts. In the Anthropocene the technological construction of the *oikos* expands from the house to the Earth – but the technological construction of the home(world) is neither easy nor predictable. This stage of species and planetary development requires a kind of evolution of conceptualisations of hospitality which are no longer fit to survive unaltered.

The planet that hosts us rests at a 'flash point, tipping point', giving new poignancy to the suggestion that

> To offer hospitality [...] is it necessary to start from the certain existence of a dwelling, or is it rather only starting from the dislocation of the shelter-less, the homeless, that the authenticity of hospitality can open up? Perhaps only the one who endures the experience of being deprived of a home can offer hospitality.
>
> (Derrida and Dufourmantelle, 2000: 50)

Though its impacts will not be spread equally (quite the opposite), climate change might constitute a kind of global deprivation in that there is no longer a Wordsworthian 'solid ground of Nature' in which to trust. This is why David Wood's early attempt to configure an ecological Derridean hospitality falters when he argues that the 'destruction of the planet, the destabilization of its life-sustaining processes, is an intrusion on our human project as powerful as the appearance of the refugee on our doorstep' (2007: 266). The trouble is that the hospitality we might show a refugee *arrivant* does not easily transfer to the scale of climate change where the conditions of everyone's doorsteps are liable to shift (though not necessarily deteriorate). While the status of *arrivant* might be conferred on some of the unpredictable effects arising from climate change, the phenomenon itself is not unexpected but rather consistently mapped, modelled and predicted. This means, as Tom Cohen reminds us, it 'is not apocalyptic at all. That is: there is no calamitous instant precisely, no revelation' (2010: 77). To put it another way, we already know that climate change might produce nations of refugees; indeed it has been argued that it has done so already. As such, their showing up on our doorstep (whoever *we* are) should not come as a surprise nor be seen as an event in Derrida's sense of the word. To rush in with a Derridean notion of hospitality in the way that Wood does recapitulates the anthropocentricism where humans are in total control of Earth's systems, borders and shorelines. As Clark points out, the ecological significance of Derrida's own description of hospitality is stymied by his seldom looking beyond systems of law and communication:

> his frontier questions of conditional or unconditional hospitality can seem foreclosed in scale, two-dimensional, for they ignore that ubiquitous border already contiguous with all other countries at the same time, a shared atmosphere.
>
> (2012: 154)

Graham's poem, as with many of those in this book, radically challenges the sense of the global host in a way that makes us 'homeless', though in a manner that Derrida's work does not fully anticipate. Her use of 'host' and 'guest' hints at the organicism which would see the Earth being the host to the human disease, uncomfortably close to the sort of misanthropic formulation deployed by Lovelock where 'Gaia's illness could be called a polyanthroponemia, where humans overpopulate until they do more harm than good' (2010: 151). Reading the poem this way calls up another meaning of the word: host as a 'multitude'. Hence the reader would be part of a host in the process of becoming its own worst enemy because, as another believer in the imbalance of a different *oikos* puts it, 'we are too menny' (Hardy, 1999: 264).

The true state of population pressure on Earth's systems is beyond the bounds of my commentary. However, I would argue that Graham's poem and the other poets in this book show that a thinking where Nature is either a benevolent host or its dark (distorted) reflection, a revenging Gaia, cannot properly address the relationships between organic life, climate, society and technology. Giorgio Agamben (2011) and Paul Krugman (2013) are amongst the many who have highlighted the issues with an analogy that says that yet another *oikos*, the economy, functions like a household. If the model of the household sometimes fails to capture the operation of national economy then also, albeit in different ways, it also runs into problems when applied to the complexity of the global *oikos*. Life at local or planetary levels does not sit well either with calculative logics or the model of careful domestic management, as indicated by the ways the very different poets I have discussed describe a regime of unpredictability and emergent properties across multiple scales: Mahon's chaos of complex systems, Prynne's viruses and vibrant materialities, Hughes's mutative and mutating myths and species. In the face of such phenomena Huxley and Goethe's stable, self-observing organic whole with which this book began can no longer hold.

Reading 'Positive Feedback Loop' in the light of the other poems in this book draws out the aporia in making us hosts of our own host(is). The threatened Earth becomes 'our guest' but this is not only a demand for care. Rather it constitutes an emphasis on the boundaries between inside and outside, system and environment; an emphasis that turns humans and their world inside-out while also acknowledging that the magnitude of this threat is not uniform for different species or societies nor indeed always best described as a threat. The poets in this book move across different scales of the organic: viral codes in genomes, parasites in organisms, (endangered) species in ecosystems. Amidst, around and within them lie various vibrant materials – mutagens, greenhouse gases, shifting geophysical processes like the thermohaline currents. These too are affected both by the operation of developing technologies and the political, economic, media and other social systems which partially dictate how humans will intervene in these biotic and metabiotic assemblages.

While, in the Anthropocene, life on Earth has evolved to a state where human instruments risk extinguishing large swathes of it, the life of these instruments – and the effect they have on the organic – is not easily subdued. The different ways of reading engendered by poetry's various formal strategies enable a recursive engagement with, and examination of, our concepts, languages, myths and structures of feeling in light of their history, their hidden traps and their future potentialities. Poetry written in the shadow of ecological crises sharpens the focus, facilitating an exploration of our orientation toward ideas of home, futurity, economy, hospitality, earth, life, evolution, adaptation, Nature and, of course, ecology, technology and biology. Moreover, poetry engages with the ways these ideas inform and deform each other in different contexts and re-readings. The results of such processes of re-engagement are not predictable but rather dynamic and emergent, contingent on shifting conditions both inside and outside the reader's mind. Reading poetry enacts another kind of feedback loop where the human may observe its environment, and the way it observes, and change itself and its environment as it does so. The effects of such feedback loops play out amongst a complex network of systems. Against this emergent awareness of the limits of agency and predictability I suggest that for too long readers have looked to poetry primarily to understand how one might dwell in the world; the point, however, is to change (with) it.

Notes

1 In 'A Disaster' a monstrous 'word' devastates the earth, killing men, bulldozing cities, poisoning seas. This word is not divine but human – 'it can digest nothing but people' and without them its powers wane though its devastation lasts (2003: 226).

2 In answer to Iris Leal's enquiry on the state of ecology, Hughes wrote that 'He [Edward Goldsmith, publisher of *The Ecologist*] believes that unless all the world's governments come to their senses instantly, and reverse all the policies that on most fronts are advancing with increasing momentum, the world has maybe thirty years. This is another way of saying, I suppose, that yes we are already beyond the point of no return' (1994a). Compare also a letter to his friend Michael Martin, sent in 1997 and shown by Martin to journalist Ed Douglas: 'I seriously feel the whole bickering struggle between commerce and husbandry will be overtaken on the grandest scale by global warming' (Douglas, 2007).

3 Every effort has been made to keep to the original formatting of 'Positive Feedback Loop'. However, the lengths of Graham's lines are such that, on a few occasions, the formatting has become distorted and several long lines that, in the original, contain no line breaks, have been allowed to follow-on into the "middle column". The following lines have been affected: 'contributions from [...] hold a' (p.206); 'An orchestra [...] other plans' (p. 206); 'everything in and out [...] into this our' (p. 208); 'positive feedback loops [...] taken in' (p. 209); 'we who began [...] upon stone (p. 209).

4 The way the tension between line and long sentence begets unexpected connections is reminiscent of another of the influences Graham acknowledges in her *Paris Review* interview, Marianne Moore.

References

Agamben, Giorgio. 2011. *The Kingdom and the Glory: For a Theological Genealogy of Economy and Government*. Translated by Lorenzo Chiesa and Matteo Mandarini. Stanford, CA: Stanford University Press.

Allenby, Braden R., and Daniel Sarewitz. 2013. *The Techno-Human Condition*. Cambridge, MA: MIT Press.

Bate, Jonathan. 1991. *Romantic Ecology*. London: Routledge.

Bennett, Jane. 2010. *Vibrant Matter: A Political Ecology of Things*. Durham, NC: Duke University Press.

Blackie, Sharon. 2012. 'An Interview with Jorie Graham'. *Earthlines* 2: 36–41.

Clark, Timothy. 2012. 'Scale'. In *Impasses of the Post-Global*, edited by Henry Sussman. Ann Arbor, MI: Open Humanities Press. 146–167.

Cohen, Tom. 2010. 'The Geomorphic Fold: Anapocalyptics, Changing Climes and 'Late'Deconstruction'. *Oxford Literary Review* 32(1): 71–89.

Colebrook, Claire. 2012. 'A Globe of One's Own: In Praise of the Flat Earth'. *SubStance* 41(1): 30–39.

Derrida, Jacques, and Anne Dufourmantelle. 2000. *Of Hospitality*. Translated by Rachel Bowlby. Stanford, CA: Stanford University Press.

Douglas, Ed. 2007. 'Portrait of a Poet as Eco Warrior'. *The Guardian*, 4 November. Available at: http://www.guardian.co.uk/books/2007/nov/04/poetry.tedhughes [accessed 13 June 2014].

Emmeche, Claus, and Jesper Hoffmeyer. 1991. 'From Language to Nature: The Semiotic Metaphor in Biology'. *Semiotica* 84 (January): 1–42. doi:10.1515/semi.1991.84.1–2.1

Gardner, Thomas. 2003. 'Jorie Graham, The Art of Poetry No. 85'. *Paris Review*. Availible at: http://www.theparisreview.org/interviews/263/the-art-of-poetry-no-85-jorie-graham [accessed 1 June 2013].

Graham, Jorie. 2008. *Sea Change: Poems*. Manchester: Carcanet.

Habermas, Jurgen. 1990. *The Philosophical Discourse of Modernity*. Translated by Frederick Lawrence. Cambridge: Polity Press.

Hardy, Thomas. 1999. *Jude the Obscure*. Second edition, New York; London: W.W. Norton.

Hughes, Ted. 1994a. '*Letter to Iris Leal*'. 1 September. Box 54, Folder 11. Ted Hughes papers, Stuart A. Rose Manuscript, Archives, and Rare Book Library, Emory University.

Hughes, Ted. 1994b. *Winter Pollen*. Edited by William Scammell. London: Faber & Faber.

Hughes, Ted. 2003. *Collected Poems*. Edited by Paul Keegan. New York: Farrar, Straus and Giroux.

Krugman, Paul. 2013. 'The Big Fail'. *The New York Times*, 6 January. Available at: http://www.nytimes.com/2013/01/07/opinion/krugman-the-big-fail.html [accessed 22 March 2014].

Lovelock, James. 2010. *The Vanishing Face of Gaia: A Final Warning*. London: Penguin.

Luhmann, Niklas. 1989. *Ecological Communication*. Translated by John Bednarz. Cambridge: Polity.

Mahon, Derek. 1970. 'Poetry in Northern Ireland'. *Twentieth Century Studies* 4: 89–93.

Moeller, Hans-Georg. 2012. *The Radical Luhmann*. New York: Columbia University Press.

Morton, Timothy. 2012. 'An Object-Oriented Defense of Poetry'. *New Literary History* 43(2): 205–224. doi:10.1353/nlh.2012.0018

Ovid. 2004. *P. Ovidi Nasonis Metamorphoses*. Edited by R.J. Tarrant. Oxford: Clarendon.

Riley, Peter. 1992. *Reader*. London: n.p.

Wengen, Deidre. 2008. 'Imagining the Unimaginable: Jorie Graham in Conversation'. Available at: http://www.joriegraham.com/wengen_2008 [accessed 22 June 2015].

Wood, David. 2007. 'Spectres of Derrida: On the Way to Econstruction'. In *Ecospirit: Religions and Philosophies for the Earth*, edited by Laurel Kearns and Catherine Keller. New York: Fordham University Press. 262–290.

Index

For Product Safety Concerns and Information please contact our EU representative GPSR@taylorandfrancis.com Taylor & Francis Verlag GmbH, Kaufingerstraße 24, 80331 München, Germany

Printed and bound by CPI Group (UK) Ltd, Croydon, CR0 4YY

08/05/2025

01864358-0005